Praise for *Putting the Public Back in Public Relations*

"Rip up your communications degree. Write off your PR job experience from the last 30 years. As Dorothy said in *The Wizard of Oz*, 'Toto, I have a feeling we're not in Kansas anymore.'

But take heart, Tin Man, 'rehab' is available—brought to you by Solis and Breakenridge in this book—to get you back on your feet and re-invent yourself. The first step toward full recovery begins on page one."

—**Jerry Santos**, Senior Vice President,
Corporate Communications, Global Crossing

"What is wrong with PR? Plenty. Every day for the last decade or more I've received more than fifty unsolicited pitches. Less than 1% ever wind up being articles. That's wasted effort for the person who wrote the release, wasted time for the journalist weeding through it all, and wasted money for the client.

It's not a new gripe, but until ten years ago it was the only system we had. Now, social media has turned everything on its head. It's changed the way readers consume information, the way reporters find and write about it, and it's high time it change the way PR professionals pitch.

Putting the Public Back in Public Relations gets it all—what's wrong with the old model and the power of the new one. Brian and Deirdre explain in clear detail how it's no longer about pitching, it's about engaging. They explain what that means and how to do it right. If everyone read this, my job as a reporter would be a whole lot easier."

—**Sarah Lacy**, journalist and author of *Once You're Lucky,
Twice You're Good: The Rebirth of Silicon Valley and Rise of Web 2.0*

"This book is essential reading for any and all communication professionals. Learning how to speak *with* and not *at* your audience is the key to success in the PR 2.0 world. Brian and Deirdre talk strategy, tactics, and what works, with detailed case studies that illuminate each point. It's also written in a clear style that everyone will be able to understand, from social media novice to advanced technology user. This is a must read for any communications professional working today."

—**Jane Quigley**, Relationship Director, crayon

"PR has changed forever and Brian Solis and Deirdre Breakenridge are at the forefront of this change. If you think PR is fine and dandy, please buy this book because without it you will be out of business!"

—**Gary Vaynerchuk**, Director of Operations, Wine Library

"*Putting the Public Back in Public Relations* is a passionate and persuasive case for rewriting the rules of public relations. Authors Solis and Breakenridge expertly combine third-party perspective with case studies and examples to paint a picture of a profession on the brink of reinvention. In their view, social media is the public relations profession's opportunity to take its place at the forefront of the new age of conversation marketing. After reading this book, that will likely be your view as well.

—**Paul Gillin**, Author, *The New Influencers* and
Secrets of Social Media Marketing

Putting the Public Back in Public Relations

Putting the Public Back in Public Relations

How Social Media Is Reinventing the Aging Business of PR

Brian Solis
Deirdre Breakenridge

Vice President, Publisher: Tim Moore
Associate Publisher and Director of Marketing: Amy Neidlinger
Acquisitions Editor: Martha Cooley
Editorial Assistant: Pamela Boland
Development Editor: Keith Cline
Operations Manager: Gina Kanouse
Digital Marketing Manager: Julie Phifer
Publicity Manager: Laura Czaja
Assistant Marketing Manager: Megan Colvin
Cover Designer: Chuti Prasertsith
Managing Editor: Kristy Hart
Senior Project Editor: Lori Lyons
Copy Editor: Krista Hansing Editorial Services
Proofreader: Kay Hoskin
Senior Indexer: Cheryl Lenser
Compositor: Nonie Ratcliff
Manufacturing Buyer: Dan Uhrig

© 2009 by Pearson Education, Inc.
Publishing as FT Press
Upper Saddle River, New Jersey 07458

FT Press offers excellent discounts on this book when ordered in quantity for bulk purchases or special sales. For more information, please contact U.S. Corporate and Government Sales, 1-800-382-3419, corpsales@pearsontechgroup.com. For sales outside the U.S., please contact International Sales at international@pearson.com.

Company and product names mentioned herein are the trademarks or registered trademarks of their respective owners.

Printed in the United States of America

First Printing February 2009

ISBN-10: 0-13-15069-5
ISBN-13: 978-0-13-715069-4

Pearson Education LTD.
Pearson Education Australia PTY, Limited.
Pearson Education Singapore, Pte. Ltd.
Pearson Education North Asia, Ltd.
Pearson Education Canada, Ltd.
Pearson Educación de Mexico, S.A. de C.V.
Pearson Education—Japan
Pearson Education Malaysia, Pte. Ltd.

Library of Congress Cataloging-in-Publication Data

Solis, Brian.
   Putting the public back in public relations : how social media is reinventing the aging business of PR / Brian Solis, Deirdre Breakenridge.
      p. cm.
   Includes index.
   ISBN 0-13-715069-5 (hardback : alk. paper) 1. Public relations. 2. Social media— Economic aspects. 3. Online social networks. I. Breakenridge, Deirdre. II. Title.
   HD59.S65 2009
   659.2—dc22
                                                    2008041937

To my wife Wendy, whose support and love served as my inspiration. To my mom and dad, for pushing me to never settle and for helping define who I am today. To my son, Dylan, thank you for keeping me company all those nights and weekends while I was writing, writing, writing. To Deirdre, who made the experience of writing this book one of the highlights of my life. Finally, to everyone whom I admire and learn from everyday: Your blogs, books, articles, speeches, and most important, friendship have helped me personally and professionally.

—Brian

To my daughter Megan who is the true inspiration behind everything I do.

To my husband, Mark, who supports all of my efforts and gives me the strength to pursue all of my dreams. To my parents, who raised me to live, love, and learn with passion and determination. To Brian, who coined PR 2.0 and made it possible for PR professionals to challenge our industry and to succeed. To my partner, Jason, who inspired me to pursue my aspirations as a writer.

—Deirdre

Contents

Foreword

It is a tradition for authors to ask a well-known person in their field to write a long, eloquent, and flattering foreword about their book. However, this is a book about the new PR, and it must reflect the current trends.

One of today?s most powerful current trends is the use of Twitter as a PR weapon—how else can you describe something that is fast, free, and approaching ubiquity?

Don?t get me wrong, I am perfectly capable of a long, eloquent, and flattering foreword as anything but that would simply be wrong. Hence, in the *lingua franca* of the times, here goes:

"Attention all marketing and PR people! Must-read new book by @briansolis @dbreakenridge: *Putting the Public Back in Public Relations*."

Guy Kawasaki, author of *Reality Check* and co-founder of Alltop.com

Preface: The Socialization of Media and PR 2.0

What is *Social Media?*

Social Media is the democratization of content and the shift in the role people play in the process of reading and disseminating information (and thus creating and sharing content). Social Media represents a shift from a broadcast mechanism to a many-to-many model, rooted in a conversational format between authors and peers within their social channels. Social Media is, quite simply, anything that uses the Internet to facilitate conversations. People now have the opportunity to broadcast their thoughts, opinions, and expertise on a global scale. In many cases, these voices are as influential as many of the most widely renowned journalists and industry experts.

Social Media is empowering people to become the new influencers, and it is forcing PR and marketing professionals to recognize and include these powerful tools in their advertising and marketing communications (marcom) strategies. However, marketers are still unsure exactly how to adapt to the new world of Social Media. Believe it or not, relatively few experts exist, even though there are many actively trying to play the role.

Social Media is powerful. It is not only changing "the game," it is also inspiring everyone across every marketing discipline to evolve or quickly become victims of media "survival of the fittest." Some professionals will make it; some won't. Others will get mired in researching ROI and reasons to justify whether there's a business case to participate. Others will waste time questioning the viability of Social Media and the need to reform, while simultaneously the world advances around them. Unfortunately, the outcome will be the gradual obsolescence of many marketing departments and advertising and PR teams.

In the mid to late 1990s, Brian Solis observed a shift in PR, which he termed *PR 2.0*—in recognition of the impact that the Web would have on PR and how the communications industry would be forced to eventually connect with customers directly while still working with traditional and New Media influencers to also reach them. This is an important distinction in the evolution of PR. PR 2.0 was born almost ten years ago, well before Web 2.0, and was inspired by the early signs of the shift in media during the Web 1.0 boom.

Long before Social Media, user-generated content originated from the very people who would inevitably rise up and use the Web as their soapbox, and who would eventually recruit readers, enthusiasts, and evangelists along away. User groups, forums, bulletin boards, and even manually created personal Web sites were the channels through which people shared their thoughts, opinions, expertise, and vision. As the Web grew, so did the ability to reach people through online tools and channels.

Do you remember Deja News? Believe it or not, Google and Yahoo! Groups are still widely used today, and these were among the catalysts for Social Media.

The communications and marketing industries are going through some of the most incredible and dramatic transformations in decades. However, only a few industries are embracing it and pushing things forward. Even though Social Media is eliciting corporate participation and engagement, not all companies believe that this is the right step. These companies hesitate because of a variety of factors, including fear, disbelief, underestimation, lack of ROI and metrics, plain old misunderstanding, misperceptions, or a combination of all these. In general, companies are conservative. They don't move quickly and are inherently resistant to change—even though the entire media landscape is already transforming radically right before all of us.

In some cases, companies are merely experimenting with Social Media because of mounting competitive or customer pressure. Some are doing a great job. Others, unfortunately, are underestimating it and applying the same old-school approach of "marketing at" people instead of engaging in conversations that will enhance the brand and customer relationships. And, some companies just don't get it at all. Many executives still view blogs as random musings, social networks as places where people troll for friends, and other social places as founts of pure narcissism. Most notably, companies fear letting go of control and acknowledging that the "wisdom of the crowd" can be a powerful group.

In actuality, companies lost 100% control of their communications a long time ago. People are discussing their brands, products, and services right now, across multiple forms of Social Media, with or without them. Plugging their "ears" and pretending none of this is taking place isn't going to help the situation or make it go away. Quite honestly, it will only make things worse for the brand. The key is to let go and embrace the chaos.

We are merely nodes in the greater network of life and business. We just need to participate to earn the attention of our customers and peers. Think about it this way: In the process of learning the new channels of influence, you in turn can also become an influencer:

- Participation is marketing.

- Participation is branding.

- Participation is influence.

As you participate and contribute content, advice, and information, you build an online portfolio of knowledge that enhances your reputation, boosts your brand, and raises the profile of the company you represent. And most important, that participation encourages customer loyalty. You earn trust, and trust is priceless.

In all honesty, most PR and marketing models are not designed to engage with people directly, nor are they equipped to do so in a way that doesn't insult those they try to reach. But this doesn't mean that the future represents doom and gloom for us. Social Media requires one-on-one conversations and unfortunately many marketers and PR "pros," until recently, have cowered in the shadows, hurling messaging in bulk at people, hoping that some would stick. This is our chance to not only work with traditional journalists, but to also engage directly with a new set of organic influencers using the media channels (traditional and social) that reach them.

PR 2.0 starts with a different mindset and approach, neither of which is rooted in broadcast marketing or generic messaging. It's all about humanizing and personalizing stories specifically for the people we want to reach. Great PR has always been about telling stories in a way that makes people identify with like-minded individuals to share information and build strong relationships.

Participation is the new marketing. And to participate, we must become the people we want to reach. The New Media landscape is creating a hybrid of PR, online marketers, market analysts, and customer advocates, to effectively and genuinely engage in the conversations that define Social Media and create relationships with customers (those formerly known as the "audience"). No BS. No hype. What we have here is just an understanding of markets, the needs of people, and how to reach them at street level (*their street*). Social Media isn't a spectator sport. To truly participate, companies must be inspired and compelled to do so. After all, we're in this to build relationships with customers wherever they go to share and discover information. This is about the masses, but at the same time it's about peer-to-peer interactivity.

We're combining the art of personalized mass marketing with the individualization of distinct, vertical, and smaller markets, also known as the *Long Tail*. This is the socialization of media, the amplification of word-of-mouth marketing, and the engagement between companies and people (for example, customers, their influencers, and their peers). We can all discover and share information in ways that bring everyone together, and we can extend conversation threads "across the chasm," bridging stories and market segments with relevance and unique benefits that matter to communities rather than to audiences.

For too long, PR and marketing have operated behind a wall, spamming media with generic e-mails and news releases. Even so, many in the industry have survived without understanding why their news or information matters to the communities they try to reach via this push. Now we have the tools at our fingertips to reach people directly. Some PR pros will fail. However, many smart, proactive, immersed, and passionate professionals will readily adapt to this New Media landscape. If you do so, you will no longer be just another PR person. Instead, your relevance elevates you to someone much more important and influential. You become the PR person who walks into a room and is introduced as more than just some "PR guy/gal." You now receive a proper introduction. "This is *the* PR pro, the one you need to meet." Suddenly, you are proud of your profession again.

In the realm of Social Media, companies will earn the community of customers they deserve. The revolution will be socialized, and it all begins with you. With this book, we intend to help guide you through this new landscape. We wrote this book to show you how to take advantage of the socialization of media, whether you are just starting out or you've been in the communications industry for years. Part I, "The True Value of New PR," is the start of your education. You learn how traditional PR, as you know it today, does not provide communications to accommodate the fundamental shift in our culture. A new layer of influencers is present, as is an entirely new ecosystem for supporting the socialization of information. The influencers and the ecosystem in which they socialize are facilitating new conversations that can start locally but have global impact. As our friend Shel Israel, coauthor of *Naked Conversations* and a technology adviser for start-ups on strategic communications issues, says, "We are building global neighborhoods."

As you work your way through Chapters 1 through 5, you'll quickly understand what's wrong with PR, how we can fix it, and the clear differences between PR 2.0 and the PR we used to know. You will also learn how PR 2.0 has a place in the Internet economy and how traditional vs. new journalism vs. Social Media is changing the art and process of influence.

Most of all, PR is about relationships. It always has been and always will. Although we discuss many changes throughout this book, it doesn't change the fact that you need to know what you're talking about, why it matters, and how and who it helps. Part I discusses how we can put the *public* back in Public Relations. Basically, we must focus on important markets and influencers. By doing so, we will have a much greater impact than if we try to reach the masses with any one message or tool (old-school PR).

Part II, "Facilitating Conversations: New Tools and Techniques," is more than just talking about what to do. In this Part, you learn how to implement best practices into a company's communications plan. This section of the book charts "unchartered" waters for many communications professionals and requires an open mind and a true understanding of the nature of marketing conversations in Web communities. You will read about the reasons why you should strike *users* and *audiences* from your vocabulary and how doing so will change your approach (and success rate) in New PR.

Part II also covers how to get into the conversations through blogging, whether corporate blogging or blogger relations with new influencers, and how to develop and sustain mutually beneficial relationship through blogging. This Part also examines other useful tools and techniques, such as Social Media Releases (SMRs), Video News Releases (VNRs), and explains why Search Engine Optimization (SEO) and Social Media Optimization (SMO) are vital to PR 2.0 efforts.

The ultimate goal of Part III, "Participating in Social Media," is to have you internalize a new approach. You will come to realize that Social Media is more about sociology and anthropology (and the social sciences in general) than it is about technology. You will also be reminded (and reminded again) that listening is key to the most intimate conversations in markets where you might not have been invited to participate in the past. In this Part, we also want to raise your comfort level with regard to marketing and Public Relations in social networks. You will gain a true understanding of social networks and micromedia (any form of online media that channels smaller chunks of "bite-sized" communications through Web communities and mobile devices), which you will come to learn is the hub for your online brand. You will also learn that PR is in the "Long Tail." Chris Anderson's (author of *The Long Tail*) concept applies to the field of PR, and certainly is not about using the news release as your ultimate tool. You reach the Long Tail through conversations in niche areas of Web communities. The Long Tail is perhaps one of the greatest concepts in the field of marketing, and in this Part you learn why it's so important to your PR 2.0 initiatives.

Part IV, "PR 2.0: A Promising Future," takes a look at our industry's future. Communications professionals who embrace PR 2.0 will gain additional influence, and they will also quickly come to realize that PR 2.0 is a wonderful form of customer service for companies. After all, listening to conversations, answering questions, and helping people enables companies to create trust of and foster relationships with a brand. When you listen, you can then use valuable information to better your company and its products and services. The last few chapters of this part introduce you to the new rules for breaking news, the future of news releases, and new metrics relevant to our industry. After all, if you do not monitor and measure your new marketing conversations, how will your knowledge remain current regarding market perceptions?

Part V, "Convergence," anticipates the future of PR, where PR 1.0 + PR 2.0 = New PR, and explains how to make it a reality today. The future is already underway, and as your professional landscape evolves, so do your roles and responsibilities. New PR is the path to better relationships with your stakeholders and the opportunity to really listen and help your customers. Convergence enables PR to excel in today's social economy, and you have the opportunity to become a champion, leading your organization to more effectively compete now and in the future. No longer will PR professionals be seen as mere publicists or spin artists. Instead, your role will increase in size and scope. You will become involved in everything from Web marketing and analytics to viral marketing, and from customer service and relationship management to cultural anthropology. Your willingness to converge will lead to new and higher standards for Public Relations and the professionals who serve the industry.

Acknowledgments

When writing a book about the transformation of an entire industry—one that is socially driven by so many incredible people who collectively work together to form one voice—the acknowledgments necessary to thank and credit everyone could be a book in itself. The creative, visionary, and brilliant minds, voices, and architects in journalism, marketing, PR, New Media, and online development have not only inspired us to write this book, but more importantly have stimulated the change necessary for the entire ecosystem for the creation, sharing, distribution, and learning of new information, thoughts, and ideas. These names include everyone we mentioned in our book as well as the scores of additional influencers who have worked so hard to carry the flag forward.

Also, we would like to specifically thank Keith Cline for his incredible advice, support, and developmental work on our book. A special thank you goes to Martha Cooley for giving us the opportunity to write this book and educate PR professionals on the challenges and exciting new changes as a result of Social Media. We'd also like to thank our production team, which includes Lori Lyons and Krista Hansing, who did an exceptional job to get this book to print. Many thanks go to the Pearson marketing team, including Megan Colvin and Laura Czaja, whose promotional support is truly appreciated. A big thank you also goes to the rest of our fantastic team at Pearson who have helped and encouraged us to write this book.

We also want to acknowledge our agency partners, executives, and colleagues who have worked alongside us every day throughout our entire writing process. They have been instrumental in our research and constantly provided excellent information and resources that have helped to shape the pages of our book. And, of course, our families, who sometimes see very little of us for long periods of time—we're thankful for your patience and understanding as we went through the writing process.

About the Authors

Brian Solis is Principal of FutureWorks, an award-winning PR and New Media agency in Silicon Valley and San Francisco.

Solis is globally recognized for his leading views and insights on the convergence of PR, traditional media, and Social Media. He actively contributes his thoughts and experiences through speaking appearances, books, articles, and essays as a way of helping the marketing industry understand and embrace the new dynamics fueling new communications, marketing, and content creation.

Solis has been actively writing about new PR since the mid-90s, discussing how the Web was redefining the communications industry—he coined PR 2.0 along the way. He was among the original thought leaders working to defend and define "Social Media" as a definitive media category. Solis is co-founder of the Social Media Club, is an original member of the Media 2.0 Workgroup, and also contributes to the Social Media Collective.

He has dedicated his free time to helping PR professionals adapt to the new fusion of PR, Web marketing, and community relations. He's a strong supporter of fusing social sciences in Social Media marketing and New PR and believes that communications always comes down to people talking to people instead of companies to influencers and then to customers.

He blogs at PR 2.0, www.briansolis.com/, one of the most authoritative marketing blogs online today.

Deirdre K. Breakenridge is President, Director of Communications at PFS Marketwyse. A veteran in the PR industry, Deirdre leads a creative team of PR and marketing executives strategizing to gain brand awareness for their clients through creative and strategic Public Relations campaigns. She counsels senior-level executives at companies including

AmerisourceBergen, JVC, Kraft, Michael C. Fina, and RCN Metro Optical Networks.

Deirdre is an adjunct professor at Fairleigh Dickinson University in Madison, New Jersey, where she teaches courses on Public Relations and Interactive Marketing for the Global Business Management program. She is the author of three Financial Times business books: *PR 2.0: New Media, New Tools, New Audiences; The New PR Toolkit;* and *Cyberbranding: Brand Building in the Digital Economy.*

Deirdre has spoken publicly on the topics of PR, online marketing, and brand building for the Public Relations Society of America (PRSA), the National Association of Broadcasters (NAB), Strategic Research Institute (SRI), Women's Presidents Organization (WPO), Tier1 Research, and at a number of colleges and universities. Deirdre blogs on the topics of PR 2.0 and Social Media strategies at www.deirdrebreakenridge.com.

Introduction

Social Media = The Reinvention of Public Relations

Pblic Relations as we know it is quickly changing. Many tried-and-true PR strategies that we know and rely on are becoming ineffective and irrelevant. We can no longer trust them to effectively reach and motivate today's influencers.

The Web has changed everything. And the Social Web is empowering a new class of authoritative voices that we cannot ignore.

This rising group includes (and is being led by) people just like you. User-generated content (UGC) has flipped traditional PR and media on its head, leaving many communications professionals and journalists dazed and confused. They wonder why everything is changing so suddenly, seemingly overnight. However, these changes do not really represent "new" concepts. The "sudden" shift has actually been more than ten years in the making.

Social Media and Web 2.0 are altering the entire media landscape, placing the power of influence in the hands of regular people with expertise, opinions, and the drive and passion to share those opinions. This people-powered content evolution augments instead of replaces traditional media and expert influence. And in the process, entirely new layers of top-down and bottom-up influence have been created. These layers dramatically expand the number of information channels (one-to-one, one-to-many, and many-to-many).

Traditional influence flowed from a news or information gatherer (for example, a journalist) to his or her audience. Blogs, social networks, online forums, and other forms of Social Media have changed the dynamics of influence. New information is now readily shared among peers. This peer-to-peer sharing—in which you, personally, and as a client representative participate—now affords communications professionals the opportunity to reach beyond their "A-list" media when telling their story. We can now also reach the "magic middle," that group of ideal customers who directly reach their peers through Social Media channels. As you'll learn throughout this book, the participant's story replaces the pushed messages of the past, now tailored for specific audiences; Social Media requires that we "share" stories that benefit all those engaged in the process by first learning what they're specifically looking for.

Monologue has changed to dialogue, bringing a new era of Public Relations. It's no longer about traditional media and analysts. PR must now also focus on the very people it wants to reach.

> *Everything is changing, and (in our opinion) it's for the better.*
> *People are blogging.*
> *Journalists are becoming bloggers.*
> *The masses are creating and sharing content via social networks.*

Bloggers are gaining recognition as industry authorities, earning the same (and sometimes more) respect and reach as traditional media (and sometimes surpassing it).

PR veterans are suddenly finding themselves searching for guidance and answers as everything they know is changing right before their eyes. A new, hybrid breed of Web-savvy communications professionals is emerging, and companies and agencies are actively seeking these new experts to effectively compete, now and in the future.

These highly sought-after New Media PR practitioners include those who blog, run a podcast or video show, communicate in popular micro-media networks such as Twitter, create profiles across several social networks and actively cultivate their social graph, customize pages with an understanding of "lite" HTML, and participate in the communities that are important to them (whether professionally or personally). Genuine experience is the desired commodity, not just a willingness to venture into new marketing channels just because you have no other choice.

Therefore, it's time to engage.

Don't worry, though. It's not too late to join and help guide the PR renaissance. You're reading this book, so you already have a head start. The principles driving the New PR movement are not foreign; they're deeply rooted in customer service, the social sciences, and community participation. When you look at it from the perspective of an ordinary person and not a marketer, you'll quickly realize that you already have experience as a consumer—one who makes purchases and advises others about their purchases. You have what you need to start the change from within.

We're writing this book for you.

Social Media will help us put the *public* back into Public Relations. With that in mind, we encourage you to jump in, but also to understand the dynamics of Social Media, the new world of influence, and the relevant tools necessary for successful participation. Our goal with this book is to make you Social Media literate and to start you down the path of becoming a New Media expert and, more important, a champion for change. We believe that this book will help you excel in your marketing career and give you the capability and confidence to help those around you, including the company you represent.

This book lays out the lessons you need to learn, direct from our experiences over this past decade of continuous evolution. The information (and, we hope, wisdom) included in this book comes from more than just our personal experiences. We have included insight from some of the most visionary, brilliant, and active authorities on the subject of PR and the socialization of media. We believe that these insights will help you understand New PR and encourage you to adapt your own professional practices to our new reality.

We all learn from one another.

PART I

The True Value of New PR

Chapter 1
What's Wrong with PR?

Although it's exciting to witness the evolution of the Public Relations industry, it is also a bit frightening. PR is evolving quickly, from the technology used, to the changing market dynamics, to the increased demands and empowerment of the twenty-first-century consumer. Most important, the principles and channels you use to reach people, whether influencers or your direct customers, are also changing. It's impossible to continue viewing the PR industry in the same way we have for years. After all, we always have something new to learn and embrace—no matter how much we think we currently know.

You might have uttered or heard this question once or twice in your career: "What's wrong with PR?" Many PR veterans are cautiously or skeptically observing the changes taking place in PR. Instead of debating what's wrong with the status quo, let's look at a different way. With Web 2.0 and the mass adoption of Social Media (discussed in more detail later), we can also ask, "What can we do better to make PR more effective in these rapidly changing times?"

The answer involves a new, forward-looking way of thinking. The answer also shows you how to enhance your own personal experience, value, and brand through engagement and how to approach Social Media for your brands. For us, it took years (in fact, a decade) to change our way of thinking about PR. But now we believe that the socialization of media and PR 2.0 have expedited all the good change that we see today and discuss throughout this book.

In the chapters ahead, we examine why and how PR has changed and still is changing, and how PR 2.0, Social Media, and marketing conversations with customers and new influencers are reinventing an industry. Over the course of our careers, we have talked with hundreds of professionals to find out what they believe are the greatest benefits of PR and what they think PR is supposed to achieve. Those conversations have told us that these professionals believe that good PR does the following:

- Provides one of the most credible forms of marketing: third-party endorsements

- Leads to effective communication, which builds trust and strong relationships with media, bloggers, analysts, influencers, and customers

- Influences and changes opinion, increases exposure, and builds a positive image and reputation

- Creates presence, enhances brand loyalty, and extends brand resonance

- Elicits response and action

These positive features of PR must remain prominent in our minds as we consider the changing markets, the advancing Internet technology, and the shifting ways in which consumers want to receive information (and, in turn, share it in their communities). Because of the technological revolution currently underway, PR can truly be one of the most powerful marketing disciplines. And although we know that PR should always result in the positives previously listed, we must now seriously consider some new factors: how to engage and communicate through the appropriate channels and which tools to use to achieve these benefits.

Challenging the Status Quo

Let's first identify what's wrong with the industry before we try to fix it. This is not a bashing session to point fingers or otherwise place blame on you, your PR and marketing colleagues, or your faithful industry associations (or to make professionals feel like they "just don't get it"). Instead, this is our way of saying that we recognize how difficult it is to embrace change. With insight and shared knowledge, however, we can move forward together. If we establish and maintain a united front, the change will be easier and more widely accepted. It will also help so many companies and their customers have meaningful, direct conversations—dialogue resulting in strong relationships and, ultimately, more brand loyalty. The change is meant to complement traditional PR, which means that first we must reflect on the status quo. Our goal, as you are reading *Putting the Public Back in Public Relations*, is to have you say, "I know what's wrong with PR, and I know what to do to fix it."

As experienced professionals, we can identify what is good within our industry and then pinpoint what is less than desirable—the PR practices we prefer to leave behind. In the face of socialized media, however, our industry has a new wave of critics. And instead of plugging our ears, we're listening and sharing what we've learned with you.

Countless articles, books, blog posts, comments, and opinions speculate about why PR doesn't work and why so many executives have a bad taste in their mouths at the mere mention of Public Relations. In this book, we show you how this conversation has been building in various communities (for example, in blogs), with some very influential people sharing their opinions.

Industry veteran, financier, and marketing evangelist (the man credited with bringing "evangelism" into the marketing department through his work with Apple in the 1980s) Guy Kawasaki sparked a thread of conversation with his blog post "The Top 10 Reasons Why PR Doesn't Work." Kawasaki followed up with "DIY PR," a guide to "do-it-yourself" PR penned by Glenn Kelman, the CEO of Redfin. With blog titles such as these, every new comment, link, and blog post ruffled feathers and bruised egos. (This is just a small glimpse at the ongoing discussions about this topic; you can also get involved in the dialogue and vest in the process of improving and changing the game.)

Truth be told, there are 1,000 reasons why PR doesn't work, but there are also countless reasons why it does work. Sometimes DIY PR works, too, but often it works to an extent that eventually requires an internal team or an agency (depending on the goals and reach of the campaign).

Kawasaki's blog post, sourcing Zable Fisher of ThePRSite, lists the top ten reasons why PR doesn't work:

1. The client doesn't understand the publicity process.

2. The scope of work is not detailed and agreed upon by both parties.

3. The client has not been properly trained on how to communicate with the media.

4. The client and the PR person or PR firm are not a good match.

5. The client has not gotten results quickly enough and ends the relationship too soon.

6. PR people don't explain the kind of publicity placements a client will most likely receive.

7. Clients don't realize that what happens after you get the publicity coverage is sometimes more important than the actual placement.

8. Clients refuse to be flexible on their story angles.

9. Clients get upset when the media coverage is not 100 percent accurate or not the kind of coverage that they wanted.

10. Clients won't change their schedules for the media.

However, paring PR to its basics to address these top ten concerns will not solve the industry-wide plague of bad PR. In fact, just addressing these concerns would make sense only to those who believe that bad PR doesn't exist.

Dave McClure, a Silicon Valley technology entrepreneur, seemed to capture it more accurately in his blog—at least, for those of us in a world that demands that we prove value and worth using metrics (and not just whether we can get along with people, trained our spokespersons well, or explained the publicity process so that executives could have something other than running a business to worry about). McClure summed up his top six reasons why PR doesn't work:

1. The PR firm doesn't understand the product or technology.

2. The PR firm is seen as a spinner, blocker, or gatekeeper to access the CEO/CTO/brain trust.

3. The PR firm hasn't been properly trained on how to communicate with bloggers or Social Media.

4. The PR firm prefers working with a few big traditional media instead of lots of smaller online media and online channels.

5. The PR firm doesn't understand SEO (search engine optimzation), SEM (search engine marketing), widgets, blogs, tags, social networks, pictures, video, or other online and viral methods—a.k.a. "all that Web 2.0 stuff."

6. Most PR folks have no clue what the hell a TechMeme is.

   (*TechMeme* is a news aggregation site for the most popular discussed technology news stories at any given moment. McClure's point is that PR people generally don't stay plugged into the evolution within their own respective industries.)

Obviously, there's no shortage of gripes about PR. If you look closely, however, you'll notice common themes. We asked a few more respected influencers about why PR works and why it doesn't. Forrester Research analyst Jeremiah Owyang continued with more reasons why PR doesn't work on his blog, www.web-strategist.com, paraphrased here:

1. Dialogue versus monologue is not fully understood. I believe that markets are two-way conversations, not message throwing. As dialogue happens, communities form and trust (or distrust) forms.

2. Marketing is about storytelling, not raw facts on the press release.

   Marketing (and communications) is not just facts (the when, what, and where), but it's telling a story, engaging the community, and being "human."

3. The community must be included in the event and message.

   In countless events that I've attended, PR firms have forgotten to welcome or invite "influential people" who will help dialogue or tell a story about the event using Social Media. Although it often makes sense to invite the mainstream media, don't forget that customers are now playing the role of media as well as analyst. I got beat up pretty bad when I asked this question: "Who should you trust more, a paid analyst or a customer blogger?"

4. More than one group in the company does Public Relations (resulting in a lack of awareness).

PR is no longer limited to the PR firm or corporate communications. Various groups and individuals will communicate with the
market. If you don't know what I'm talking about, it's important to
understand Brian Oberkirch's Edgework concept.

Brian Oberkirch is a marketing consultant focused on Social Media
and product development. His Edgework concept is inspired by the
very media evolution that we highlight in this book. It's based on
the idea that PR can also complement outbound influencer and market relations with two-way dialogue.

You can understand from this discussion that PR and the way we need
to communicate with people are changing. No matter what business
you're in, you can do a number of things to help you improve, manage,
and measure PR. This list of 20 PR gripes is a game changer and can serve
as the foundation for improving PR and elevating its value among those
who have been burned by previous experiences.

PR for PR People

So you've heard some reasons why PR fails (from us and from people
who join us on a quest to better an industry). *This is the part where you can
take your fingers out of your ears.* The gripes about PR that we've heard for
years, our own involvement in the discussion, and the dialogue among
people who share similar concerns—all these conversations are important.
They set the stage for the chapters ahead. We affirm that we can all learn
something about our own communications. It's similar to driving: No
one admits to being a bad driver, but the roads and highways are full of
them.

If you read carefully, you'll realize that our suggestions or answers to
the "What's wrong with PR?" question are just the beginning. By internalizing and remembering them, you will see and think about things
differently:

- Remember that just because you show up to work doesn't necessarily mean anything. It may simply equate to you keeping your job.

- If you expect to represent anything, whether in an agency or in a company, spend a significant portion of your time figuring out why it matters to people—on your own time. This is the difference between PR and good PR.

- Figure out who your customers are and where they go for their information. This forces PR to mirror sales strategies to reach the people who could benefit from the product or service. Different people go to different places for information. First determine where you want to be, and then work backward from there.

- Read the blogs, magazines, newspapers, forums, newsletters, and so on—this is where customers are actively engaged. Then understand how to translate what you do in a way that matters. This is the only way to be successful in running PR in the "Long Tail." People within your target markets share experiences, pains, and wants that are unique to each group. By reading, you're participating. And by participating, you're better staged to engage more effectively than the rest of the flacks.

The Long Tail, written by Chris Anderson, describes a niche business strategy in which businesses realize significant profit by selling small volumes of hard-to-sell items instead of focusing on large volumes of blockbuster items.

- Don't speak in messages. Instead, spark conversations based on the unique requirements of each market segment and the people within them. And please, don't spin. We all hate when politicians do it. If you find yourself consistently selling or spinning instead of evangelizing, you might be in the wrong place in your career.

- Traditional PR still matters, but you also need to embrace Social Media (after you've had a chance to participate as a person and not as a marketer). This is the future of PR. Understanding how it works and what it takes to participate will ensure that your experience is relevant to the communications needs of businesses during the next decade.

- Broadcasting your "message" to your audience with top-down PR campaigns no longer works in New Media. You have to engage people through the diverse segments that represent your target markets.

- When working with reporters, bloggers, analysts, and other influencers, spend a significant amount of time understanding what they write about, to whom, and why. Then align your story accordingly. One story no longer applies to the masses.

- When you understand what it takes to make the story more compelling to the various markets and the influencers who reach them, then, and only then, think about news releases. One news release no longer carries across the entire spectrum of customers. Figure out the core value proposition and then write several different flavors based on the needs and pains of your target customers, addressing how you will help them do something better, easier, and more cost-effectively.

- Set goals with the executive team of the company you represent. Based on the previous points, you have to ensure that your activities align with their business strategy. Ask them to define success month-to-month so that you can all agree, in advance, what it takes to move forward. Create the PR program that will help you achieve these goals. If anything beyond your control stands in your way of success, do what it takes to fix it. If your spokesperson is horrible, either train him or her or tell the spokesperson that you need someone else. If the product or service isn't wowing people, find out why and learn what it takes to compel people to use it.

- Communicate progress regularly, document milestones, and showcase successes. PR often suffers from a lack of "PR for the PR." If you don't demonstrate success, who will? By communicating progress, status, and feedback, you can consistently prove your value to those who underwrite the PR program.

Company Executives

You can't fairly assess work that you don't understand. We also offer our advice to company executives who need to understand the difference between PR and *good* PR, and how to be an effective partner in the process.

Understand PR Capabilities and Limitations

First, understand what PR is and what it isn't. Businesses often expect PR to perform miracles just because they confuse it with advertising, online marketing, media buying, search marketing, and so forth. PR can't *guarantee* legitimate coverage in industry publications, no matter how tight the relationship. If PR promises it, they're lying. We leverage relationships daily to encourage consideration of "stories" packaged in a way that's most relevant to them. If we took advantage of our contacts to force coverage whenever we needed to deliver on a promise, it would mark the beginning of the end of our relationships.

Although we won't compare PR to each branch of marketing, we agree that *PR is not advertising.* Reporters and bloggers don't stop what they're doing to write about your company just because you send them a news release. They're bombarded by PR people from all over the world. Stories are cultivated. If you respect your contacts, do your homework and help highlight the value of a story—coverage is imminent. If you want guaranteed exposure, buy an ad.

Don't Undervalue PR

When done correctly, PR is extremely valuable to company branding, which results in immeasurable benefits in the long haul. Customers have choices, and if you're not consistently vying for their attention, it's pretty easy to fall off their radar screen when they evaluate options. Too many companies try to nickel-and-dime PR, to the point of absurdity. Don't get us wrong: Expensive PR doesn't equal success. But shortchanging PR is usually a first step in the wrong direction.

Maintain PR Participation

PR is not a switch. It doesn't go on and off whenever you have the time or budget to throw at it. The market moves too fast, and if you're not actively participating in it, you'll quickly find that company sales and site traffic will begin a downward spiral that might not recover.

Plant the Seeds

In most cases, coverage doesn't just happen. PR is similar to farming: The more seeds you plant, the more crops (in the form of coverage over time) you will grow (as long as you spend time watering, caring for, and feeding those seeds and new shoots). Although some things force information out quickly (for example, hard news), other stories take time. And when those "slower" stories appear, they help raise brand visibility, drive some people to buy, and also spark others to consider writing about them (which, in turn, influences the cycle to repeat). Don't assume that all this coverage happens just because you are a popular company or have a killer product. Even the best companies and solutions need great PR to rise above the noise.

Use the Best Spokesperson

Just because you created the product doesn't mean you're the best person to sell it. We've worked with some of the most passionate executives who just don't click with the people they're trying to engage—no matter how hard they try. Suck it up and get a spokesperson who will connect with the people and who will help grow your business.

Recognize Campaign-Specific Factors

Understand that PR is only an umbrella for the specific communications initiatives that will help you reach complementary, simultaneous goals. For example, corporate branding and product marketing require different campaigns.

Use an Array of PR Tactics to Reach Your Full Audience

No matter what industry you're in, realize that the most popular blogs, newspapers, and magazines are only one part of the process. Your market is divided by adoption and buying behavior and documented through many means: a bell curve rich with chasms, pyramids that further divide and classify them, quadrants that demonstrate competitive advantages, ladders that represent how people use the technology to participate in online media, a "cluetrain" that shows how people carry it through the Long Tail as the new conductors, and, hopefully, the guerilla tactics that propel the hockey stick and eventually force you to evaluate what to do from "inside the tornado" to continue the success. For those who just read that sentence and are shaking your heads wondering if you just missed an inside joke, let us explain. We referenced the most often cited and the most popular business and marketing books, graphs, and tactics that help companies carve up their markets and define how to reach them at every step of the product life cycle. Yes, this was meant to be funny...but it does show that one program no longer serves the masses when you deconstruct it by the markets and the people who comprise them.

This means that you have to embrace both New Media and traditional media in PR. In the tech space, for example, TechCrunch, Mashable, Venture Beat, ReadWriteWeb, and other channels will yield measurable traffic so great that most of the time it knocks out company Web servers. Every executive wants these channels. CEOs cry if they can't get coverage on them. But by no means do they carry your value proposition to the entire collective of people who might embrace your product and help sustain your business for the whole game.

These channels represent early adopters and pragmatists. However, other worlds of global micro communities rich with horizontal and vertical publications and blogs can carry your story to the more conservative groups of people who collectively converge as the primary base of recurring revenue. In this case, it's less about traffic and hits as metrics for success and more about quality, registrations, purchases, referrals, and so on that define business growth.

Involve Yourself

Engage in Social Media. We live in a "social" economy, and the only way to succeed in it is to participate:

- Listen to what your customers and the customers of your competitors are saying.

- Blog about industry-relevant topics, not just company accomplishments. Social Media is not just a new tool in the marketing belt. It is a new opportunity to engage customers and cultivate relationships. Be a resource for your community. Comment on other blogs, too. Be part of the conversation.

- Embrace online video and watch how creative, genuine, and cool content becomes incredibly viral. Words can carry the message just so far, but video is an opportunity to showcase the product while entertaining viewers.

- If possible, host a podcast, livestream, or Webcast to share new updates, customer successes, ideas for new product uses, and so forth. Embrace and cultivate the community.

- Bookmark and share relevant links using the popular social tools available.

- Cultivate user-generated content.

- Write Social Media releases in addition to traditional releases.

- If relevant, build transparent profiles in the social networks where your customers can find and support you and where you can find and support them. Go where your customers are.

- Share images, demos, and behind-the-scenes footage using services such as Flickr, Zooomr, and YouTube.

- Hire a community manager. Having someone actively represent the company in all things social will complement New PR by providing proactive information and support to people looking for guidance in the communities they frequent. Don't market to them—have conversations.

Although this is just an ultra-simplified list of how to jump into the world of Social Media, your initial participation will increase your curiosity, knowledge, and online savvy. You can expect your community profile to increase exponentially with your participation. But first you have to get your feet wet.

Support Your PR Program

Support your PR program and feed it as you do any other branch of the company. Respect it when it works and let your team share in the success. Don't focus on the shortcomings. Extend congratulations as goals are achieved.

Keep Your Allstars

If you find a PR person who truly lives and breathes the company and the product, never let that person go. These Allstars are a rare breed and deserve support and promotion.

Communicate Regularly

Meet with your PR team regularly to communicate realistic goals and measure progress. Paint a real-world picture of what success looks like each month and listen to the reports to see whether those goals are indeed attainable. You get out of PR what you put into it.

Establish Metrics

Agree upon metrics in advance. Executives often lose sight of what PR is designed to do. The right coverage is invaluable, even when it doesn't translate directly into visible hits, traffic spikes, or sales. Super Bowl ads, for example, rarely pay for themselves in the short run. Realize that a proactive, intelligent, and consistent PR program will contribute to the bottom line. It shouldn't be solely responsible for company success or failure. Metrics can be in the form of specific targets every month, registrations, lead generation, links, and, now, conversations.

In the past, a PR person looked at a campaign with a well-known and highly accepted approach: You evaluate the target demographics, develop strategic messages, conduct an audit or focus group, revise messages, determine the broadcast mechanisms to push your content, go live, monitor the response, evaluate the ROI, and repeat the process with enhanced information.

However, communicators who have embraced Social Media and the idea that sociology is a prominent focus, not just the technology that facilitates the process, take a much different approach.

Brian shed some light on this topic when he blogged about an excellent example of a company whose communication team knew the value of dialogue and engagement. Skullcandy (www.skullcandy.com) is a popular Generation Y brand that makes electronic products, including MP3 players and headphones, that can run circles around Sony, Bose, and Phillips. Everything Skullcandy does is reflective of those they want to engage and embrace—from embeddable widgets with valuable content, downloadable music, custom artwork, and peer-to-peer street teams to blogs, communities, events, and social networks, all combined with traditional marketing. Skullcandy makes the customer the center of everything. And it could do even more to reach customers with the right social tools, proactive participation, elevated outbound strategies, and voices.

Here's an example of a tweet scan from Twitter engaging a community of people in the Skullcandy brand:

Seanieb64: My Skullcandy canal buds pair #2 have lost the left channel again I'd rather get these, and I will http://tinyurl.com/5w3xz6 (2008-04-11 23:21:44) Reply

concafe: Nuevo post: Skullcandy todo de rosa las chicas (http://tinyurl.com/6y8nxq) (2008-04-10 09:14:21) Reply

litford: wicked sick MP3 watch by Skullcandy: http://snurl.com/23zmt (2008-04-10 00:40:55) Reply

Noticiasdot: New blog post: Los cascos y auriculares de Skullcandy todo de rosa http://tinyurl.com/552xtn (2008-04-09 17:42:39) Reply

MosioQuestions: Where can i find skullcandy earphones on sale? Crystal -crystal1987 www.mosio.com/q (2008-04-09 14:41:29) Reply

angryfly: Picked up a pair of SkullCandy Full Metal Jackets while I was out for lunch... these things sound way better than the apple earbuds... (2008-04-08 15:23:21) Reply

Chorazin: I'm returning my Skullcandy FMJ iPhone earbuds. Cord too short and not that comfy. (2008-04-07 13:12:38) Reply

fetalsage: I love my new Skullcandy headset :D (2008-04-06 19:56:19) Reply

chriswall: My last pair of expensive headphones (http://tinyurl. com/6kuhbc) or the shures ? Or the Skullcandy iPhone FMJ.....sheesh here we go again (2008-04-06 15:03:40) Reply

cavlec: @cfred: I <3 my Skullcandy Proletariats. (2008-04-02 18:18:42) Reply

nickle4urdreams: I am a COMPLETE idiot. My Skullcandy canalbuds have been on top of my TV for about 2 weeks, while I've thought they've been lost... (2008-04-02 05:14:44) Reply

Chorazin: Mmm...my iPhone Skullcandy FMJ earbuds are the shiznit. I <3 Skullcandy. (2008-03-31 18:54:32) Reply

Noticiesdot: New blog post: Skullcandy: auriculars Rasta http://tinyurl.com/38mdd4 (2008-03-31 18:48:33) Reply

T_Infin: is enjoying his Skullcandy. (2008-03-31 13:55:12) Reply

justinpeacock: checking out the hip/ghetto Skull Candy headphones: http://www.skullcandy.com/ I want the ones with the bullets on the headband! (2008-03-31 13:21:51) Reply

T_Infin: just bought some Skullcandy headphones (2008-03-30 23:47:31) Reply

The Skullcandy example shows how PR is changing—more than 180 Skullcandy blogs exist, proving that the brand's customers are its surrogate sales force.

We think the change in PR is for the better. It will take some intense readjustments in thinking, resources, and participation by all. Most important, it requires you to become more than just a communicator. You need to evolve into something more significant than just a publicist. You can be more effective and valuable as a genuine enthusiast for who and what you represent. We want you to become a part of the New PR movement that carries forward all the good of the past, but also moves ahead with a realistic sense of how today's brands need to communicate in the market. Welcome to the world of PR 2.0 and the socialization of media—a new standard to advance the PR industry and the communication professionals who abide by today's rules of conversation.

Chapter 2

PR 2.0 vs. Public Relations

A great deal of confusion has always surrounded the meaning and true value of public relations. Over the years, questions have also surfaced about the credibility and integrity of the professionals who represent the industry. In this chapter, we examine the rise of PR as an industry, its evolution through the years, and the role and reputation fluctuations practitioners have experienced from then to now. From this discussion, you'll understand that traditional public relations lost its focus somewhere along the line, and it's no longer okay to be complacent. PR 2.0 offers a second chance to put the *public* back in PR. Let's take it!

Good Old Days

In the early 1900s, Ivy Lee and Edward Bernays, who were recognized and respected PR visionaries and are still to this day, are considered the purveyors of the PR we know and practice today. These forward-looking luminaries took the role of strategic counselors and both created and defined the art and science of modern PR—although their original motives were more aligned with strategic propaganda and manipulation. That was almost 100 years ago, but many of their tools, including the news release, are still widely used today. And although many of their early philosophies and contributions are still used to further evolve the PR industry today, we believe that *right now* is the time that experts recognize as PR's greatest renaissance.

Ivy Lee initially developed the first working news release; you can praise him or dislike him for it. Lee believed PR was a "two-way street"— that is, he believed that communications professionals were responsible for helping companies listen to the people who were important to them and communicate their messages to them. This practice is absolutely critical in the twenty-first century.

Edward Bernays, who is often referred to as the father of PR, was most certainly our first theorist. Interestingly, Bernays was a nephew of Sigmund Freud, and Freud's theories about the irrational, unconscious motives that shape human behavior were the inspiration for how Bernays approached public relations. What's interesting to us is that he viewed public relations as an applied social science influenced by psychology, sociology, and other disciplines to scientifically manage and manipulate the thinking and behavior of an irrational and "herdlike" public. Yep, we just said *social sciences*. More on this later—but just remember this as you read on: *PR is about people, not about the tools.*

According to Bernays, public relations was considered a management function—even back then. It was always meant to measure public attitudes; define the policies, procedures, and interest of an organization; and execute a program of action to earn public understanding and acceptance. Bernays' work also shaped public opinion related to the companies he represented. As we all know, this isn't the first use of *promotion* or *spin,* but PR has become synonymous with those words. Basically, some of Bernays' earlier PR practices were—and still are—the source of and inspiration for the PR 1.0 publicity and "hype" machine.

So what?

Isn't it PR's job to control the message? Not every product or service can be perfect, right? We're publicists and, as such, we're supposed to "sell it."

Okay, sounds nice. But what are we really saying? You can't have an opinion as a consumer? You're not intelligent enough to offer feedback? Your experience doesn't matter?

In the new world of PR, people are flipping the world of influence in their favor by embracing Social Media and sharing their voices with all those who'll listen. Newsflash: *People are listening to each other!*

This hype philosophy remains pervasive today. In fact, a majority of companies and professionals still approach PR via this very framework—even though the philosophy is all changing right before our eyes. Many of Bernays' thoughts (which fueled his books *Crystallizing Public Opinion,*

Propaganda, and *The Engineering of Consent*) were on the cusp of predicting what PR is currently facing in the dawn of Social Media. And Social Media is reintroducing the opportunity for sociology, anthropology, psychology, and other sciences to inspire a new, more meaningful platform for marketing.

Skepticism Creeps In

Through Lee and Bernays, the foundation of PR was built decades ago. And as the years went by, criticism and skepticism mounted. By the time we entered the industry about 20 years ago, uncertainty was already swirling about the PR industry and PR professionals as strategic partners involved in true management functions. Smart consumers also became increasingly skeptical over the years. PR was—and still is—viewed as a necessary evil and is undoubtedly the least understood and sometimes least appreciated marketing discipline. In our early experiences, PR was viewed as a function that took place outside the boardroom; many executive management teams even referred to PR professionals as "flacks" and "spin doctors." Unfortunately, this attitude still exists today.

PR is only good for generating news releases, spamming reporters, and selling ice to Eskimos, right?

Um, no.

Chris Heuer, a new media and Social Media raconteur, recently participated on a Vocus Webinar panel with coauthor Brian Solis that focused on a new tool sweeping the PR industry: the Social Media news release. Originally introduced by Todd Defren of SHIFT Communications in 2006, the Social Media news release is a new take on the traditional release. It incorporates and leverages many of the social networks and social tools available today, and puts them into an online format for use by bloggers, new media journalists, and even consumers.

During the panel session, Heuer stated, "Quality is missing at the end of the day. Many feel animosity toward PR people because they spin; they put lipstick on a pig." Heuer went on to say that consumers today would trust their neighbor or a blogger more than a PR professional.

Are PR professionals the new lawyers?

PR Industry Response

We realize that some of the negative comments heard today result from laziness, and PR practitioners have been working for years to change this damaging image. We believe that this image was perpetuated by people who never truly understood the meaning and value of PR.

There's no PR for the PR. And perhaps, for the most part, there's a reason for it.

What are we going to do about it?

Part of the problem with PR is that many associate it with spin, hype, or pure BS. Then there are executives who see its only value in the news release, which is essentially only a communication tool. And if PR professionals and the industry are being judged by the news releases they write, what does that say about us? Take a snapshot of several releases. They're often written poorly, riddled with jargon, full of hype, puff pieces (and sometimes irrelevant) with less-than-newsworthy information ... the list goes on.

We're here to tell you that PR, whether back in the early days or today, is about people. Although not always practiced properly, PR has always been about building relationships with the public through meaningful communication. It never should have been about anything else.

For years, PR professionals have been using PR as a means to create "messages" for "audiences," not realizing that, by default, they were often shooting over the heads of the very people they were trying to reach.

By driving New PR from a social-centric position, however, companies can identify the right groups of people, determine their needs, uncover their channels of influence, and use the tools and words that will reach and compel them. PR 101 will tell you that's the way it should have been done all along. That's common sense, right? You'd think so, but no.

Think about it. Reread the first sentence in the preceding paragraph. Just by practicing PR according to this methodology, you elevate the value of PR and become an expert in the process.

If we could reintroduce perspective, meaning, and value back into PR, PR practitioners would be recognized not only as the communications experts that businesses need to land invaluable coverage in media, but also those who can also authentically influence markets instead of manipulating them.

What would people think about PR then?

Individual PR Practitioner Response

The ideal PR professional of the twenty-first century is not only a market expert, but also an informed, socially adept conversationalist—and we all know, or should know, that listeners make the best conversationalists. This new breed of tech- and market-savvy PR people (*you*) will be skilled at observing, facilitating, and maintaining relationships, and creating and fostering trust and credibility with myriad groups of people who populate and define the landscape of new influencers and customers we need to reach.

The effects of these enhanced relationships and increased trust will be directly visible and measurable by those in charge of monitoring the brand communication, resonance, and ensuing loyalty.

How Did We Get Here?

Let's first look at the historical landscape of communications and technology, to build a bridge to the future of communications. And, just so we're clear, *the future is here now.* Let's explore!

The era of the dotcom boom and then the resulting bust was particularly damaging to the image of the PR industry and its professionals. This was a time when executives from companies wrote business plans on bar napkins, and these same individuals and their companies were being promoted in the news and gained publicity in some of the top media outlets in the country. From *The Wall Street Journal* and the *New York Times* to *BusinessWeek* and broadcast outlets such as CNN and network news, e-brands with little substance became media darlings. Internet and PR spin became abundant, and when the dotcom bust inevitably occurred in 2001, the media, the analysts, and the market suffered embarrassment and shame at having covered companies and contributing to their global visibility. Many PR professionals and their agencies suffered the "black mark" and lost their credibility. Valuable media contacts no longer trusted those individuals, unable to take them seriously again.

It also was a blow to the greater PR industry. Even though tech PR wasn't the only catalyst for PR's downward spiral, it represented one example of the many contributing factors and offending industries that amplified the problem instead of fixing it.

The first thing you learn as a PR professional is to uphold your integrity and credibility at all times. For many, the dotcom bust was an extremely hard lesson to learn.

Wait. Isn't all press good press? Haven't you ever heard the saying "There's no such thing as bad press"?

If all PR is so bad, how did it ever survive and continue to prosper? PR professionals can earn a substantial income. Agencies are profitable. So what's the problem?

PR contributes to the brand personality, perception, and resonance of a company. It is the voice. It shapes the company's personality. It helps keep companies, products, and services on the radar screens of their customers.

When you think of things in this light, you can quickly understand why "bad PR" isn't "good PR."

Let's come back to the Web for a moment. Sure, the dotcom bust simultaneously deflated the PR balloon and left people with a bad taste in their mouths. There were actually calls by senior corporate and marketing executives to temporarily move emphasis away from the Internet. So in a sense, the Web basically also took a hit, along with PR, but time would prove that the next Web would provide the foundation for a renaissance in PR.

After the dotcom bust, we entered a more humble, humiliated, yet landmark phase of the Web. Companies focused on increasing Internet functionality instead of on BS.

Internet technology experts such as Tim O'Reilly predicted that a more useful Web would emerge, one that would not only be more pervasive in our daily lives, but that would also be driven by us, "we the people."

This was the beginning of what eventually became known as Web 2.0.

Let's go back to that bridge mentioned earlier.

Web 1.0 wasn't all that bad. The Web is still here. PR is still here. In Web 1.0, some pretty incredible revelations inspired new marketing strategies and ideas that lay the foundation for more effective communications.

For example, the Web opened up an entirely new medium for publishing and broadcasting content. Traditional media recognized this early on and jumped in. New players also emerged to establish authority. As the tools to create Web sites emerged on the market, we started to see the formation of mainstream citizen journalism, which many later recognized as Social Media.

In the 1990s, Steve Sanders of StevesDigicams.com started a Web site on which he discussed and reviewed all things related to digital photography. He wasn't a traditional journalist or a professional camera reviewer; he was just an enthusiast with the ability to share his words with millions. Sanders ultimately became recognized as one of the leading voices on the subject of digital photography, and every major and minor company realized that they needed to pay attention to him. PR followed.

Simultaneously, Web-based communities gained traction—and users, enabling people to share information and connect with each other online in ways not possible before. As our friend Shel Israel puts it, it sparked "global neighborhoods."

Yahoo! Groups and other forums allowed people to build dedicated online communities to host conversations around topics or companies and to collaborate on projects. Epinions.com and other, similar sites allowed people to discuss products and services online as a way of helping other people make more informed decisions based on real-world experience.

Amazon.com not only proved that online commerce could work, but also allowed people to leave reviews on product pages, thus introducing peer-driven perspective to the Web equation.

In addition to traditional media, everyday people joined the revolution to publish and share information on the Web. They communicated with each other and also built their own audience to create individual authority.

This is around the time that Brian marked the beginning of *PR 2.0*. He, along with other Web enthusiasts (who also happened to be marketers), realized that new channels of influence were rising.

Ten years in the making, PR 2.0 is simply a reference for reflection, inspiration, and education.

Where Are We Going?

PR 2.0 was born through the analysis of how the Web and multimedia were redefining PR and marketing communications, while also creating a new toolkit to reinvent how companies communicate with influencers and directly with people.

PR 2.0 is the realization that PR now has an unprecedented opportunity to not only work with traditional journalists, but also engage directly with a new set of accidental influencers. We can now talk with customers directly (through social networks, wikis, micromedia communities, online forums, groups, blogs, and so on).

With Web 2.0, the ability for everyday people to publish content and build authority exploded. We officially entered the era of Social Media. Simply put, Social Media comprises the tools for people to create, share, and publish content online.

One of the most pervasive forms of Social Media today is blogging. Blogging has erupted over the past couple of years. According to blog-tracking network Technorati, 112.8 million blogs already exist today. Most blogs are written by regular people, "citizens"—and, hence, the genre *citizen journalism*. Social Media, more platforms, and networks were born to allow people to contribute additional forms of content such as text, video, audio, and pictures, which is also known more broadly as user-generated content (UGC).

But with blogs and social networks creating new influencers, PR has to change to reach the right people.

The new model of PR looks something like this:

- PR > Traditional Media > Customers
- PR > New Influencers > Customers
- PR > Customers
- Customers > PR

PR is evolving into a hybrid of communications, evangelism, and Web marketing, strung together by the teachings and benefits of sociology, anthropology, and psychology.

Now is the time for companies to learn how to use the Internet for marketing and PR campaigns that spread useful information: more substance, less hype. These times could indeed represent a new golden age of PR, when PR professionals are once again considered strategic partners. We are at a new dawning, with PR 2.0 and new and powerful Social Media applications at our fingertips. The tools people use to share content online are the same tools we can use to reach them.

Social Media also forces PR to see things differently. No longer can one set of messages to one audience serve a purpose. Social Media has forced PR to focus on the mainstream as well as the Long Tail, a group of niche markets reachable via dedicated channels. We now have the real ability to put the *public* back into public relations. The *public* means communicating to many different groups, even those hard-to-reach niche communities on the Web. PR starts to look less like a typical broadcast machine and more like a living, breathing entity capable of also participating in conversations with publics. These conversations (through direct-to-consumer communication) contribute to more meaningful engagement and brand visibility, and help people make purchasing decisions. These conversations also represent an opportunity to foster brand loyalty.

The tables have turned. In PR 2.0, we no longer rely solely on promoting products through third parties. We can take off our marketing hats and have real conversations with people. PR professionals are learning to advise brands that they can reach customers in many ways, through traditional channels *and* socialized media. We have made a complete circle that brings value and insight back into the marketing department, to concentrically construct more enlightened and accurate marketing initiatives. We are right back to the renaissance of PR and what Ivy Lee saw early on. Two-way communication is going on, and it feels good. A new age is born.

Recently, Brian was invited to moderate a panel at the Web 2.0 Expo titled "PR 2.0: Dead as a Doornail, or Still Alive?" Although the session was well attended, Brian couldn't believe the theme—or the title. In fact, we believe that PR 2.0 has yet to reveal its true promise and potential for changing an entire industry. Brian observed that any notion of its demise is premature and misleading. We share this experience here, however, because it showcases the confusion that exists between company executives and marketers during this landmark time of change.

In the tech world, traditional PR, defined as print and broadcast focused, has already been viewed as out of fashion. The rest of the economic sectors are beginning to catch up, but technology shows again why it's always on the bleeding edge. Many tech companies believe that traditional media is dying and that blogs and social networks are *it*. They believe that news releases are passé. But are they? Are deadwood media and reporters no longer relevant, or do they still have reach? How does PR operate today, in a world full of direct communication with customers via Web sites, e-mail, blogs, and video?

The easy answer is that PR has to go where the customers are, using the channels of influence that reach them. Subscribing to PR 2.0 or new PR philosophies, we now know that these channels will span traditional, social, and new media landscapes. We will look to influencers, and we can also look at reaching customers directly. But not one campaign, news release, or other PR trick of the trade will do a complete job.

Brian Cross from Fleishman Hilliard's Digital Group reinforced this notion in an interview in 2007 that was later published in Deirdre's book, *PR 2.0: New Media, New Tools, New Audiences.* He discussed the PR 2.0 tools and the basic building blocks with three distinct layers:

> The top layer is "your assets." So, for example, consumer generated media is your asset, whether it's a post, a blog, or a photo you uploaded or a video or link to a document. Anything that you take and share with people, what you put out there, is an object. As for the next layer, the middle layer, an area where people can vote, comment, subscribe, share rate, and collaborate. The bottom layer is for the tools, whether that's Wizard, wiki, blog, tag, IM, a poll, and so on. The third layer is the one that is always going to change. This is representative of the future. There will always be new tools. Even though the tools will continually change, PR professionals will always start the conversation, facilitate that conversation and then, of course, monitor the conversation.

Although we agree with Cross in principle, his last statement showcases the false assumption that companies can always control the conversations and message: "Even though the tools will continually change, PR professionals will always start the conversation, facilitate that conversation and then, of course, monitor the conversation."

What we're seeing now and predicting for the foreseeable future is that influencers still drive (and will drive) notable influence. But people also have the ability to start conversations that force PR to respond.

We believe that PR 2.0 is defined by the evolution of industry practices forced by the shift and the process of influence. We pose these questions:

- What if PR professionals took the time to read the publications or the blogs they pitch?

- What if PR actually used and believed in the products or services they represented?

- What if PR could be compelling without its reliance on hyperbole?

- What if PR understood the dynamics and interworkings of the Web?

- What if PR became the people participating in online communities among the very people they were trying to reach?

If this were the case, perhaps it wouldn't be PR any longer ... well, at least not the PR of the past or PR as we know it today. We're sure every PR person will nod his or her head in agreement, saying, "Yeah, PR needs to get it" ... as if they didn't contribute to the state of the industry.

The truth is, we're all guilty. So, what can you do?

- Face it.

- Accept it.

- Move forward.

- Change.

- Continually learn.

This is the premise of the PR 2.0 philosophy we've been talking about since the first boom. New PR is not formed or fed by Web 2.0—even though anything 2.0 seems to steal the spotlight these days. The reinvention of PR and the embracement of new influencers is a manifesto for improving our profession in a new age of communications. It is PR redux, a milestone that documents how PR has evolved more in the past 10 years than it has in the last 100 years. This new milestone is our chance to not only work with traditional journalists, but also engage directly with a new set of powerful and insightful voices by interacting with customers directly (because now we have the capability and the opportunity).

Suddenly, PR is no longer just about audiences. It's now about people. And with Social Media gaining mainstream acceptance, it will only expose those weak in PR and force our industry to improve. Unfortunately, the way it stands now, the body count will be high. But that's for everyone else. You're reading this book. You are among the new catalysts for change, and in the process, you're going to become more successful than you thought possible in PR.

New PR is about people and relationships, not just new tools. The game is changing, and it's survival not only of the fittest, but also of the most capable and sincere. PR in the era of Socialized Media requires a fusion of traditional PR, Internet marketing, Web-savvy market intelligence, and the ability to listen and engage in conversations without speaking in messages.

PR 2.0 represents the evolution of industry practices forced by the shift and the process of influence in a social economy that has created a new layer of influencers. Although we're not proponents of labels, these differences require explanation, and these labels will, we hope, facilitate your understanding.

New PR is a milestone that documents the shift of PR from a broadcast machine to community participation. It is no longer about audiences. It is now about people, as so eloquently stated by Jay Rosen in his poignant essay "We Are the People Formerly Known as the Audience." (Rosen is a well-known journalism professor at New York University and most certainly a thought leader on influence and the role people play in it.) This time it's about sociology and the cultivation of relationships. Whereas content was king in Web 1.0, conversations and community and participation therein are "the new black."

Let's just take out the BS and hype, and let's start understanding what we represent and why it matters to those we're hoping to reach. While we're at it, let's also take some time to read the publications and blogs that reach our customers. This is about understanding markets, the needs of people, and how to reach them.

This is PR for the mass market and for reaching those people who comprise the Long Tail—reaching out to the disparate markets that collectively represent your customer base. And no steps can be taken without first listening. Consider the difference between PR and PR 2.0:

- News releases vs. engaging with communities

- Spin vs. relevance

- Speaking in messages vs. genuine conversations related to the subject matter of peers

- Wire services vs. social/conversation tools and networks

PR cannot exist if we don't carry the confidence of those who trust and empower us with the brand of the company we represent. PR is evolving, and to survive we have a lot of learning and listening ahead of us. We have quite a bit of work to do in PR (let's just say that the PR industry itself needs some PR right about now) because CEOs, investors, and business leaders at the events we speak at and attend obviously feel less than confident that PR actually brings value to the table. PR has come full circle, and we all have the opportunity to rise to a higher level. The new movement leads to better conversations, useful information to make informed decisions, better relationships, and a newly developed trust in the profession—and the ability to earn the trust of customers. Relationships should have always been the foundation of PR, and the New PR renaissance reinforces this solid foundation.

Chapter 3

PR 2.0 in a Web 2.0 World

Y ou might be asking, "What do people mean when they refer to the Web 2.0 world? How does PR fit in, and how does Web 2.0 complement PR?" These are all valid questions. If you were to research the origins of Web 2.0, you would find that Tim O'Reilly coined the term. O'Reilly was a huge supporter of free software and the open source movement. His company, O'Reilly Media, is known as a technology transfer company focused on "changing the world by spreading the knowledge of innovators" (in the words of Wikipedia). After the first O'Reilly Media Web 2.0 Conference in 2004, the term became widely recognized and communities developed online to enable collaboration, sharing, and creativity among users. These communities included social networking sites, blogs, and wikis. Web 2.0 brought a new way for groups of people to converse, and it presented an opportunity for them to gather and then share information collectively.

This was the rebirth of the Web. It was also a catalyst for officially inspiring the reinvention of public relations.

The New Collaborators

Web 2.0 introduced a read/write Web, a new paradigm where hosts and participants could contribute to a more collaborative Web landscape and experience. But it's not the tools that make Web 2.0 or New PR what it is today; it's clearly the many people who collaborate and share information every day in their communities and who demonstrate how the latest tools can facilitate conversations and foster relationships across the Web. Web 2.0 introduced the Social Web, which is about people communicating with each other using the tools that reach their respective online communities. Online conversations and the discovery, creation, and sharing of content is the foundation for Web 2.0, Social Media, and New PR.

New PR's goal is to understand the communities of people we want to reach and how to engage them in conversations without marketing at them.

The Social Web induced the realization by smart companies that the people and respective brands that "let go" and share control of how messages and communications are received and perceived, create and foster a more active and respected community through communication and the participation in direct conversations with their peers and customers. In a Web 2.0 world, "command and control communication," which is dictated and prescripted communication, has diminished because companies are realizing that this type of communication no longer belongs in today's marketplace. In this "new world," companies augment and "let go" of the push and broadcast mechanisms associated with traditional marketing and message control, enabling customers to internalize information and, in turn, share their reaction and interpretation.

Understand that you're not giving up the ability to share your messages and broadcast them. People now have a powerful voice and, in many cases, have the ability to steer your messages within their realms of influence, picking up steam and voices along the way.

You, as a participant and also a content creator, have the ability to shape perception through the process of the information you say about yourself, what they hear, how they share that story, how you respond, and how you weave that insight into future conversations.

Listen and read before engaging in or launching important outbound initiatives. Follow the dialogue. Learn from it. Help shape conversations productively. Answer questions. Become a resource. Listening teaches us everything—from where to start, to how to improve our communications processes, and even how to improve our products and services to better meet the needs of customers.

In the Web 2.0 world, brands are more embraceable, shapeable, and approachable than ever before. People are actively participating in the social Web—sharing, finding, and writing about the things that are important to them. Brands are frequently the focus of conversations. The interactivity of the new Web makes brands personal and portable, making their reach fairly unlimited and requiring participation from brand representatives to help shape and steer them through discussions. With the openness and collaboration of Social Media, successful brands need to establish trust and build relationships with stakeholders. People do business with people they respect. Brands today must show their human side by participating directly with the people they want to reach in the networks where they're active.

Since Brian introduced the idea of New PR in the mid-to-late 1990s, the PR 2.0 manifesto has quietly spread through a natural evolution via an intelligent set of influencers, which hasn't been fast enough to appease outspoken critics. Traditional and new influencers are looking for meaningful information delivered in their preferred approach, and PR 2.0 is the platform that will finally be the catalyst for change. It took Social Media and Web 2.0's migration into the mainstream to finally accentuate the need to improve PR's foundation and also nurture the community needed to help PR professionals learn how.

The New PR movement has met resistance over the years. Change isn't easy to embrace, especially when processes have existed relatively unchanged for many years. However, the Web changed everything well before Web 2.0, and it's inspiring a new level of commitment—one that fuses the role of PR with market expertise, product and brand enthusiasm, and customer empathy. The technology that socialized Web 1.0 and gave way to Social Media is giving communicators a new toolkit to reinvent how companies communicate with influencers, and directly with people, in a more open and honest way.

PR Redux

PR 2.0 was, and is, the PR industry's chance to improve our craft and escalate our value by directly engaging and participating with traditional voices as well as those new influencers who have emerged as leading authorities through the use of socialized media. Web 1.0 actually inspired the concept (although many communications professionals think Web 2.0

did) and the new channel of information distribution it represented. Web 1.0 changed everything. It forced traditional media to evolve. It created an entirely new set of influencers, developed a completely different mechanism for collecting and sharing information, and reformed the daily routines of how people searched for news and information.

PR 2.0 is a philosophy and practice to improve the quality of work, change the game, and participate in a more informed and intelligent way. As mentioned earlier, we envision fusing the intelligence of market analysts, the mechanics of Web marketing, the credibility of market influencers, and the conviction and reach of passionate evangelists. This remains PR 2.0's goal.

PR 2.0 was not inspired by Web 2.0, but it was influenced by it—just as it was by Web 1.0, search engine marketing (SEM), and Social Media. New PR is driven by learning, practicing, and sharing, which alleviates and untangles the conflict between traditional, social, and new media as they wrestle with influence challenges. It truly is PR redux, with leading PR professionals marching forward with a true working knowledge and honest conviction to improve an industry long plagued and hampered by the lack of PR for itself.

We'd like you to help reinvent PR and become a more successful communications professional in the process. The issues with PR and the struggle for survival and credibility aren't just a notion that came to us through our own personal experiences. Every so often, journalists and other influencers strike back against PR for its inauthentic, disingenuous, and "spamlike" ways of pitching them. For example, Chris Anderson, Editor-in-Chief of *Wired* magazine, opened many eyes with his blog post "Sorry PR People, You're Blocked." On October 29, 2007, this was Anderson's way of telling lazy PR people and the PR industry that something just wasn't working:

> I've had it. I get more than 300 emails a day and my problem isn't spam (Cloudmark Desktop solves that nicely), it's PR people. Lazy flacks send press releases to the Editor in Chief of *Wired* because they can't be bothered to find out who on my staff, if anyone, might actually be interested in what they're pitching. Fact: I am an actual person, not a team assigned to read press releases and distribute them to the right editors and writers (that's editor@wired.com).

So fair warning: I only want two kinds of email: those from people I know, and those from people who have taken the time to find out what I'm interested in and composed a note meant to appeal to that (I love those emails; indeed, that's why my email address is public).

Anderson then listed about 100 PR professionals' e-mail addresses. We respect Chris Anderson and his work. Brian appropriately responded to Anderson's post in November of 2007 on his blog PR 2.0:

Chris Anderson, Editor in Chief of *Wired* and also author of *The Long Tail,* is someone whom I deeply admire and respect. We've linked to each other in the past and, for the most part, I agree with his views and observations.

Every now and then Anderson discusses the state of PR and when he does, it causes nothing less than a full blown blogstorm that reverberates across the entire industry. But, what matters is that we all learn from it.

In his latest post, he makes a pretty powerful statement, "Sorry PR people, you're blocked."

If you don't read anything else in my post, please just learn from what Chris says here, "So fair warning: I only want two kinds of email: those from people I know, and those from people who have taken the time to find out what I'm interested in and composed a note meant to appeal to that."

What's it going to take for PR to reflect that sentiment and honest plea for relevance?

It should be common sense. But it's not. Common sense is all too uncommon in almost everything we do these days. I really wasn't going to blog about this, as there has been plenty of very astute, as well as unbelievably lame, commentary on the subject.

Taking a step back to observe the landscape, the cumulative response represents both sides of the spectrum and everything in between. The net result should be that we as PR people need to do things better.

I promise to fix this problem among those with whom I work and can reach. I will also work with others whose voices are trusted among PR practitioners and their peers within the communities in which they seek guidance. We will do everything we can to help teach those PR people who truly desire to learn and truly understand the ramifications of their actions, good and bad, how to be successful while respecting the rules.

Everyone else, a.k.a. the lazy PR flacks, well, they're on their own.

Yes, they represent the larger epidemic of what we, the few but proud PR folks who try to do things better, have to contend with day in and day out—the worldwide poor reputation of PR. Public relations, when you think about it, really is the furthest thing from PR these days. I mean, honestly, very few of us are out there building relationships with the public or people, for that matter. Most of us don't bother to spend the time to really learn about what we represent, why it matters, and how it's different than everything else out there. And without that understanding, how could we possibly figure out the channels and context necessary for it to reach the people that would need to hear the story?

This is the reason why many PR people aren't, or will never be, ready to make the transition to Social Media. After all, if reporters and bloggers don't want to talk to us, why would we bring the same foolish BS and spam tactics to our customers?

I join a growing group of people who really do want to change, build relationships, and be of service to you, our customers, as well as to the people who employ us.

Let's look at the game, however, because PR is only one of many functions in the greater scheme of content distribution.

It is a job that many people perform every day in order to earn a living. Like any business, there are shining stars and lazy flacks that ruin it for everyone else. But it is still a job and people are still just people. We all have a$$hole bosses or clients that push and push us in order to prove our value and earn our paychecks regardless of how much we push back. In many cases, like in everything else, most just grin and bear it. We also have coworkers that are just in this to collect a paycheck. Even though the timer is ticking until they leave the business, their contribution only damages the damaged PR reputation in the meantime.

Many of us are measured in volume, inbound links, traffic, sales, or by the stack of coverage that all collectively determines our ability to keep our jobs. Don't get me wrong. There are plenty of snake oil salesman in this business, and in every business for that matter, but those who truly want to do things differently choose to separate themselves from the crowd.

There are those that are overly ambitious and just don't know better. Then there are those who are trained by decades of outdated communications philosophies, formulas, and bullsh!t metrics that send them out into the real world only to get baptized by fire for every mistake they make—while taking down the brand they represent in the process. And in the realm of Social Media, these lessons are the equivalent of public flogging in the town square, except this time, the world is watching.

There have been many responses to this subject; however, what every single one of them is missing is that sense of internalization that demonstrates that "we" get it. Maybe most don't believe that some of us could get it, but boy, do we get it. Then again, how does everyone else know we really get it?

I can guarantee you that I will still get my scheduled call from Cision (formerly MediaMap) offering to renew my unbelievably expensive subscription to the "industry-leading" media database that, as they *swear,* provides me with every opt-in contact who wants to receive information associated with key topics, products, and industries.

But it's the difference between building lists and building relationships.

Could we take the time to make sure that what we want to share is actually important to you?

Yes, absolutely.

Should we spend more time reaching out to people individually than blasting matrices comprised of those who are simply grouped by "key words?"

I mean, it should be obvious. But most PR people, veterans included, are just groomed to make the numbers. But yes, we really need to adopt and live the "less is more" and "quality versus quantity" mantras we hear all the time. More importantly, we need to also push back and ensure that our clients and bosses understand what the collective group of fed-up journalists and bloggers are saying that they will no longer tolerate the status quo.

It's all about humanizing not just the process of receiving information, but also the process of sending it.

This is business and every cog in the machine has its associated benefits and downsides. For every reporter and blogger that's inundated with lame pitches and unsolicited press releases, I can show you two flacks that are equally spammed with requests for updates and the status of coverage from execs in order to prove their worth. The problem is so much deeper than PR spam. It goes back to the very reason why companies invest in PR in the first place, and in the process, they mostly miss the point of publicity altogether. They all believe their news matters to everyone else and that you have nothing better to do than take our release and run with it.

Get me the *Wall Street Journal*!

Why aren't we in the *New York Times*?

You do have these relationships, right?

We all choose who we ultimately work with and we earn the relationships we deserve. But at the end of the day, the onus is on PR leaders to do something about it—at least from our side anyway.

Chris Anderson didn't tell us anything we didn't already know. He only brought a bigger magnifying glass to class in order for us to more effectively see the ills of our business. We still have things we need to change and until we do, these public lists are only going to increase in frequency and volume.

Attention PR people, here are your life hacks or PR hacks in order for you to do your job better and stop pissing people off (and ruining it for the rest of us in the process).

1. Remember, this is about people.

2. What do you stand for? Answer that first before you try to convince people that are busier than you why they should take time to stop what they're doing to pay you any attention.

3. It's more than doing your homework. To some, doing homework is building lists. Figure out what you are representing and why it matters. How does it compare to other things? What do people need? What are their pains?

4. Practice saying it aloud in one to two minutes or less to a friend or in front of a mirror. Seriously. It works. If you don't get it, no one else will.

5. Less is more. Find the right people, not just because you read their profile in a database, but because you read their work and understand their perspective.

6. Engage in conversations outside of when you need something.

7. Build relationships, not lists.

8. Humanize the process and remember that this is about people.

9. Stop whining and making excuses. You are responsible for your actions, so arm yourself with what you need to be successful.

10. Isn't it weird that it's always 10? Stop sending press releases without summarizing what the news is and why it is *important* to the individual person you're sending it to.

11. Ah, thank you Spinal Tap. This one goes to 11. Remember, the future of PR is on you. If you're not in this to do your job better, then ask yourself why you're here. If you're not actively contributing to things improving, then you're part of the problem.

As Anderson's statement and Brian's thoughtful response affirm, there's no room for mass, meaningless, one-way communication. It historically hasn't been accepted in PR and certainly will not fare well with the New PR movement today—especially in an era of a more social Web. New PR has an opportunity to reinvent itself (with the help from people such as you) because Social Media provides us with the tools and the channels to reach people directly. Through this process, you become part of the media paradigm and your communication and influence can become powerful.

Anderson's post lit up the blogosphere and traditional press. Yes, one post sparked online conversations that spawned hundreds of articles in response. That's the power of a social Web and tools that power it. Anderson reached people, and they responded. The new Web is forcing a more "conversational" methodology when reaching out to influencers— both traditional (press) and new (everyone with access to Social Media tools).

Don't get caught up in the tools that define the Web 2.0 landscape. Tech darlings Twitter, Utterz, Digg, Wordpress, Blogger, Jaiku, Facebook,

Yelp, FriendFeed, and Bebo are just tools and communities in which people share, learn, and communicate. The *approach* you take to engage them sets you apart. As the earlier example showed, influencers—whether they're traditional journalists, bloggers, or enthusiasts—all seek information in specific formats through their preferred methods of contact. In the era of Social Media, broadcast PR, in of itself, isn't going to work anymore.

Communicating *With,* Not *To*

PR today encourages collaborative communication, enabling people to find, enjoy, and share useful information. No pitching or blasting news releases. It's the art and science of marketing without marketing. The emergence and proliferation of a socially powered Web created a conversation ecosystem, and we're now responsible for learning more about what we represent and how it's important to those with whom we want to connect.

It's no secret that the PR industry has inadvertently positioned itself as a necessary evil or the "stepchild" of marketing communications.

Again, this is our chance.

Social media is the product of Web 2.0 technology, and it's important because it represents the democratization of news and information. But remember that PR 2.0 isn't Social Media, and Social Media isn't Web 2.0. These are distinct movements that can complement and inspire each other. To sum up, PR 2.0 does incorporate the tools that enable the socialization of media, enabling smart folks to reach other folks directly. Social media frames "media" in a socialized context, but it doesn't invite PR (as it exists today) to market through (or to) it. However, worthy individuals can participate in conversations.

You are worthy!

You're reading this book. You're worthy. You're learning what it takes to communicate transparently and honestly with the people who matter to your business, using the tools they use to communicate. You can also balance PR with the traditional elements that still work.

The best new media practitioners are using social tools to conduct PR 2.0 transparently. At the end of the day, it's about the conversations you start and participate in, not about how many people in the industry understand how you did it.

Web 2.0, PR 2.0, and Social Media aside, reporters and customers share in their desire, and their demand, to hear from you as a person who took the time to think about and present information to them their way—individualized content and the tools that get it there. What's going on right now is tremendous, and we're living through history in the making. This is our opportunity to force a renaissance of a worn and beaten profession and transform it into something much bigger and more meaningful. PR 2.0 is about bringing value and prestige back into the profession, and creating a new breed of communications professionals for a new century. PR 2.0 can thrive in today's ever-evolving and highly competitive online social climate. The two movements are complementary, and together they lead to a powerful arsenal of communication practices and applications that foster trust and build better relationships among stakeholders.

It all starts with you—you are a new influencer.

Chapter 4

Traditional vs. New Journalism

The ability to opine, report information, and track daily news in the twenty-first century has changed. The traditional journalists of years past are not the only "reporters" interested in covering the news and offering their opinions about events affecting their lives. Everyday people are now part of the equation. Armed with digital cameras, camera phones, handheld video cameras, podcasts, blogs, and social networks, we've entered the era of citizen journalism and user-generated content.

Today's major news outlets recognize the significance of citizen journalists and rely on their active participation in the news-reporting process. CNN's iReport is just one of the great examples of how the news media turns to the public to report and provide firsthand accounts with photos of events worldwide. Easy to access on the CNN Web site (www.cnn.com), iReport invites and encourages everyone to report: "See it first. Your stories. No boundaries. You won't believe what people are uploading." From the Tibet protests to the tornado destruction in Atlanta, Georgia, CNN turns to bloggers for play-by-play photo news. As of April 2008, iReport.com stated that 80,532 iReporters exist worldwide, with 1,108 of them on CNN.

Citizen journalism is also paving the way for individual voices to rise to a level of influence that, in some cases, eclipses that of most traditional media. These voices are amplifying and also realizing their effect. Blogs, podcasts, and video blogs are crystallizing into a new breed of media networks and are engaging audiences in an entirely new and immersive way.

Journalist vs. Blogger

With the changes and evolution in the news-reporting process and distribution of influence, largely caused by the socialization of media, we're sure that many people ask or are asked these questions:

- What's the difference between a journalist and a blogger?

- Is a blogger a journalist?

- Is a journalist a blogger?

- Are bloggers really that important to our communications program?

Many have not yet found consistent answers; after all, they are a bit elusive. Although you might think the questions should be simple to answer, ask anyone these questions and you'll quickly find that the conversation usually spins down a maze of confusing avenues. We answer these questions later in this chapter, but first you need a little background to set the stage.

When we were in school, there were journalism and PR/communications programs, as there are today. Whether you were aspiring to be a newspaper or magazine writer or a PR professional, this was your given course. Deirdre remembers having to write several news releases in Associated Press (AP) style for her journalism classes. Her professor made her class read the *AP Stylebook* from cover to cover and then tested the entire class on every little detail, from grammar, punctuation, and spelling to how to use surnames and titles appropriately. She still has that book in her office today, as does coauthor Brian.

This same type of writing carried forward into our careers with the drafting of the inverted pyramid style of news release and other types of PR writing, including byline articles, case studies, PR plans, and whitepapers. The *AP Stylebook* was our bible, and we carried it everywhere. We were told that journalists worldwide accepted the guidelines in the *AP Stylebook* and that if we wanted to get our news releases and articles published, we must always strictly abide by its rules and never deviate.

Journalists were also classically trained in how to research, interview, write, and fact-check stories. If we learned anything in school (and also experienced during the early years of our careers), it was that journalists have earned their rights to be called journalists based on intense education and the strict ethical guidelines they follow in the reporting process. The Society of Professional Journalists (SPJ) Code of Ethics[1] has ethical standards for journalists to ensure that they:

- Test the accuracy of information from all sources and exercise care to avoid inadvertent error. Deliberate distortion is never permissible.

- Diligently seek out subjects of news stories to give them the opportunity to respond to allegations of wrongdoing.

- Identify sources whenever feasible. The public is entitled to as much information as possible on sources' reliability.

- Always question sources' motives before promising anonymity. Clarify conditions attached to any promise made in exchange for information. Keep promises.

- Make certain that headlines, news teases, and promotional material, photos, video, audio, graphics, sound bites, and quotations do not misrepresent. They should not oversimplify or highlight incidents out of context.

- Never distort the content of news photos or video. Image enhancement for technical clarity is always permissible. Label montages and photo illustrations.

- Avoid misleading reenactments or staged news events. If reenactment is necessary to tell a story, label it.

- Avoid undercover or other surreptitious methods of gathering information except when traditional open methods will not yield information vital to the public. Use of such methods should be explained as part of the story.

[1] SPJ Code of Ethics, April 2008, www.spj.org/ethicscode.asp.

- Never plagiarize.

- Tell the story of the diversity and magnitude of the human experience boldly, even when it is unpopular to do so.

- Examine their own cultural values and avoid imposing those values on others.

- Avoid stereotyping by race, gender, age, religion, ethnicity, geography, sexual orientation, disability, physical appearance, or social status.

- Support the open exchange of views, even views they find repugnant.

- Give voice to the voiceless; official and unofficial sources of information can be equally valid.

- Distinguish between advocacy and news reporting. Analysis and commentary should be labeled and not misrepresent fact or context.

- Distinguish news from advertising and shun hybrids that blur the lines between the two.

- Recognize a special obligation to ensure that the public's business is conducted in the open and that government records are open to inspection.

Although the *AP Stylebook* is still updated today and, according to Wikipedia, is "a style and usage guide used on newspapers and in journalism classes in the United States," writing has significantly changed between the days of traditional journalism and the concept of new journalism and Social Media. The writing styles and forums of new journalism are definitely different, and information is exchanged and shared more expeditiously, with more individual flair, enthusiasm, and passion. It's personal, and when it's personal, it takes a different voice than what we're used to reading. Contrary to the standard AP style of writing, Social Media is encouraging a more conversational tone, and it's affecting everything from blog posts to online articles, to news releases.

Blogosphere Rising

A dramatic shift is taking place in which blogs are increasing and traditional media networks are thinning. This isn't just our opinion; it's a reflection of where advertising dollars are flowing.

The Newspaper Association of America released figures in Q1 of 2008 that show an accelerating decline of newspapers, with total 2007 print advertising revenue tumbling 9.4 percent to $42 billion, compared to 2006. This is the most substantial drop in revenue since 1950 when the industry started tracking annual revenue. Online advertising for traditional media networks actually grew from 18.8 percent to $3.2 billion, compared to 2006. However, that's significantly lower than the 31.4 percent growth the year before and isn't close to replenishing the losses from print advertising. Online advertising revenue currently represents 7.5 percent of total newspaper ad revenues.

The current mantra driving the Social Media revolution is this: If the news is important, it will find me. It's an arrogant statement, but it isn't incorrect. With feeds, alerts, instant messages, social networks (Facebook, MySpace, and bebo), micromedia (Twitter, and tumblr), and activity streams (friendfeed and chi.mp), information is actually finding people directly and, in many cases, before they can find it on their own. Blogs and new media networks and communities are competing for your attention, indirectly and directly.

Yes, blogs are more than ranting diaries—a common misperception and underestimation, yet a popular assessment of anything written online by a citizen. According to Technorati, a popular online directory for blogs and their rankings, 112.8 million blogs and more than 250 million pieces of tagged Social Media exist. These blogs cover everything from technology, fashion, and entertainment to sports, lifestyle, business, and everything in between. The World "Live" Web encourages bloggers to link and comment on other blogs, and it encourages readers to also participate through comments, referrals, and, perhaps, blogging—creating online conversations and threads that actively power Social Media 24/7.

The reality is that blogs offer some of the most honest and hands-on information, insight, and advice, and usually deliver it quicker than many traditional media sources. We can say emphatically that you need to invest your time in reading blogs and participate in Web communities that are important to you both personally and professionally. You will gain invaluable perspective, and it won't take long until you feel compelled to contribute your own two cents.

Blogs can make a difference in your life. Identify people who can provide valuable information, and engage them in enjoyable, rewarding, and mutually insightful conversations along the way.

It's Not Just for Kids Anymore

Bloggers have earned the title of "citizen journalists" whether we like it or not. But you'll quickly come to refer to them as bloggers or even influencers. The barrier to entry has been lowered so dramatically that anyone can share thoughts, ideas, opinions, observations, and arguments. The capability to create and publish content is so great that content creators have become media contributors, not just consumers. Therefore, blogs, camera phones, tags, pages on social networks, and so on have become part of the citizen media movement with undeniable force. Savvy marketers are creating specialized campaigns that reach not only traditional media, but citizen media, or bloggers, too. In PR, this is commonly referred to as blogger relations or influencer relations. And we're happy to report that citizen journalists, and even journalists-turned-bloggers, can now deviate from the traditional style of journalistic writing to accommodate the communication of PR 2.0 and New PR.

For example, Erick Schonfeld left Time Inc.-owned *Business 2.0* for a blog. But he didn't leave for just any blog. He left for one of the biggest in the world: TechCrunch. He recently hit a posting milestone (600) and published his thoughts on the collision of journalism and blogging. Here's an excerpt from "Six Months in and 600 Posts Later ... The Worlds of Blogging and Journalism Collide (in My Brain)."

For me, blogging and journalism began to blur long ago. I took over the *Business 2.0* blog (which became the Next Net) from Damon Darlin, now technology editor at the *New York Times*. That was back in May 2005, one month before Michael Arrington started TechCrunch—which just goes to show that Michael and I have been on the same wavelength from the start. Of course, back then, he took blogging much more seriously than I did.

At *Business 2.0,* my blog was always a side project—although it grew to 50,000 feed subscribers. I was paid to write, package, and orchestrate articles for the print magazine—in addition to other sidelines, which included organizing mini-conferences and dabbling in Web video. Eventually, blogging became more important to the magazine—all writers and editors had to start one. But it could never quite shake that extracurricular tinge.

Working at TechCrunch is a completely different experience. For one thing, I no longer write long-form, narrative journalism. There is not much time for storytelling (except for weekend posts like this one). It is mostly breaking news, reporting facts, and providing analysis. At TechCrunch, I am completely focused on blogging, 24/7. With a few exceptions, no single post is very difficult to write (unlike an in-depth magazine article that can require 50 interviews and weeks of travel, for instance). But taken as a whole, blogging is actually harder. That is because the blogging never stops. Just ask my wife and kids, who now mock me by repeating back my new mantra: "I'm almost done, just one more post."

Putting out TechCrunch is like riding a bullet train. When I jumped aboard, it was already going 150 miles per hour. Six months ago, the main TechCrunch site was attracting about two million visitors a month and it was ranked No. 4 on the Technorati 100 list of the most linked-to blogs. Today, six months later, we are within spitting distance of three million visitors a month (2.9 million, to be exact), and last week we overtook Engadget for the first time to reach the No. 1 spot on the Technorati 100. (We'll see how long that lasts, the Huffington Post is right on our tail).

So what is the TechCrunch formula? It is hard to say other than obsession. The main TechCrunch blog is written by four of us—Michael, Duncan, Mark, and me. (When I began, there were five, but Nick Gonzalez decided to opt for the comparatively saner hours of a startup.) Despite our small size, we are a global organization. When not traveling, Michael and Mark write from California, Duncan writes from Australia, and I write from

New York. Somebody is always online—often all of us. Michael literally never sleeps. It is really unhealthy.

What we do at TechCrunch is actually pretty simple. We write about Web startups and the larger tech companies that try to either copy or acquire them. Depending on the day, I could be liveblogging the launch of the Amazon Kindle, arguing about free speech in the Internet age, uncovering secret projects at Google, giving Yahoo! unsolicited acquisition advice, or writing about a hot new startup.

There is always something else to write about, and not enough time to cover it. But we live or die by how fast we can post after a story breaks, if we can't break it ourselves. We hardly have time to proofread our posts, as anyone who's come across one of the frequent typos in TechCrunch knows. Luckily, our readers love to point out our mistakes in comments. They are our copy editors and fact checkers. (We love you guys.) Our philosophy is that it is better to get 70 percent of a story up fast and get the basic facts right than to wait another hour (or a day) to get the remaining 30 percent. We can always update the post or do another one as new information comes in. More often than not, putting up partial information is what leads us to the truth—a source contacts us with more details or adds them directly into comments.

Some people question whether TechCrunch is even a blog anymore rather than a professional media site. But that distinction is becoming increasingly meaningless. The truth is that we are both. We compete with traditional news organizations, but with a small fraction of their staff. That is our competitive advantage. We certainly cover the news and do original reporting, but we also discuss news reported by others and are not shy about voicing our personal opinions. We are as much a filter as a source.

There is something about blogging—the immediacy, the give and take, the point of view—that helps it compete with traditional media for attention. And we don't want to lose that. We like to speculate, argue, and debate—sometimes in ways that traditional journalists may think is unseemly. That's okay, as long as our readers keep coming back for more.

Because what is a blog? It is a conversation with readers. And you don't have to start a conversation knowing all the facts. But it helps if you end up with more than you start out with, and if you turn out to be right more often than wrong. Otherwise, people will stop listening to you—the same as they would with any media source.

To refresh your memory, not only are we providing you with the background on the rise of Social Media and citizen journalism, but we are also pointing out the differences between bloggers and journalists.

- What's the difference between a journalist and a blogger?
- Is a blogger a journalist?
- Is a journalist a blogger?

We're still on the road to helping you discern the differences and values of each, so let's continue.

Number Crunching

Many bloggers are now privy to valuable information that was once the sole domain of traditional news media. That access, combined with the ability to instantly publish information, means bloggers are scooping reporters more often than not. Let's be fair, though. As we pointed out at the beginning of this chapter, the best journalists are in a completely differently league than most bloggers. They're trained in the art and science of journalism, they adhere to values and ethics that bloggers are only starting to think about, and they understand the differences between fact and opinion and the value of sources and fact checking. Although many journalists have successfully crossed over to blogging, citizen media has blindsided newspapers, magazines, broadcast journalists, and the parent media companies and networks, causing them to lose mindshare.

Several services track the top blogs and the Web metrics for each. Technorati, for example, lists the top blogs by analyzing and measuring the inbound links to any given blog and produces a ranking based on authority.

Other services, such as Compete.com and Alexa, provide analytics and rankings based on traffic. Many other free tools exist, too. However you measure things, the top blogs are outperforming many traditional media outlets, receiving millions of readers on any given day.

So who are the top blogs? According to Technorati, the top 10 blogs as of March 2008 are as follows:

1. **TechCrunch**—A blog covering Web 2.0 startups

2. **Huffington Post**—The Internet Newspaper

3. **Engadget**—Gadgets and consumer electronics news

4. **Gizmodo**—Gadgets and consumer electronics news

5. **Boing Boing**—A directory of wonderful things

6. **Lifehacker**—Tech tricks and tips for getting things done

7. **ARS Technica**—The art of technology

8. **Mashable**—Coverage of social networks

9. **icanhascheezburger.com**—A playful community that spotlights the Internet phenomenon of LOLcats

10. **Daily Kos: State of the Nation**—Political analysis on U.S. current events.

Notable blogs close to cracking the top ten list include these:

- **ReadWriteWeb**—Technology news, reviews, and analysis
- **TMZ**—Celebrity gossip
- **ProBlogger**—Blogging advice, tips, and tricks
- **Perez Hilton**—Celebrity gossip

The current number one blog, TechCrunch, is a quintessential example of citizen journalism. Michael Arrington started the blog only a few years ago. He is a lawyer and also a start-up founder. He's not a classically trained journalist, but he has proven that "we" can earn a significant global audience with the right content and mindset. And, TechCrunch is now syndicated by the *Washington Post* online. Many other top tech blogs have also signed distribution deals with top media brands.

Do Unto Others

With the rapid rise of blogs, calls for standards and reform are firing in from the journalism industry, as well as the people, companies, and brands affected by sloppy, overly opinionated, misleading, hostile, biased, motivated, or incentivized blog posts.

We look at the blogosphere as an area with dynamic communication that stumbles and also thrives. Many believe that just as journalists are held to a code of ethics, bloggers should be held accountable and responsible for their content. This is an incredibly delicate and controversial topic because the fuel that powers the continued evolution of Social Media is the raw and untamed voices of people. Some bloggers do intentionally adhere to best practices and ethics as a way of building their community of readers and partners. However, standards and ethics are currently embraced on an individualized basis because a standards body does not exist; therefore, no one is governing the blogosphere.

Charlene Li, a social computing analyst and consultant covering the social Web, began discussing a blogging code of ethics in 2004 on Forrester's Groundswell blog. A sample "Blogger Code of Ethics" included the following points:

I will tell the truth.

I will write deliberately and with accuracy.

I will acknowledge and correct mistakes promptly.

I will preserve the original post, using notations to show where I have made changes, so as to maintain the integrity of my publishing.

I will never delete a post.

I will not delete comments unless they are spam or off-topic.

I will reply to emails and comments when appropriate, and do so promptly.

I will strive for high quality with every post—including basic spellchecking.

I will stay on topic.

I will disagree with other opinions respectfully.

I will link to online references and original source materials directly.

I will disclose conflicts of interest.

I will keep private issues and topics private, since discussing private issues would jeopardize my personal and work relationships.

Although different from the SPJ's Code of Ethics, it was a great start. The Social Media community also realized that bloggers could assist and learn from each other to help mature the evolution. The Social Media Club, founded in 2006 by Chris Heuer, Kristie Wells, coauthor Brian Solis, and others, offered the first official collection of Social Media practitioners the capability to learn and share best practices. The group has since spawned chapters across the United States and all over the world. In October 2006, the San Francisco chapter, led by Heuer, Wells, and Solis, explored the topic of blogger ethics and disclosure. A post by Heuer set the stage for the discussion, which is still relevant today.

Talking About Disclosure: A Social Media Club Roundtable

I think about disclosure or talk about it with someone almost every day. Often it is in regards to whether or not I am able to disclose something because it has to do with advice I am giving clients, which happens all the time if you write about the field in which you work. If I am *able* to do so, then the question becomes whether I *should* write about it. Rather than just thinking about it on my own, I thought it best to organize a conversation among those who care about this issue here in San Francisco. ...

The issue of disclosure came to the forefront recently with the Edelman problems with the Wal-Marting Across America blog and then two other "flogs" that were being written by Edelman employees. The thing is, I did not want people to think I am just calling out the utter failure of the Social Media consultants at Edelman to do the right thing because I work as an independent contractor with Fleishman Hillard, a competing PR agency who used to do Wal-Mart work (I was never involved with that account). Look how much text I had to use to disclose that one portion of my interest in it. Then consider the 20 or so minutes I have spent editing that disclosure to make sure it sounded right, addressed the important points and fit into the story. I have a lot to say on the Edelman story, but so much else has already been said. I think I will be talking about it for a long time to come, because their failure to be transparent and authentic is a huge lesson for corporations which hopefully won't be repeated, but most likely will.

My newfound emphasis on the topic of disclosure, however, came from my friend Mike Arrington's little dustup with traditional journalists at the Online News Association conference, which Jeff Jarvis writes about here [www.buzzmachine.com] and Mike writes about here [www.crunchnotes. com]. The subsequent post by Nicholas Carr called "A Glass House" [www.roughtype.com] really struck a deep chord with me. I know Mike and I don't believe he is purposely trying to deceive anyone, but he does have a competitive streak and many other interests across the Web 2.0 landscape, which puts him in a precarious position. From my discussions with many people, there are no truly easy ways to make disclosures and there is no standard accepted practices for how to disclose and when to disclose. As I have consulted my clients over the years, it is often the perception of impropriety that is the problem, not the actions themselves. ...

This is why I immediately resolved to do something about it and began to organize a Social Media Club Roundtable called "Talking About Disclosure." What I hope we get from the event is a great discussion about the best practices around disclosure of interests in pursuit of a common understanding of how to properly apply the principles of transparency and authenticity. The conversation has already begun, with great articles written by Jason Calcanis (older but relevant post), Shel Holtz, Matthew Ingram, and Todd Defren. We want to bring that conversation into real time, with a focus on the solution. Also, we want to move from conversation to action, so we are hoping that we can produce a set of guidelines to recommend as best practices for people to use, which will ultimately be a part of the pledge we ask members to make when joining Social Media Club. We also will address WOMMA's lack of action on the Edelman fiasco, which is a point Shel Holtz makes in his post [blog.holtz.com]— though I don't know what we can do differently.

Lisa Stone brought our attention to a post by a former Edelman employee on Blogher [blogher.org] at our workshop yesterday in which Lisa points out some of the key requirements around disclosure that need to be addressed by a blogger.

What kind of commitment should bloggers make to their readers? I'm one of the people who thinks every blog owes its readers four answers, whether the blog is a corporate blog, a news blog, or a personal diary:

1. Who are the bloggers?
2. What are the bloggers doing?
3. Why are the bloggers doing this?
4. Why do I—the reader—care?

The Wal-Mart blog flunks every question. . . .

Don't ever squander the trust you have with your audience by not being completely truthful. The public (aka audience) will revolt if you do, and they will speak up and call you on it. Even though there are a number of a**holes in the world with their personal axes to grind who may attack for the sake of being able to do so, most people won't buy into that crap— particularly if you have continuously proven your trustworthiness over time while building a great relationship with your audience....

The Social Media Club met on October 25, 2006, at CNET's head-quarters, with the following outcome of the initial discussion:

Talking About Disclosure Round Table Recap

Wow! What a great conversation tonight over at CNET's headquarters here in San Francisco—thanks again to Joel Sacks and Rafe Needleman for hosting us there. . . .

As for the meat of the matter, it was quickly clear that the issue of disclosure is one that impacts everyone, and everyone understands its importance in the broader context. When one person makes a bad decision, everyone is impacted so it is an issue that everyone wants to work on together.

There were a few key points that emerged from my perspective:

- I started off the conversation talking about this era needing to embrace the 3 T's (as opposed to the old focus on the 3 C's— content, contact, community), which are Transparency, Truth, and Trust.

- There are a lot of grey areas, so absolute rules are hard to come by here; we should strive for greater understanding of best practices (which is the purpose of Social Media Club).

- Disclosure is somewhat situational in nature and will vary by geography and culture.

- The biggest issue is seemingly one of media literacy among media consumers as much as it is an issue for those producing media.

- Everyone is biased in some way; journalists are not immune as we are all human—bloggers need more appreciation of how they can be influenced.

- We all get free drinks from time to time (including everyone who attended tonight), but that usually is not enough to be bought.

- We need to find a great and easy-to-understand metaphor/story about what is okay and what is not okay.

- We have more to figure out and map than one discussion could allow.

... At the end of the conversation, Mike Arrington made a proposal that:

We begin a dialogue and process that we all agree to adhere to the outcome of in regards to what is the proper, ethical way to handle disclosure—even if it is not the one I want, I will agree to abide by the group's decision. We also need to have a method of resolution for challenges to ethics where the process can begin in private first so that people cannot use such challenges to create controversy and generate increased page views and notoriety through baseless accusations. (paraphrased, not quoted)

... Rafe Needleman (reporter for CNET and the Webware blog) suggested we keep our initial efforts focused, perhaps, just on Technology Bloggers so we can avoid some of those muddier grey areas, and I think he is probably right about that.

This post was written in 2006, and the Blogger Code of Ethics is still in development. If you search "ethics blogosphere" in Google today, you will find that the top results are the conversations that drove the original topic in 2005 and 2006. Not much has changed, and maybe this is because the governing of ethics in the blogosphere won't be mandated by an official body. Perhaps we're learning that society will dictate when something doesn't fly, and it will push back and expose those who do not blog authentically, genuinely, or accurately.

More mistakes will occur. Bloggers who choose to ignore the benefits of ethical standards will earn the attention and support of the community they deserve, as will those who aspire to higher roads.

And Then Some

We escorted you on this little journey behind the evolution of Social Media and the ongoing culmination of the blogosphere, and we also provided you with insight into discussions about the many distinctions when it comes to journalists and bloggers. Now everyone is scrambling for survival and recognition of their "reporting." Those who "get it" are already competing for the future. To answer the questions we posed at the beginning of the chapter:

- Journalists who blog are bloggers, unless they are held to the journalistic ethics of a given media property. For example, *USAToday* has adopted a Social Media platform, opening up reporters to their audiences and enabling conversations between readers and authors, and among readers, too. In this case, they are both journalists and bloggers.

- If journalists write online without integrated Social Media elements such as comments, trackbacks, and so forth, they are still traditional journalists.

- Citizen journalists who blog and share content via Social Media are not journalists; they are usually classified as bloggers.

However, the most important gem is that traditional journalists will embrace the socialization of information. Media networks are learning from the value of citizen journalism, not just from a technology infrastructure, but more from a conversational format. It's not just the value from the original article or the post; it's the dynamic, "the magic," that happens in the comments section that is a reflection of the enthusiasm and passion of the community, especially when the author also joins in the dialogue. The value of Social Media is also demonstrated in the extendibility of online conversations across the blogosphere and the related threads that connect people and thoughts around the world.

Social media is a powerful medium and is inspiring the evolution of journalism and communications. Whether you're a journalist, a blogger, or a PR professional, participation is marketing, and it is the foundation for building and sustaining meaningful and valuable relationships. A bright future is emerging for the citizen journalists who learn ethics and gain the accepted credibility they desire. And journalists who embrace blogging will discover that twenty-first-century reporting offers them the incredible potential to provide even more exclusive information for audiences that will look to them for the most current news, information, and trusted opinions. And, most importantly, they have the potential to build a community around hosted content and shared ideas.

We're also seeing an evolution at the scholastic level. Many universities are starting programs and encouraging instructors to embrace Social Media, teaching students everything from the art of blogging and producing online content to how to engage bloggers and online media.

As an industry, we're maturing. We're starting to "get it" collectively. We produce content. We digest content. We also share content. Social media empowers everyone, and it doesn't discriminate. Journalists versus bloggers is no longer the argument we should spotlight. The new discussions will be how we embrace Social Media to improve the quality, the reach, and the conversations around the topics that matter to us.

Chapter 5

PR Is about Relationships

In the realm of Social Media, conversation is king, and only active engagement and listening can lead to meaningful relationships. This is the new era of influence, and you have the tools and channels to emerge as a new influencer. PR 2.0 is rooted in democratized content, strengthened by enthusiasm and market intelligence, and powered by conversations.

As much as we talk about how to participate in Social Media or PR 2.0, it's meaningless if you don't take a few steps back to remember that, regardless of the technology, beneficial conversations are about trust, respect, mutual benefits, and positive experiences. We also can't stress enough that the most rewarding dialogue has always been one-to-one rather than one-to-many (a.k.a. spam or broadcast PR). Spam is taboo, and for us the terms *spam* and *Public Relations* don't belong in the same sentence—but unfortunately, they usually are these days.

People Need People

PR, as we know it, is usually associated with the process of creating messaging, distributing it via wire services such as PR Newswire, BusinessWire, or Marketwire, and sending messages to "beat" reporters and analysts via e-mail (usually generated via a list service). And although one-to-one relationships still exist with key influencers, those relationships don't scale in a way that encourages PR professionals to spend the time necessary to embrace those who aren't "A-listers." Psychologically, it's the same in almost every organization. If you invest in one-on-one relationships—meaning you call or meet your influential contacts directly—it's because you feel you *need* to. And if your relationships are solid, you feel confident that you can leverage them when needed. You also do things differently for them (for example, taking the time to prepare the story in a way that matters) because you don't want to lose the relationship. However, we don't see this across the board.

Although you should make things personal, you might not because you perceive the less-influential voices as, well, less valuable. So you decide to send them information in the hopes that they'll receive it and publish it because you took the time to send it to them. Unfortunately, things just don't work that mechanically. Reporters, regardless of their authority, are inundated with messages from hopeful PR types who believe that their news is "newsworthy." There's just not enough time in the day to cover, let alone respond to, every inbound request.

And now you have the realm of Social Media, in which user-generated content is becoming influential in its own right and, in many cases, more significant than many traditional reporters' messages. So if reporters who are classically trained in the art and science of journalism are already experiencing fatigue and intolerance, how do you expect to integrate PR 2.0 philosophies and tactics to reach people directly? After all, these are the last people who want to be showered with superlatives and hyperbole. They want things that matter to them because that's what helps them in some way. PR 2.0 is about becoming the resource and "go-to" organization because you understand that you're not really a PR or marketing person all the time—you're a human being with interests, needs, questions, and aspirations just like the next person. PR 2.0 is about people to people and long- and short-term relationships. You must realize that the metrics for transforming one person into an evangelist far outweigh the resources required to repeatedly throw spaghetti on the wall in hopes that it just might stick.

That's an almost overwhelming sense of responsibility and transformation required for most people. But that's why you're here. Reporters and analysts are at one end of the media landscape and A-list bloggers (regardless of industry and marketplace) are at the other. The "magic middle" of the blogosphere is the disparate group of underlying influencers who truly represent the people who talk to your customers. When they blog, they don't individually send an immeasurable or insurmountable volume of traffic or cascades of riches. However, the magic middle collectively forms the foundation of long-term customers who are looking for specific solutions. This is what's described as the Long Tail of niche markets, as documented by Chris Anderson, editor-in-chief of *Wired* magazine and author of *The Long Tail*.

You also have people who might be both generators and great democ-ratizers of content. Many of these individuals represent the magic middle and also carry to the right of the bell curve. These folks represent your tar-get demographic at every stage of market adoption. PR 2.0 recognizes each unique congregation, whether they're edglings, early adopters, mass market, late-market majority, or laggards. People now have access to Social Media to share their insight, and they're recognized for it.

PR 2.0 = New Relationship Strategies

New PR understands its importance in the grand scheme of influence, sales, service, and evangelism to fold these necessary and valuable contacts into our relationship strategies. One-to-one PR is a completely different game from what we're used to playing. We're usually measured by the hits we generate rather than the relationships we forge—and the value each has to the corporate bottom line. Instead of just targeting a person individually, perhaps through e-mail instead of a mass blast, you need to investigate that individual's preferred form of communication, his or her likes and dislikes, and, most important, the topics that individual usually covers and why these subjects matter. As a communications professional, you should be familiar with how to gather this type of information—how to do your "homework" on each contact, similar to what you would do in your traditional media relations work. It's no different with PR 2.0.

Remember, the genuine conversations that we are discussing can also be a form of strategic marketing without it being a marketing initiative in itself. You can't expect to speak through messages using a news release to people who are willing to listen patiently every time. As Chris Heuer says, "It's not conversational marketing, though. It's not something we do *to* people. It's what we do *with* people." Heuer is absolutely correct, and we couldn't agree more.

For example, the micro blog Twitter (www.twitter.com) is one of the most powerful conversation tools among early adopters (a.k.a. edglings). A blurb from "David Carr Is Lost in a Dream of Yesterday" (March 2008) on Stowe Boyd's blog (www.stoweboyd.com) describes a little about the edglings:

The people formerly known as the audience, we, the edglings, have decided that the newspapers (and other old school media) are not going to manage the news hole for us. We want to decide how many inches to apply to McCain and Obama today, or how many inches to use for the NCAA finals. The formulas and incantations of newspaper people have less and less meaning, here, on the Web.

A-list tech blogger Robert Scoble recently publicly posted his frustration with e-mail on Twitter, requesting that people (especially those in PR) pay attention to his ideal methods of contact. Scoble also asked PR people to examine other tools and creative approaches to catch his attention. Scoble wrote, "It's amazing that in this age of Twitter that people still send email. I hate email. I hate direct Tweets. I hate Facebook messages." He then immediately followed with, "PR people are the worst in the email regard. Speaker planners are close. I don't answer a lot of my email anymore."

First Impressions

The line that resonated most with us was Scoble's view of PR people: If they were forced to do their work in public, their entire method would change. Scoble's words are a strong reinforcement for PR people to consider the best way to start the relationship. That means understanding how busy, influential people want to engage in conversation. He's absolutely right. For too long, PR operated behind the curtain, hurling over news bits in waves instead of focusing on individual conversations. Social Media and user-generated influence change the very foundation on which PR is built, forcing communications professionals to step from behind the curtain to engage with the people they're trying to reach.

The beauty of communicating through certain forms of micromedia (tools such as Twitter, Seesmic, Utterz, Jott, Pinger, YouTube, Flickr video, and so on) is that your content is intentionally and forcibly truncated. For example, with Twitter—a tool for sharing short updates with friends and followers—you are forced to summarize your story in 140 characters at a time. (Just to give you perspective, the preceding sentence is 155 characters, counting spaces, or 27 words.) Some communicators can't cut down a 700-word news release, let alone edit their message down to a fixed (low) number of characters.

Many of you might not be able (yet) to imagine developing strong, meaningful messages in 140 characters or less. But even if you take Twitter out of the equation and replace it with Jaiku or even Facebook, all these social networking platforms share a preference for brevity. If you can summarize your story in a way that's compelling and specific to the audience, you can do it across the board, regardless of limitations or platform. The practice is invaluable because it helps you condense your story into a value-focused package that is specific to your targets, without insulting the public along the way. This is how you put the *public* back in Public Relations and truly start to push forward a 100-year-old industry that has persevered without resistance until now. This is how you truly communicate with the right people, at the right time, in the right way: with meaningful information that they require, understanding that influencers might be traditional reporters or analysts, bloggers, and other people who happen to represent the communities you want to reach.

To help you understand Scoble's concern about the best way for people to reach him, we have included highlights from his conversation on Twitter. Normally, Twitter conversations start from the bottom of the dialog and work their way up. The conversation includes tweets from:

- **Kami Huyse,** APR, the principal of My PR Pro. She frequently writes about Public Relations and communications. Her background is in crisis communication and reputation management, executing Social Media campaigns, conducting focus group research, and media relations.

- **Francine Hardaway,** a PR veteran and principal at Stealthmode Partners. She is an avid pundit and user of social tools and an exceptionally riveting blogger on the subject of Social Media, politics, and tech.

- **Todd Defren,** a principal at Shift Communications, a $10 million firm with offices in San Francisco and Boston. He is best known for his founding of the Social Media news release. He also debuted a Social Media newsroom template in 2007.

- **Robert Scoble,** a well-known blogger (if not the most famous) and technology evangelist, and the co-author of *Naked Conversations: How Blogs Are Changing the Way Businesses Talk with Customers.* He is also recognized globally for his blog, Scobleizer, which came to fruition during his tenure at Microsoft. He currently works as a video blogger for *Fast Company.*

- **Chris Brogan,** who advises businesses, organizations, and individuals on how to use Social Media and social networks to build relationships and deliver value.

- **Rick Mahn,** an independent IT infrastructure and services consultant, and an avid tech and Social Media blogger.

- **David Parmet,** a Public Relations professional since the early 1990s. According to his blog, he does everything from conventional media relations to work with bloggers and other Social Media denizens, business development, and strategic planning.

Scobleizer: @webword: Mike Arrington is a hard guy to get a hold of, especially when he's digging through 100 new hot companies. But he watches Twitter.

Scobleizer: @tildesley: the best way to get ahold of me? Blog comments. Twitter. Pownce. Kyte. Facebook. Phone (my number is always public).

Kamichat: @Scobleizer: How long before your tweets become spam? Already I have rejected some followers due to their highly spammy tweetstream

Scobleizer: @hardaway: Facebook messages are still private. I answer my public "wall" posts first. Public first, private second. That way I get scale

Hardaway: @Scobleizer: Thanks for letting us know the communications protocol for this week :-) Two weeks ago it *was* Facebook messages.

Rickmahn: @Scobleizer: Thanks for an idea for a blog post! I love twitter. TDefren: @Scobleizer, @davidparmet Lack of transparency is a shield for crappy PR.

Davidparmet: @Scobleizer: We're (pr peeps) aren't all that bad....
Chrisbrogan: @Scobleizer: agreed in the "get in contact" mode. What about the "more details" mode? What do you prefer for "payload"?

TDefren: @Scobleizer: Agreed that PR benefits from transparency: outs the bad PR, ensures only hi-quality stuff filters thru. But r u bleeding edge?

Scobleizer: If I want to get a hold of Mike Arrington, for instance, I know that writing a Tweet about him will get his attention far faster than email.

Scobleizer: Or people asking me to blog. Very low quality stuff. If PR people were forced to do their work in public their entire method would change.

Scobleizer: If something really needs to be private than email is great. But most of my email doesn't need to be private.

Scobleizer: I always answer things in public space first. Why? Because those communications scale.

Scobleizer: PR people are the worst in the email regard. Speaker planners are close. I don't answer a lot of my email anymore. If I did, I'd never do.

Scobleizer: It's amazing that in this age of Twitter that people still send email. I hate email. I hate direct Tweets. I hate Facebook messages.

What you just read *is* the conversation, and it's taking place with or without you. Scoble's discussion with his followers is an example of how you can ask a direct question that will lead to honest answers from your peers. These types of "tweets," or public messages, enable the transparency necessary in a blog, micromedia, or any social network or community that makes people adhere to the rules in the community. Scoble provided excellent information for PR people who want to build relationships with him and get prompt answers. If you listen to the conversations and follow the rules of engagement, the relationship will grow from there. In this instance, it's clear how Scoble and Defren felt about contact with PR people and how lack of transparency leads to "crappy PR."

The most important lessons here are that you should:

1. Pay attention to the wants and needs of the media and citizen journalists.

2. Shift your daily routine to observe those who matter to the brand that you represent as it will evolve.

3. Determine the preferred method of contact for each.

As a PR professional, you can no longer rely on the databases to which your PR teams subscribe and the profiles and preferences they purport. You're not in the broadcast spam or mailmerge business. You're talking, reading, and listening to the very people you want to reach, whether they're bloggers, reporters, pundits, or customers. You need to watch and listen to the people with whom you want to interact. If you want to reach people, you need to figure out what they want to see and where and how they want to see it. And you must be intelligent, informed, and genuine in your approach. If you want to see a positive reaction, show that you did your homework.

This is Social Media, which means that every aspect of media, from creation to reading, to sharing, is *social.* And, as in any social setting, you must observe and respect the community you want to join and contribute to. In many ways, you become a sociologist and market expert so that you can not only observe, appreciate, and understand how to immerse yourself in a community, but also intelligently participate in the ongoing conversations that matter to you. *This is a shift from pitching to participating, from selling a story to telling a story.*

This is how you build relationships. As mentioned earlier in this book, PR 2.0 requires PR professionals to participate in the communities they seek to influence and learn from. In fact, participation is the foundation to establishing a relationship with any community. However, old-school PR practitioners often find it difficult to initiate such participation, and some want to reject the concept itself. We refer to this as cultural voyeurism. Marketing and PR professionals are reluctant to engage in the conversations for many reasons, usually because they don't know how, don't believe they need to, or they are not empowered to do so. If you don't engage, you can't get to the reward—the relationships that build great alliances, support strong communication, and take brands to new levels of awareness.

Relationships Trump Tools

About a year ago, Brian wrote an article titled "Social Media Is about Sociology and Not Technology." The recognition of people versus the tools is more critical than ever. Many people understand and present existing and emerging social tools for us to use as mechanisms for "engaging" in "conversations." And although we've said that participation is marketing, let's add another level to that statement: Informed, mutually beneficial, and genuine participation inspires relationship building.

However, many purported Social Media experts and communications professionals are merely engaging in cultural voyeurism, at best. They look from afar and roam the perimeters of online societies without ever becoming a true member of any society. This means they don't really understand what, where, or why they're "participating." Instead, they are "jumping in" only because they have something to say and have access to the tools that will carry it into play. Unfortunately, this is a representation of the greater landscape of Social Media marketing. To keep communities intact and unaffected by outsiders, it's time to reevaluate and study the sociology of Social Media.

The future of communications requires the consideration of sociological principles when integrating Social Media into the marketing chemistry. This is one of the most important points where you simply need to stop and think about things. As in all marketing, the most effective campaigns start with listening, reading, watching, and observing. In the world of Social Media, this is not an option. It's dependent on sociology and the study of people and cultures online before you even think about engaging them in conversation.

"Listening" is the key to engagement in Social Media, and sociology refers to it as *observation*. By observing, either directly or virtually, you become a social scientist so that you can feed back intelligence and insight into the marketing loop. We consider two basic types of observations:

1. **Unobtrusive**—The observer is detached and does not take an active part in the situation:

   - *Observer as participant*—The observer's role as a researcher is known to the community, and the observer participant interacts with the participants but makes no pretense of being a "real" participant.

   - *Complete observer*—The observer hides his true identity, but participates without divulging his intentions.

2. **Participant**—The observer joins a group and studies it as an inside member:

   - *Complete*—The observer hides her identity. This type of observation can raise concerns, including what some view as ethical dilemmas. The most common concern is that observations might become compromised because the complete observer participant is more likely to become sympathetic and lose objectivity.

   - *Participant as observer*—The observer does not hide his identity and is truthful about his goals and objectives.

In most Social Media marketing initiatives we have observed (whether we were asked to assess a company's program specifically or just watch a very public campaign as a "student"), we haven't seen much more than the "latest and greatest" tools that can get them in front of bubbling and active social networks and communities. This is the equivalent of setting up camp next to a village just because you can (that is, just because you have the tools to do so) and expecting the village to integrate you into its society. It just doesn't work that way.

Sociology provides you with an understanding of how social forces shape individual attitudes and behavior. Sociologists study society and social action by examining the groups and social institutions people form. In Social Media, these communities take the form of social networks and the communal groups within them. People form their associations, friendships, and allegiances around content, objects, products, services, and ideas. How they communicate is simply subject to the tools and

networks that people adopt based on the influence of their social graph—
and the culture within.

Sociologists also study the social interactions of people and groups,
trace the origin and growth of social processes, and analyze the influence
of group activities on individual members and vice versa. The basic goal
of sociological research is to understand the social world in its many
forms. Social Media, and marketing in general, can only benefit from
intelligence. And at the very least, it removes the risk of "marketing at"
people and instead naturally shapes a more honest, intelligent, and
informative approach.

Quantitative and qualitative methods represent two main types of sociological research:

- Quantitative methods, such as social statistics and network analysis, investigate the structure of a social process or describe patterns
  in social relationships.

- Qualitative methods, including focused interviews, group discussions, and ethnographic methods, reveal social processes.

Social Media is much more than user-generated content. It's driven by
people within the communities where they congregate and communicate.
They create, share, and discover new content. They're building online cultures across online networks and using the social tools that they learn
about every day to stay connected. And the societies that host and facilitate these conversations cultivate a tight, unswerving, and mostly unforgiving community and culture. What traditional marketing and PR
standards might consider harmless activity is completely reset and highly
discouraged in the world of Social Media—driven by the community rule
that proactively strives to flag disingenuous content. For example, if you
try to leave a promotional comment on a blog post as it relates to a competitor, send a marketing message to a topic-focused group on Facebook,
or anonymously defend your brand with "campy" and hollow message-
riddled responses, you'll quickly understand the meaning of *unforgiving*
used earlier in this paragraph.

As Shel Israel, co-author with Scoble of *Naked Conversations,* describes it, people are populating global neighborhoods, and the power is moving from institutions to the people.

Technology is just that: technology. Tools will continue to change as software applications and technological infrastructure advance. Networks will continue to evolve. The number of media through which you can distribute content will grow. Through all this change, however, the people you want to reach likely won't change.

PR 2.0 requires you to realize that the communities you want to reach are more than just "audiences" that you can observe from a distance. You simply *cannot* get answers or run a meaningful Social Media program through cultural voyeurism. Social Media marketing requires observation that will dictate your engagement strategies. In the beginning, you'll use a combination of social and traditional tools to discover, listen, learn, and engage directly with customers to help them—not to market to them. But you should assist them in making decisions and doing things that they couldn't do or didn't know how to do before. Most important, the lessons learned in the field should be fed into the marketing department to create and run more intelligent, experienced, and real-world initiatives across all forms of marketing, PR, sales, and advertising.

PR 2.0 All-Stars Collaborate

Everything starts with information and the empowerment you gain from being informed. Traditional PR practitioners present a story to specific media that reaches prospective customers and work with that media outlet to get a message to an intended audience—hoping that the particular media outlet will be motivated to act in the traditional PR practitioner's interest. However, you're no longer limited to such "butter churn" traditions. Instead, using the principles and practices of PR 2.0, you can also search the blogosphere using tools such as Technorati, Blogged.com, Google BlogSearch, and the blogrolls of other bloggers to identify those citizen journalists (a.k.a. bloggers) who are actively writing stories relevant to your market. These folks might not be journalists.

In fact, they might be your customers and peers who just also happen to blog. However, don't pitch to either reporters or bloggers. Instead, read their earlier work and observe their patterns of coverage to effectively package your story to best fit their preferences. Relationships are built on interaction, and sustainable relationships are always mutually beneficial. Therefore, don't rely on pitching as your only interaction with these precious contacts. Instead, be sure to comment on other articles they have written, offer assistance with other related stories, and even contact them when you don't need something (perhaps just to check in or share ideas, unrelated stories, or updates).

Yes, this is the way it should have been all along. PR 2.0 only opens you up to a new layer of influencers who choose to be contacted in similar ways to their traditional predecessors. So PR 2.0 is a return to basics—placing the *public* back in Public Relations. Remember, however, that this is a necessity: You must put people at the center of your activity. If you don't, the conversations will take place without you. And if you do it wrong, you'll find a very public and prominent backlash against you and the brands you represent.

Social networks are where people communicate directly with each other in the particular online communities in which they congregate. Popular networks include Facebook, Bebo, MySpace, hi5, Ning, Twitter, LinkedIn, Jaiku, and content social networks (such as Flickr for pictures, YouTube for video, Utterz for multimedia, Digg for stories, Delicious for online bookmarks, and BrightKite for location-based networking). Each network has myriad subcultures within it and requires social observation before connecting with the network (and its subcultures) directly. Before jumping in, participate in these networks as a person, not as a marketer. Doing so will enable you to get a sense of the culture through immersion. *Do not,* however, get trapped into cultural voyeurism.

To determine which communities are valuable to you and your brand, search relevant keywords in each of the communities to see where and how they're discussed. This helps you learn where and how to focus your time and activity.

It's time to put aside the pitch and focus on relationships with people—a practice that can bring unprecedented interaction, personalization, and value. The only way to truly succeed with New PR is to become a reliable resource—one of information and knowledge for those who either directly or indirectly affect your brand's bottom line. Relationships will enable you to earn the trust, respect, and online friendships that you desire.

According to Social Media and PR 2.0 marketers, *conversations are markets, and markets are conversations* (and, therefore, the foundation for conversational marketing). Conversations are feeding communities, and communities are markets for relationships. In PR, relationships are the currency required to prosper. For these relations to increase in value over time, they must be cultivated from both sides.

PART **II**

Facilitating Conversations: New Tools and Techniques

Chapter 6

The Language of New PR

You've successfully made it to Part II, and it's now time to integrate PR 2.0 principles into your workflow. As you move forward, make sure that you have the right mind-set and use the proper terminology. For example, you need to understand pitching to an audience versus participating with the people who matter to your story. Because PR 2.0 transforms pitching into conversations, you want to strike *messages, audiences,* and *users* from your PR vocabulary.

The evolution to PR 2.0 requires you to participate at a more informed and human level. You need to see the target markets as the very people whom you want to engage, which requires peeling back the layer known as the "faceless audience" to reveal the people beneath. What we've learned through this process is that our perceived audience isn't captive— or necessarily in the same theater. They populate various groups and communities across multiple landscapes, which requires a heightened sense of observation and significant legwork (getting to them even before you engage in a conversation) to identify and reach them. *They're not users. They don't speak in messages. And they aren't fans of the pitch.*

And So It Begins

It's time to wean yourself away from using the words and practices associated with *pitching messages* to your target *audience* and *users.* These commonly used marketing terms no longer fill the theaters, stadiums, auditoriums, and stores, and aren't appropriate in online communities. The thought of not being able to say these words again, when you refer to groups on the Web, might seem entirely impossible at this point in your career. However, keep an open mind and you will see how PR 2.0 and New Media change the way you need to approach people through your marketing terms, concepts, and overall workflow.

Deirdre has been writing about Internet vocabulary since her first book in 2001, when she advised communications professionals to get up to speed with new terms (at the time), including *broadband, hits, cookies, firewall,* and *FTP.* Years later, after Deirdre published *PR 2.0,* communications professionals have even more unfamiliar terms to learn, including *micromedia, Really Simple Sydication (RSS), wikis, podcasts, mashups,* and so on. But in *Putting the Public Back in Public Relations,* this is the first time we're saying to "lose" certain words, even though they will still exist in their traditional realms.

Four words—*pitch, message, audience,* and *user*—have been a part of your traditional PR strategy and planning. You think about these words at the onset of every campaign. Brands speak in messages as they position themselves in the market, and these messages carry over into every touch point, whether it's a news release, direct-mail piece, corporate video, interview, or keynote speech. You have been targeting those messages for years, directing them at your target audience and users. However, audiences as you knew and referred to them traditionally no longer exist. They're immune to general, mass-targeted, impersonal messages. Web communities evolve and thrive based on those individuals who congregate to share their thoughts and opinions, and receive insight and feedback from others. The new world of Public Relations will focus on developing unique stories for the various groups it hopes to reach and inspire.

Let's explore this idea a bit further. Brian has been in tech PR since 1991, and Deirdre has been practicing PR as a general counsel since 1988. We're both guilty of using the now "forbidden" terminology for a very long time. In Brian's early career, users really were users in the tech business, and when he was researching who they were, they would ultimately become the audience for marketing initiatives. Not everyone (a.k.a. potential customers) was tech savvy at the time, so referring to "people" just didn't cut it. And it was never intended to be naïve or derogatory; it was just a specific and effective category. However, look back at the early 1990s. If you consider the number of groups on the Internet and the way in which people preferred to receive their information, the Web was not the most traveled channel—that didn't happen until the mid-1990s.

Fast-forward to 2008, and now the Internet reaches more than 80 percent of the U.S. population. And users are a series of collective groups of
people across different walks of life. It's no longer about tech. Users are
now the "users" of all products, from home and beauty products, to consumer electronics, to everything imaginable. But please, let's try something different in the era of Social Media. Let's try looking at the people
who could benefit from our story, who are all different in their likes, dislikes, and behaviors.

In Each Seat, a Different Person

As we introduced earlier, there are numerous conversations on the
Internet about these people who are "formerly known as the audience."
Jay Rosen, a professor of journalism at New York University, discusses
this topic in his article "The People Formerly Known as the Audience" on
his journalism blog PressThink.

The People Formerly Known as the Audience

By Jay Rosen

The people formerly known as the audience wish to inform media people of
our existence, and of a shift in power that goes with the platform shift
you've all heard about.

Think of passengers on your ship who got a boat of their own. The writing
readers. The viewers who picked up a camera. The formerly atomized listeners who with modest effort can connect with each other and gain the
means to speak— to the world, as it were.

Now we understand that met with ringing statements like these many
media people want to cry out in the name of reason herself: *If all would
speak who shall be left to listen? Can you at least tell us that?*

The people formerly known as the audience do not believe this problem—
too many speakers!—is our problem. Now for anyone in your circle still
wondering who we are, a formal definition might go like this:

The people formerly known as the audience are those who *were* on the receiving end of a media system that ran one way, in a broadcasting pattern, with high entry fees and a few firms competing to speak very loudly while the rest of the population listened in isolation from one another—and who *today* are not in a situation like that *at all.*

- Once they were your printing presses; now that humble device, the blog, has given the press to us. That's why blogs have been called little First Amendment machines. They extend freedom of the press to more actors.

- Once it was *your* radio station, broadcasting on *your* frequency. Now that brilliant invention, podcasting, gives radio to us. And we have found more uses for it than you did.

- Shooting, editing and distributing video once belonged to you, Big Media. Only you could afford to reach a TV audience built in your own image. Now video is coming into the user's hands, and audience-building by former members of the audience is alive and well on the Web.

- You were once (exclusively) the editors of the news, choosing what ran on the front page. Now we can edit the news, and our choices send items to our own front pages.

- A highly centralized media system had connected people "up" to big social agencies and centers of power but not "across" to each other. Now the horizontal flow, citizen-to-citizen, is as real and consequential as the vertical one.

...You don't own the eyeballs. You don't own the press, which is now divided into pro and amateur zones. You don't control production on the new platform, which isn't one-way. There's a new balance of power between you and us.

The people formerly known as the audience are simply *the public* made realer, less fictional, more able, less predictable. You should welcome that, media people. But whether you do or not we want you to know we're here.

Rosen makes several excellent points to support why the people who frequent Web communities today can't be referred to as the audience of your marketing pasts. Today people are in control as they drive their own communication. Audiences, as you typically knew them, were lumped into general categories. However, with choices so vast, PR in the Long Tail has the ability to reach individuals and influence their behavior—whether it's an opinion, a referral, or a purchase. In addition, the audiences of the past did not typically have access to the power of the press. Now people in Web communities are listening and learning, yet at any given time, they are ready to influence their peers by publishing their own interpretation, insight, opinions, and meaningful information. And finally, the audiences of the past might have craved messages. However, the people formerly known as the audience now control the information they want to consume—when, how, and with whom they want to speak, *sans* the media broadcast mechanism.

Josh Bernoff of Forrester crafted another great post to support the proper use of terminology. He declared, "I'm sick of users.... The more I write and read about social media, the more frustrated I get with the term 'users.'"

I'm Sick of Users

By Josh Bernoff

The more I write and read about social media, the more frustrated I get with the term "users."

When I started in the business twenty-mumble years ago, writing software manuals, people who used software were unusual (and had to be masochists). We spent a lot of time talking about users. The word user was helpful—it helped us to keep in mind that there was a poor slob on the other end of what we were building.

Those times are long gone. We know users are important now. Disappoint them and you lose. So why do we still have to call them "users," which puts the emphasis on the technology they are using?

Yes, I know "users are people, too." But you know what? **All people are users now!** (With nearly 80% Net penetration in the US this is pretty close to true.) Users put up with computers. People just do stuff.

Nobody talks about users of dishwashers, or users of retail stores, or users of telephones. So why are we talking about "users" of computers, browsers, and software?

Try, just for a day, to stop using this word. You'll be amazed at how differently you think about the world.

Web users become people looking for information. Application users become employees trying to get stuff done. Users of your Web site become customers. (Forrester's group focused on usability of Web sites and other technologies is called the Customer Experience Team. I like that.) User-generated media becomes amateur media.

And most importantly, social media users become people connecting with other people. Once you think about it that way it becomes a lot easier to understand. And it focuses you on the relationships, which will always be around, not the technologies, which are always changing.

It's amazing (to me) the clarity this brings to writing, and to thinking. Words matter.

Jimmy Guterman [Guterman is editorial director of O'Reilly's Radar group and the editor of O'Reilly's Release 2.0] took the pledge to stop talking about users at O'Reilly. Way to go, Jimmy.

So now you take the pledge. Right here in the comments section of this blog. Or, on your own blog and link to this.

I promise to avoid the word user whenever possible.

I will think of people who use technology as people, customers, and friends. I won't use them, and they won't use me.

The Web sparked a revolution in PR, which set the stage for an overdue shift in how PR pros approach marketing and talk about it, too. Now, in the dawn of Social Media, PR has no choice but to embrace something it resisted for far too long: transparency and participation, with the full understanding of a New Media approach.

It's not just about consumers. It's also about improving how we reach out to the press and bloggers. More than ever, we must reach them through a more aware and meaningful story that's specific to the people who rely on them for information. Media and citizen journalists are demanding that the impersonal or irrelevant pitches cease. Quite honestly, it's been a long time coming, but now they've even escalated their disdain for bad PR by publicly creating blacklists and publishing the names of PR people who refuse to change their ways. For example, just after *Wired*'s editor, Chris Anderson, made his blacklist of PR people, Gina Trapani of Lifehacker took similar action. According to *PRWeek*'s article on May 14, 2008, Trapani felt several PR pros violated her rules for pitching stories by sending e-mails to her personal e-mail address. When she published her list of PR spammers on a wiki, prspammers.pbwiki. com, Trapani created a firestorm of conversations regarding her public approach.

For many years, this shift has represented a significant challenge to the PR industry. PR professionals have been behind the scenes focusing on strategy and planning, while pushing junior people into the trenches, lobbing "pitches" at target "audiences" and hoping for big hits. Today most daily outreach relies on blasting targets based on lists generated through services such as Cision, formerly MediaMap, among others. It's a game of percentages based on mass e-mail pitches using a customizable form letter so that each e-mail appears to be personalized; and, for the most part, it has satisfied PR's quest for coverage until recently. With a list of 300 targets based on keywords, PR could expect to see 10–20 responses, with a decent conversion to coverage. If reporters didn't want to receive e-mails in the future, they would reply with something as simple as "unsubscribe."

However, PR has slipped into complacency. It has relied on blasting news releases and impersonal pitches to share news and information, when a less-is-more, human, and direct approach is more effective. The pitch as you know it is essentially dead in the Web world. It is intrusive. It is impersonal. It is perilous. To many people, the pitch has become synonymous with spam.

Even when discussing marketing in terms of audiences and users, such terminology implies a one-to-many approach. When you focus on people, it begets a one-to-one communications strategy—as we've emphasized before, shifting from monologue to dialogue. However, it's more powerful than just focusing on individuals. We can expand our focus to reach different groups of people and those gatekeepers who also reach them, linked by common interests.

When you look at groups of people respectively, you're forced to change your migration path to them. Each group is influenced, inspired, and driven by unique channels and communities. Figuring out who you want to reach, why they matter to you, and why you matter to them is the minimum ante required to buy into this game. The next step is to reverse-engineer this process of where they go for their information and discussions to learn how to reach them. And although several horizontal media might overlap, the vertical avenues are dedicated. This is the difference between broadcast PR and a focus on the hubs of influence that directly reach your customers—at a peer-to-peer level.

Yeah, but What's in It for Me?

So while you're deleting words such as *users* and *audience* from your vocabulary, let's also go ahead and eradicate *messages* when discussing customers and people. People are not motivated by messages. They want to hear how you can help them do something better than how they do it today or how this is something that they couldn't do before, taking into specific account their daily regime.

Although participation is marketing and conversations are markets, messages are not conversations and no market exists for them. Furthermore, no audience exists for your message, either. Here's an example of what you shouldn't say when you are looking to engage in dialogue:

> Hi, my name is Brian and I'm an innovative, visionary, and captivating person who is trying to revolutionize the world of communications so that the industry can monitor the evolutionary paradigm shift occurring as the democratization of information and user-generated content spans across the chasm, while riding the cluetrain, influencing early adopters, energizing the market majority, and engaging the global microcommunities that define the Long Tail in this Web 2.0 world.

Ugh. The people who speak this way are not the ones you want to engage in communication, and certainly not the ones who will provide valuable information. So when you are approached with this type of communication, move on—quickly. The bottom line is that after you take the time to listen and read, you're ready to move past the cultural or Social Media voyeurism. A traditional marketing approach is not in your best interest. For instance, when you begin to build your personality profile or brand in different social networking communities, it's highly doubtful that you would say, "What should I write in my profile so that I can convey the right messages to my audience or users?" On the contrary, your profile is an expression of the real you or your "real" brand—the voice of the person or company who reveals a very human side through conversations.

At the end of the day, PR is about people. Yes, it's about Public Relations and not about spam, mass marketing, and impersonal and blind pitches that only dig the entire industry into a deeper hole. As you become a part of a community, you'll quickly realize that there's much to learn about each of the conversations, the information, and the communities you want to reach. You'll often find that you'll change your story based on the insight garnered from simply observing. Clearly, this is the difference between speaking in messages and making your story relevant. When you are truly engaged in dialogue with other community members or speaking with media influencers, you are not thinking about messages that you want to convey; instead, you are more focused on what information you can provide to help someone else.

The forbidden words will appear from time to time, but you now know that you don't have to rely on *pitching messages* to target *audiences* and *users*. Your thinking has evolved beyond these vocabulary words to accommodate your new approach to engaging people on the Web. This entire process is invaluable to the new world of marketing—traditional and Social Media alike. It forces PR to think like a peer or a customer and less like a marketer or a competitor.

As a consumer, you don't make decisions based on *messages*. You consider information that relates to you as a person and as a customer.

The notion that one message compels one audience is also antiquated and dangerous. Again, you don't make decisions based on one source.

Markets are composed of people, and people differ. Although some mainstream channels do reach them, there are also other, more direct avenues of influence and communities where you can engage your customers in conversations (many of which are thriving, courtesy of Social Media and the socialization of information). Research (as mentioned earlier, legwork) can only help.

There is no one tool, one release, or one story that will motivate your customers to take action. It all starts with becoming the person (and different people) you're trying to reach and then reverse-engineering the process. Listen. Read. Learn.

Stop thinking like a "PR" person and start approaching marketing as both a consumer (whether it's B2B or B2C) and a market expert. This is how you demonstrate that what you represent matters to the people and why they should engage in conversations with you. Doing so will change how you see things. It will change how you approach people. It will change how you write news releases. It will change how you distribute and share information. Most important, it will give you the means to engage transparently and genuinely.

The process shift from pitching to conversation-based interaction cultivates relationships, strengthens customer service, and increases brand resonance and loyalty. It's important to humanize the story and become a part of the conversation instead of just trying to sell your way into it.

Chapter 7

Blogger Relations

At this point, you should be feeling more comfortable with the PR changes that we've discussed, and we hope much of this is becoming clearer to you. We're working together to help you not only put the *public* back in Public Relations, but also to inject *personalized* relations into your PR practice.

As a communications professional, you should naturally engage in dialogue and embrace the notion that conversations will lead to information sharing, peer-to-peer exchanges, and better relationships. Unfortunately, a significant percentage of people (whether bloggers, reporters, or analysts) still think that PR professionals are merely spin artists who focus on pitching, blasting, and cranking out poorly written news releases. We recognize the criticism, and we're on the road to change this perception. Contacting people without caring or knowing about their interests and passions, or without knowing what you're talking about or why it should matter to your contacts, should be the furthest thing from your mind. Whether you grew up with PR 1.0 or you're just starting out in PR today, you want to be on the right path to great conversations. The exposure of a few "bad apples" has led to the negative perception of the practice.

We know this goes without saying, but as a friendly reminder, "Don't be that PR person who speaks and who doesn't think about the value or meaning of the communication to the receiving party." Chances are, at one point in your career, you might have directly or indirectly contributed to this stereotype. So it's up to you to do something about it—not just for yourself, but for the betterment of the entire industry.

The New Influencers

New PR brings with it new influencers in addition to the voices who have helped guide consumers and decision makers over the years. Things aren't necessarily getting easier for you in the wake of this evolution.

If anything, these new influencers are challenging the very foundation of PR, forcing you to revisit—and often repair—the process of how you share news and information.

Believe it or not, we still arm-wrestle with influencers and feel the need to defend PR. In many cases, however, they're right. It's not just the process of sharing information in the hope of earning coverage to reach others. It's the very infrastructure of how we carry the information forward. This might have a lot to do with relying on important outreach through people who are either too junior to engage with industry veterans or who are not concerned with educating themselves on why they're reaching out in the first place. Because this is a long-time complaint, we realize the perception exists. It's time to rely on passionate and skilled professionals who know how to communicate, engage, and create dialogue for all the right reasons.

Bloggers Are People, Too

You were trained in PR from day one to abide by the rules of media and analyst relations. In the genre of the new influencer, the addition of blogger relations and the ability to humanize the process of our storytelling will help us succeed in the art of Public Relations. Bloggers are influencers in their own right. Before we delve into this topic deeper, we want you to realize that even though we're talking about blogger relations, you shouldn't forget that you're still reaching out to *people*. This is similar to talking to reporters. It's all based on building, investing in, and cultivating relationships. So similar to media relations, blogger relations are built on respect, understanding, communication, and information (among many other things).

The difference between bloggers and journalists is only the medium they use to reach people. Hold on for one moment. That statement is loaded, and it's definitely worth thinking about it. We know we should say that the difference is a formal education in journalism, experience in the print (or online) business, and circulation through traditional channels. This is why blogging is one of the great disruptors in media. Blogging, at its very foundation, gives a voice to anyone who has an opinion and the capability to access the Web. Generally, the blogosphere is simply powered by regular people, like you, who might be journalists, enthusiasts, pundits, or purely writers looking to share their views.

Blogging Is Not Just Blah, Blah, Blah

Blogging is an important evolution not only in citizen journalism, but in publishing in general. It is so much more than the composition of self-important "ranters" or those merely publishing an online diary. The blogosphere extends far beyond those individuals who simply keep an online presence to satisfy their own egos. Similar to anything that has the capability to connect with and build an audience, blogging is just an online printing press with the inherent capability for others to discover and stay connected to relevant content and the communities that help them thrive. If you overlook the opportunity to build relationships with these people and those who follow them, you're intentionally withdrawing yourself from a vibrant and expanding channel that your customers rely upon for information and guidance.

Opinions Can Be Revolutionary

Do the roots of blogging go as far back as the American Revolution? In the 1700s, pamphleteers published opinions about political issues, sermons, arguments, and essays relating to the history of the period. Whether they were published in newspapers or on single sheets of paper (these were pamphlets that told stories), they took the form of strings of writings that were characteristic of arguments, rebuttals, and even counterarguments.

Sound familiar? The seeds of PR and the importance of sharing an opinion began long ago and today show up in the form of the blog. People who write about and study the pamphleteers equate their personal writings to the style of Web logs, or the blogs that you see today. After all, it's the difference between personal publishing and personal Web sites—the real difference is only the medium of delivery. Technology changes, but people don't. PR and the public opinion of the past are alive and living in the spirit of the blog and in the many bloggers who carry the tradition forward.

As one of the main drivers in the new world of Social Media, blogging has done nothing less than change everything in the PR profession. However, we are still questioned by clients and executives of the companies we represent about why we place such great emphasis and resources on bloggers (in addition to top-tier press). We do so because we realize that blogging can move the needle for companies and brands, boost sales, and also enhance customer service.

Oh No, They Didn't

Examples abound of how companies are using bloggers to successfully reach their customers and gain awareness and consumer interest. Johnson & Johnson (J&J) did just this with their Baby Camp event in April 2008. The objective of Johnson's Baby Camp was to invite about 50 of the most influential mommy bloggers to a three-day retreat to share the latest parenting trends and information. J&J encouraged the attendees to blog about the event, but this was not mandatory. J&J had a full day of activities for the mommy bloggers, from cocktails and gaming to dinner and campfire nightcaps. J&J realized that attracting the attention of the mommy bloggers was critical to the company's future. However, communicating and starting new relationships deserves a different approach and requires a different set of communications rules. For example, J&J quickly learned that its outreach had some fiery backlash. We included a short snippet from Erin Kotecki Vest's (the blogger known as Queen of Spain) blog about the event. (You can find the entire post at http://queenofspainblog.com.) Vest is the Election '08 producer, BlogHer in Second Life producer, and BlogHer's acting project manager for BlogHer.com. She also writes for the Huffington Post and MOMocrats.

So You Want to Talk to Mommybloggers...

BY ERIN KOTECKI VEST

So basically there are these big 'ol corporations who are just salivating to get their money grubbing claws into women online. Oh, wait, I take that back—they are ignoring those of you who are childless, of color, breastfeeding, in need of childcare, lesbian, or anything other than Christian. Which leaves us with what—White. Straight. Jesus-Loving. Breeders.

White, straight, Jesus-loving breeders online *are* a big f*!!?** deal. Apparently we're the only ones who can communicate a message and influence other white, straight, Jesus Loving breeders to buy! buy! buy! buy! At least that's the message I'm getting, you?

It's a damn shame these companies, marketers, PR flacks and social media opportunists don't actually READ the blogs of the Moms they target. They would learn an awful lot in a very short period of time if they did.

They would learn you might not want to ask the Mom with the newborn to ditch the baby and screw that whole breastfeeding thing to come *try their products* for a weekend. They would learn you might not want to ask the *Jewish Mom* to come celebrate Easter or say, attend an event during Passover.

Oy Vey is right….

Yes, this might be an abrasive example of how underestimating bloggers can backfire, but it is also representative of how passionate they are for maintaining the integrity of their community and the sensitivity of the overall art of influencer relations.

Not exactly the write-up that J&J expected, and it immediately put damage control into action. J&J's PR team quickly acknowledged their misjudgments and reached out to the bloggers who complained. J&J also delivered personal apologies as guests arrived at the event. Despite the backlash, J&J's Baby Camp turned out to be a successful event overall that many of the mommy bloggers enjoyed.

Word Spreads

Robert Scoble, considered one of the most influential technology bloggers in the world, blogged about the same event and had these comments to add.

Johnson and Johnson "Breaks Into Jail" with BabyCamp

BY ROBERT SCOBLE

When I worked at Microsoft the PR team had a saying they told me often: "don't break into jail."

In other words, don't screw up a good thing. Or, don't do something that'll get you bad PR.

Which is just what Johnson & Johnson did over the past week.

They are throwing a "BabyCamp" for mommy bloggers. Sounds great, right?

But a couple of problems.

1. You can't bring your baby. Dumb.
2. They scheduled it at the same time as Blogher. Double dumb.
3. They disinvited a couple of bloggers, one who had a baby, and another who was speaking at Blogher. Triple dumb.

Scoble's wife, Maryam, blogged her thoughts about the J&J event, some of which are excerpted here.

Goin' to Camp, Johnson's Baby Camp

BY MARYAM GHAEMMAGHAMI SCOBLE

The event was called "Camp Baby" and they were reaching out to Mommy bloggers most of whom had attended excellent Blogher events and were used to having child care available at the events, and since it was a Johnson & Johnson's event for God's sake, I thought I should and could bring my baby with me. Since there was nothing written about the details of child care, however, and the registration website seemed to be closed off due to the capacity being full, I thought I would research the blogs and see what other moms were doing. That's when I read about one of the mommy bloggers being disinvited because she wanted to take her baby with her. How could you invite a nursing mother to an event about babies and expect her to come sans baby? A company that makes baby products should know their audience better. Johnson was losing a great opportunity to reach out to nursing mothers and in fact was shunning them.

That wasn't the only thing though, another mommy blogger was being disinvited because she couldn't attend the full program as she was speaking at the Blogher conference which happened to be taking place at the same time as Camp Baby. Having the Johnson's event coincide with a very popular mommy blogging event was bad enough, but inviting a speaker from this event and treating her well could have given Johnson an opportunity to expose their company to all the audience at the Blogher event. Instead they were kicking the speaker out of their program. Another clear marketing loss.

Reading these posts made my heart ache for whoever was behind organizing this event. It was clear they had their heart in the right place. They wanted to reach out to mommy bloggers and let them have a great time while giving them an opportunity to try out some of the company's products. It was obvious they had worked very hard to organize this event, but it seemed they had made a couple of mistakes which had backfired in a blazing blogstorm. Being an event planner and having made mistakes in my own time, I wish I could tell them, hey people are much harsher online than they are in person. Just pick up the phone and reach out to them. The key to dealing with bloggers is all about the personal touch. You'll see that they are only human and will be much nicer to you in person. And as my husband had said, this was a great opportunity for any company to show how they can handle a PR crisis, make friends with bloggers by reaching out and learning from their mistakes and come out even stronger.

These examples illustrate how the value of personalization in cultivating relationships counts for everything. Please don't let this scare you away from reaching out to bloggers. But as in anything where people are concerned, we earn the relationships we deserve. In this instance, Maryam gives the best advice, and we, too, agree that J&J had good intentions. And although intention counts, actions speak louder than words. The key to dealing with bloggers is not just to rustle them up and get them to an event for feedback on J&J's products, but to really learn who they are and what matters to them, and to build a solid relationship from there.

Blogging will be the very institution that forces the reinvention of PR. And it's for the better.

Not Every Blog Is Created Equal

Certain bloggers in every market segment have the sheer numbers of followers behind them to not only influence the people you want to reach, but also to drive reporters in traditional media to cover the same topics. *BusinessWeek*, the *New York Times*, *The Wall Street Journal*, *Newsweek*, *Time*, *Forbes*, *Fortune*, and *USA Today*, among many well-respected publications, devote editorial resources to monitoring the blogosphere. Part of the reason is that these publications understand that blog readers are very loyal and enthusiastic. The loyalty shows in the Internet metrics and analysis each month. Although some might not have sizable volume, many smaller communities can pool together to make a big difference.

If you're unfamiliar with the almost immeasurable level of clout that many blogs carry today, they have substantially grown from pockets of disparate musings, personal experiences, enthusiast rants, and editorial opinion pieces to full-blown reporting across every category that you can imagine. You can find influential pundits defining and stimulating activity in every demographic possible. The interconnectivity among bloggers has formed an incredibly powerful network of authority that changes how people find information and make decisions in every facet of life.

Many tools enable you to rank bloggers and determine their authority based on any given subject. You're able to analyze the amount of online traffic using tools such as Compete.com or Alexa.com. You can use referring links via Technorati and find ensuing conversations (memes) by using BlogPulse. It's also very easy to see the number of subscribers to a blogger's feed through Google Reader or Feedburner. You can also get a feeling for how well certain bloggers grasp the industry they represent via tools such as Radian6 and BuzzLogic.

Remember, you don't have to focus on just the top-ranked bloggers— they're not the only game in town. In fact, they might not always be the most beneficial or necessary target in your overall communications strategy. Top-ranked bloggers usually represent the thought leaders who are held in high regard by their readers, with many creating a dedicated following that look forward to every post. When they cover a topic, it elicits a flurry of online traffic almost instantly, inciting a series of online discussions that usually extend across the blogosphere (sometimes lasting several days to several weeks).

As an example from Brian's technology business area, one of the top targets is TechCrunch (www.techcrunch.com), which can send nearly 10,000 visitors to any given Web site within 24 to 48 hours. Of course, Brian would never say to overlook this group. Obviously, they lend credibility to your brand or the brand you represent—as long as the exposure is representative of the story you helped to cultivate. In our experience, however, this group typically jumps from topic to topic and product to product, with very little investment in dedication or loyalty, simply because its focus is driven by activity. For the right product, story, or service, a decent percentage of these bloggers, and their readers, will keep their partial attention with you (as long as they like what they see).

During a recent discussion at the TurnPRon conference in San Francisco, where Brian presented on a panel discussing the future of Public Relations, the moderator asked why he should "waste" his time chasing down every blogger who covers his markets when he could just focus on the top. He referred to this as "the cream of the crop, as they are the true influencers out there." Although there is an A-list for every market, and the A-list helps with the credibility of a brand, it does very little for generating new customers or enhancing brand loyalty. The true influencers are the peers of your customers. The best communications strategies will envelop not only authorities in new and traditional media, but also those voices in the Long Tail. They help carry information and promote discussions among your customers directly in a true peer-to-peer approach.

This group is often referred to as the *magic middle,* a group of passionate people dedicated to writing about topics and issues relevant to them personally. The magic middle, as originally defined by David Sifry, the founder of Technorati, are those blogs with 20 to 1,000 active inbound links. These are the bloggers who tend to inspire real-world customers to explore and experiment with new products and services based on the word of their peers. For example, Deirdre admits on Twitter that she's checked out numerous companies based on recommendations by her favorite bloggers. And in some cases, it has led to the sale of a product that wasn't even on her radar. The same is true for blogs.

One Hot Topic

Blogger relations is a popular topic of discussion these days, not just on the blogosphere, but also within the HR departments of PR agencies and businesses that understand its importance. It's something new and is perceived to require a different skill set than most PR and communications professionals are used to (but don't necessarily lack). Therefore, new job positions are opening up in an attempt to hire people who understand the art of blogger relations. And if that doesn't work, some companies are just hiring anyone who blogs, sometimes regardless of industry and communications experience. Many believe that if you blog, you must understand company value propositions, marketing, customer relations, and, ultimately, why all this matters to the people you're trying to reach, right? Well, not exactly. Several companies that we work with, or simply know of, have hired bloggers to handle blogger relations even if they haven't engaged in the process before. They immediately assume that bloggers know the game, so they must understand how to get posts written on their behalf.

From personal experience, we can tell you that anyone halfway decent in media or blogger relations will agree that the discipline has less to do with the mechanics of publishing media and more to do with storytelling, an understanding of what you represent, why it matters to certain people, and a genuine intent for cultivating relationships. We'd love to simply say that blogger relations is about common sense or PR 101, but somehow in the world of marketing communications, we forget to act like the very people we're trying to reach and instead push messages at them to get their attention.

To genuinely approach blogger relations, or media relations, you must first deconstruct the process of the media ecosystem and reprogram yourself to tap into the basic building blocks of what makes good content and sparks conversations. This, in turn, helps define why people should take the time to speak with you.

Similar to the news release, the PR industry has been stuck in a rut for so long that the industry is content with the existing manufacturing line of building news, writing reports, "schmoozing," and simply broadcasting messages to anyone with an inbox. As we've noted throughout this book, PR is experiencing some of the greatest innovations and advancements in quite some time. But instead of embracing a new-and-improved commitment for creating and sharing news with people, PR is taking it on the chin by using the same old marketing ethics and tactics to broadcast messages (spam) to recipients. Again, this is about people and personal relationships, and the realization that less is more.

In a Nutshell

First and foremost, successful blogger relations are built on respect. It all starts with understanding what *you* stand for. We're not convinced that every PR person actually takes the time to fully "get" what he or she represents and why it matters to the rest of the world. And more important, how will it help others to make a decision and help them do something more effectively than they could before? For this simple reason alone, we challenge you to a quick test. And yes, the clock is ticking!

If you had to tell us in one sentence why we should write about you and why our followers or readers will care, what would you say?

It's not as easy as you think. It's amazing that many "PR pros" can't pass this test. Brian, who is also an avid writer outside of PR, is pitched every day and has been for years. It still blows him away how few people take the time to read what he writes and match their products and services to the most important part of his writing—his loyal followers. This is the listening and reading part we emphasized previously.

The next step is to really think about why you should reach out. What is it about what you represent that will compel others to share it with their communities? Remember, bloggers have a responsibility to their readers to maintain credibility, along with the trust of the community. In today's attention economy, bloggers must actively compete for readers' precious time, so you can bet that good bloggers will be selective. We have a strong suspicion of what you might be thinking: "Who has time to do this? Dedicating one-on-one time with bloggers in addition to traditional media exceeds the number of hours in a day." We'll say this as clearly as possible: *Make the time.* Prioritize the people you want to reach (and, no, you won't find them through a database).

As you move forward with your campaigns, you should never be limited to either blogs or media, nor should your campaign just focus on the top list determined by any single service. You need to be where your customers are discovering, sharing, and talking. Blogger relations is all about people and relationships, and sometimes the greatest influencers are those who are already among the customers you hope to reach.

Going back to the earlier J&J story and also our belief that bloggers will be instrumental in helping the evolution of Public Relations, we're currently witnessing this play out online well before you even finish this book. As noted in a couple examples, many bloggers are going as far as blacklisting certain PR people or companies who they think spam them without taking their preferences into consideration. And it's not just about blacklisting them in one place; they're leveraging the reach of the blogosphere to share these lists with each other as a form of public humiliation and education. Therefore, we need to improve how we do things across the board.

However, bloggers can benefit from maintaining a strategic and advantageous relationship with the right PR professionals. Love them or hate them, good PR people can still be a helpful part of the news and information process. They can and will work for you. Our earlier example of Chris Anderson running the names of lazy PR flacks in a public forum is definitely one way to send a clear message. Social Media is fueled by people and their peers, so running things in the blogosphere definitely becomes very personal. However, there are also other ways to ensure that PR people "think" before approaching bloggers. One way is to send positive feedback to those who do it right. Another way is to send notes to management about those who do it wrong and remind them how to do things correctly. Or just block the individual from contacting you again (but in the process, let the person know why).

Yes, it takes time for bloggers to respond rather than ignore things. It also takes an extraordinary level of patience and understanding. However, it helps PR professionals adapt and learn. Using the Chris Anderson example, one blog post might have inspired hundreds of people to do things better. Bloggers can also work better with PR people by clearly stating somewhere—perhaps in their blog or a social network (remember the discussion between Robert Scoble and several of his followers)—how they want to be contacted, what they are looking for, and advice for cutting through the clutter. It's not about submission forms—they are not helpful.

We are all in this to help each other and learn together. And those who aren't ready to discover or embrace evolution will seal their own fate. From the large companies, such as J&J, to the individuals building their own personal brands, the blogosphere has so many influential people who can help you meet your PR objectives. Approaching them the right way and constantly offering insight and valuable information will make bloggers receptive to exploring a relationship with you over time.

In the rapidly shifting era of blogger and media relations, we can expect one thing to occur as we forge ahead: mistakes. It happens to the best and the worst of us. This is about relationships and creating a value cycle from PR to bloggers, journalists, and, ultimately, the people you want to reach with your news. Relationships are cultivated and should be mutually beneficial because of the extra time we take to personalize our contact. As stated earlier, there's a difference between spam and prequalified blogger outreach, and it's all rooted in genuine intent and execution. Nothing beats homework and real one-on-one conversations that show some important credentials:

- You know who you're talking to and why what you represent matters to them and their readers.

- You specifically packaged the story to their preferences.

- You are an expert in the field in which you work, and you are knowledgeable about the playing field and the players who also define the space.

- You're positioned as a resource instead of as a PR spammer.

If you can keep these four important points in mind, you will do well with the bloggers. They will be more receptive to your information, and they will want to share it with their faithful followers.

Chapter 8

Social Media Releases (SMRs)

In 2006, the news release celebrated its 100th birthday. During those hundred years, the news release changed little until the advent of broadcast TV (which led to a quicker pace of change). However, the mass proliferation of the Web has changed the news release radically. News releases primarily still "look and feel" like they did 20 to 30 years ago. But unfortunately, over time the content of news releases has moved toward more superfluous language and meaningless information (boilerplate and filler).

A Bit of History Never Hurt Anyone

Ivy Lee created the very first news release on October 28, 1906, when an electric service car on the Pennsylvania Railroad jumped a trestle and landed in the Thoroughfare Creek. Unfortunately, 50 people lost their lives that day. The *New York Times* deemed this new approach (the news release) successful, and the Pennsylvania Railroad was praised for its openness and honesty with respect to the event.

As a result, many have called for the death of news releases, especially during the past couple years. The complaints are common: Releases are usually populated with jargon, buzzwords, hyperbole, and unnecessary detail, all united by self-serving (and usually made-up) quotes. And although the Public Relations landscape has changed significantly during the past 100 years (as discussed throughout this book), the traditional news hasn't necessarily reflected those changes.

The Old Way

You are probably quite familiar with the following traditional news release.

Company X Launches World's First, Industry-Leading, Innovative Thingamabob That Will Change Our Lives for the Better

Fantasy Land -- Sept. XX, 2007 -- So and so, a leader in such and such, today announced the world's most groundbreaking, revolutionary, and never-before-seen widget, which will change the lives of everyone who uses it. Not only is it versatile and ubiquitous, but it scales across the marketing bell curve and into the Long Tail. It is a disruptive game-changing solution that forces a paradigm shift and, yes, it's just that simple to use.

"We are excited and thrilled and happy and delighted that our new groundbreaking widget will change your life," said a company executive who didn't say this quote, but instead simply signed off on it after his PR person wrote it for him. "There really is nothing out there like it. We have no competition. This is something everyone needs; they just don't know it yet."

It's troubling to see how releases such as this one populate the wires and search engines. You can only imagine how many revisions and contributors the marketing and executive teams went through to ensure that every useless piece of industry-speak made the final cut. The end product usually omits the most important part of the story: what it is, who it's for, why it's different, and why it's valuable and beneficial to the people to whom it's targeted. However, all hope is not lost. In the era of PR 2.0, news releases are experiencing a revitalized life, perhaps leading to a fresh and even more diverse future.

A New Way

In October 2007, Brian published a new take on the traditional release to help PR professionals experiment with different, effective templates for reaching a variety of people. The template was based on years of experimentation, evolution, and analytics to fine-tune what worked every time.

News Release Example: Convey Your News without Excessive Wording or Hype

In a Perfect World -- Sometime in the Near Future -- Brian Solis (note how Brian is not indicating that he is a leader here, nor should you) drafted a new outline for wire-ready and static online news releases to help PR and communications professionals tell a more meaningful story in a way that helps convey the true value of the news—without insulting the people who read it.

This new template can include a list of bullets (note that wire services cannot incorporate bullets, only dashes), quotes, and links:

- News releases can tell a story to customers that specifically demonstrates why the news is valuable to them.

- These releases can include SEO (search engine-optimized) keywords to improve their pickup by Google and Yahoo! and so on.

- Traditional releases can also complement SMRs and blog posts simply by linking to them.

- The difference between a traditional release, new media release, and an SMR is intent, media, socialization, and distribution.

Or, the news release can be written as an article you want others to view as a story, not as a promotion. Basically, it can explain more thoroughly why the information is important, how what is written about is unique, and whom it benefits and how. The key about this paragraph news release is that it needs to be honest, and it must demonstrate that the writer actually analyzed the needs of the market he or she is trying to reach.

A supporting paragraph, in this case, is going to help round out the story. In this case, usage examples will help strengthen the story and potentially inspire people to take action. These releases can be distributed in various ways, such as via traditional wires, free wires, static Web pages, and in blogs. They can be written for journalists, bloggers, and analysts, and for the very people we're hoping to reach.

Provide genuine and interesting quotes that say something other than "we are excited...."

Brian Solis of PR 2.0 weighed in on the world of news releases: "Some journalists prefer to cut and paste from a well-written news release, whereas others just need the facts without the spin. However, what's new here is that you can have a variety of flavors of each news release to tell a story in different, genuine ways for journalists, bloggers, and customers in different markets. Just keep them interesting and relevant."

Links, too, are now more important than ever. If the link is too long, just input it into www.TinyUrl.com and get this shortened format in return: http://tinyurl.com/3ctn2s.

Blog: www.briansolis.com
Web site: www.future-works.com
RSS feed: http://feeds.feedburner.com/Pr20
Market background: http://del.icio.us/briansolis
Artwork: www.flickr.com/photos/briansolis

About This Template

What you should not to do here is repeat information. As noted earlier, avoid excessive wording. (If this is to cross the wire, why pay for the extra words?) Say something that qualifies the company to offer perspective about the information that you are presenting (for example, the company's market share/standing). You should also provide more details about the company (such as interesting facts, market demographics/share, and history) that set the company apart from its competitors—and of course, you should include news that supports the story.

Also, include some traditional and new media formats for contacting you more effectively.

Contact:
Brian Solis
PR 2.0 / FutureWorks
408-720-8228 Ext. 101
brian [at] future-works [dot] com
LinkedIn: www.linkedin.com/in/futureworks
Facebook: http://tinyurl.com/38su71
Twitter: www.twitter.com/briansolis
Vcard: http://tinyurl.com/3242wm

Be Part of the (R)evolution

News releases today are more than just text, buzzwords, and spin. They come in various flavors and serve different purposes. We believe well-written news releases are far from dead. When developed strategically, their opportunities, appeal, and benefits are only expanding in conjunction with the groups of various influencers and consumers who rely on them for relevant information.

According to Outsell, Inc., in November 2006, 51 percent of information technologists sourced their news from releases found on Yahoo! or Google News instead of from traditional trade journals. Although this might be expected in the technology industries, we can assure you that this statistic is probably equally significant across a variety of major industries. This means that news releases are no longer limited to journalists, bloggers, and analysts; they are now also read directly by customers to help them make important decisions. People are now relying on news releases as a direct source of information, so let's take this opportunity to tell the story that matters to them. We need to deconstruct 100 years of tradition and rebuild something that will actually work in today's attention economy.

No rule states that we can use only one news release template. And as you learned in Chapter 6, "The Language of New PR" (which we believe was probably an eye opener or even a rude awakening), an *audience* no longer exists for your *messages*. Markets consist of groups of disparate (the Long Tail) yet connected people who look for value and benefits in different ways. Therefore, a good story requires personalization. Don't forget that journalists, bloggers, and analysts are people, too. So if you humanize the process of writing releases as well as the content you create, you might enhance readers' ability to connect with and share the information.

The socialization of the Web has resulted in myriad news release formats that serve different audiences and different purposes: traditional releases for media; SEO releases for customers; SMRs for press, bloggers, and also customers; and video news releases (VNRs) for broadcasters, and now just about everyone.

Perhaps one of the most discussed innovations in the 100-year-old news release is the SMR, which has rallied as much support as it has controversy. Because many PR professionals were reluctant to embrace the changes in the industry, they didn't recognize the need for a new type of communications tool. PR professionals were also confused about its use and purpose, which to this day are still misunderstood. However, we have come a long way. For many, it's no longer a matter of *if* or *when* you should use the SMR, but instead how it becomes a part of your approach and daily practice.

Before we dissect the SMR, it's important to review the evolution of the news release. We begin with the traditional release, follow that with the customer-focused release, proceed to the SEO release, and then move forward to showcase the latest new shiny object in PR: the SMR. Another important template that fits into the evolution of releases is the VNR. However, today the industry is calling for a VNR redux, or VNR 2.0. We highlight the value and appropriate use of VNR 2.0 in Chapter 9, "VNR 2.0."

Let's start by reacquainting ourselves with basic principles for good, well-written news releases. These ten principles (more definitely exist) serve as the foundation for New Media releases:

1. Elevate the message.

2. Inform, don't persuade.

3. Write with balance.

4. Include traditional and New Media.

5. Be informative.

6. Provide resources and add links.

7. Use available Social Media channels to open up and distribute dialogue.

8. Listen.

9. Converse.

10. Learn.

Traditional Releases

Many reporters and bloggers use standard news releases to build their stories. Let's help them help us in the process. When expanding your news or story into a press release, it's important to recognize that most of the wording templates that are used, as noted previously, might not serve as the best foundation. But there's room for a well-written release that conveys value, benefits, and a story that's relevant to each recipient. However, this is easier said than done. Most news releases are driven by product development, which can cause an inward and narrowly focused view from life inside the company. The final release usually winds up riddled with adjectives, industry jargon, and hype, with very little value stringing everything together.

The best releases will be outward focused and reflective of the state of the market, how you fit into it, and what's in it for the potential stakeholders (customers).

We also strongly recommend eliminating the "canned" quotes. We all know you're excited and thrilled at whatever you're announcing. But if the quote isn't genuinely from the person saying it and bears little or no value to the implications of the news, it only takes away from the announcement—it's okay to leave it out.

The best advice is to make the release read like the article that you would ultimately like to see, worrying less about structure and format and more about news, the story, and the supporting facts (and media elements) that help writers build the story more effectively. With the standard news release, try to keep the announcement between 400 and 500 words.

Customer-Focused News Releases

Companies and marketers can use distribution services to complement releases written for journalists and bloggers, to reach customers directly through traditional search engines and news aggregation services such as Techmeme. Recently, BusinessWire and PRNewswire have consistently ranked in the top 100 sources for news in Techmeme's Leaderboard (a news tracking service for the technology industry). This means that a significant number of influential bloggers are referencing original news releases in their posts related to news and market information.

The trick for this new breed of releases is to write them as the article you want to read. Keep it clean, clear, pseudo-impartial, and definitely focused on benefits for specific customers. Basically, you need to humanize the story.

SEO Press Releases

Distribution of news releases via a wire service such as PRNewsire, BusinessWire, and MarketWire offers additional value in the form of SEM (search engine marketing). Integrating keywords, phrases, and embedded links optimizes their "findability" and rank within traditional search engines such as Google and Yahoo!. In this case, the greatest targets for SEO releases are actually customers, not journalists.

As noted previously, customers use search engines to find solutions, and news releases often provide them with objective information that aids them in the decision-making process.

Many say that if you're not on the first two pages of search results, your company is losing the battle for online mindshare. SEO releases contribute to the authority of related search results, but keep in mind that other factors also contribute, such as keyword buys, keywords on your Web site, affiliate strategies, and other tools and campaigns. When drafting the release, ensure that your top keywords are included toward the front of the release, especially in the headline and subhead, as well as in the boilerplate. Choose up to three words and repeat them throughout the release, especially in the boilerplate. Search engines seem to pay more attention to the bolded words and to the repeated words in the first half of news releases.

It's also extremely helpful to use those keywords as anchor text to link back to strategic landing pages on your Web site. Make sure those pages are also keyword optimized. It's important not to overuse each word or to overlink.

Keyword density, the number of times a keyword or phrase appears compared to the total number of words in a page, is optimized between 2 percent and 8 percent, according to experts. We've erred in the middle of that range. Without ruining the flow, include industry and product names and categories in place of generic descriptors such as "the product," "the solution," and "the company" throughout the release. We want to match our keywords to correlate with the real-world patterns of how people search. Also be sure to link rich media or multimedia so that your keywords show up in content-specific search engines, too.

These resources are helpful in determining the best keywords for your business:

- SEO Book
- WordTracker
- Google AdWords
- Google Trends
- BlogPulse Trends

The ideal length of this release is usually fewer than 400 words.

Social Media Releases

As we've mentioned, the latest new shiny object in PR is the SMR. This, along with Web video and online VNRs, is one of the greatest breakthroughs in the 100-year-old history of news releases. Originally introduced by Todd Defren in response to Tom Foremski's call for the death of press releases, the SMR represents a new socially rooted format that complements traditional and SEO news releases by combining news facts and social assets in one easy-to-digest and improved tool.

Chris Heuer helped lead an effort to propose a standard for the construction and distribution of SMRs by creating an official working group, dubbed the "hrelease project." Stowe Boyd reminded disingenuous, lazy, or opportunistic PR people that they're not invited to participate in Social Media (and rightfully so) if they do so as marketers. Included in this working group was also Shel Holtz, who hosted the original NMRcast and who continues to demonstrate the value of SMRs. Shannon Whitley also worked to help PR pros "get it." Many other professionals continued to march onward, educating PR professionals, bloggers, and consumers on the subject.

Brian joined Heuer from the onset of the working group and has since spent most of his free time defining and defending the reasons for the SMR's existence in blog posts and at conferences worldwide, while simultaneously practicing the use of the tool himself. Instead of being a spectator, as many of the critics we've come across, Brian has been a player on the field, helping to define the opportunities, landscape, and best practices, and demonstrating when to apply restraint with the use of the SMR, which requires careful consideration. Today the SMR continues to evolve and is heading toward official standardization, led by the International Associations of Business Communicators (IABC).

Giving everyone what he or she needs in a relevant way requires a different approach. Almost every news release distributed today goes out without video or audio, and many still do not include links to additional information or supporting content. And although these multimedia pieces represent underlying components of SMRs, it's not just about multimedia content; it's about connecting information across social networks, the people looking for it, and the conversations that bind them together. SMRs also help bloggers and online journalists more effectively write a rich media post using one resource that provides them with everything they need.

Picture an everyday blog post with a headline, an intro paragraph, news facts, genuine quotes, and supporting market data (with links) combined with embedded socializable content. This might include video from Viddler, pictures from Flickr, screencasts hosted at YouTube, supporting documents piped from Docstoc, the use of social tools to bookmark, relevant tags for indexing and discoverability, subscriptions via RSS, company contacts via LinkedIn or Facebook, and, most important, the ability to use compartmentalized components of the SMR as building blocks for a new story (embed codes). SMRs can also include other social elements such as trackbacks (the ability to host a list of other posts to reference the SMR as well as the ability to host and facilitate comments). They're also findable within Social Media search engines such as Technorati, Google Blog Search, BlogPulse, Yacktrack, and Ask Blog Search.

Similar to SEO releases, SMRs offer a new and perhaps unforeseen benefit. SEO releases provide assistance to customers seeking solutions through search, and SMRs offer similar benefits through social channels. The difference lies in how people interact with it and discover it, and also the tools they use to share and rebroadcast it. Basically, an SMR should contain everything necessary to share, discover, and retell a story in a way that complements your original intent and context.

However, SMRs should not cross the wire. They should be hosted on a social platform, such as WordPress, Blogger, or Moveable Type. The platforms can easily become extensions to company online press rooms or to specific company blogs but provide a dedicated channel for SMRs to complement traditional releases, SEO releases, company blog posts, and all other outward-focused communications. Any customizable blogging platform will more than likely serve as an effective—and social—platform. Remember that a traditional Web page isn't necessarily social, so any published SMRs on a standard Web site will most likely not appear in social search.

What SMRs Are Not

Although the SMR represents an exciting mechanism to socialize news, let's recap everything that the SMR is not:

- It is not a mechanism to fix what's wrong with most news releases.
- It is not designed to replace a traditional news release.
- It's not exclusively for journalists or bloggers.

- It is not created for PR to build new value for itself. (That goes for Social Media in general, too.)

- If it is advertised by wire services, it is not a true SMR, and neither are the multimedia releases these services offer (although they do have value).

- Even though a great template exists, SMRs can take many forms and include a variety of content plus social tools.

- It is not about BS or spin, and it's not a communications tool that's meant to control the message.

SMRs represent the opportunity to share news in ways that reach people with the information that matters to them, in ways that they can easily use to digest and, in turn, share with others through text, links, images, video, bookmarks, tags, and so on, while also enabling them to interact with you directly or indirectly.

Around the Water Cooler (and a Sample SMR)

Holtz's New Media agency, Crayon (www.Crayonville.com), recently led a Social Media campaign for Coca-Cola's Virtual Coke program. The program focused on a competition that asks consumers to submit ideas about a virtual vending machine that dispenses online "experiences" versus carbonated sugar water. The individual with the winning idea received a trip to San Francisco to observe the Second Life development wizards at MillionsOfUs, an agency specializing in virtual worlds, implement the chosen design.

They used an SMR to spark conversations about the campaign. The release contained all the elements that enabled bloggers, the media, and consumers to follow and build their own stories:

- Bulleted list of news facts

- Bulleted list of accepted quotes

- Short boilerplates about the Coca-Cola Company, Coke Short Side of Life, and Crayon

- Contact info

- Multimedia

Download / photo: Michael Donnelly, director, Global Interactive Marketing, the Coca-Cola Company (coming soon)

Download / photo: Joseph Jaffe, president and chief interrupter, Crayon (JPG format, 10KB)

Download / image: Virtual Thirst prototype (Virtual Thirst images are available for viewing via a YouTube embed at www.virtualthirst.com.)

Web page: Traditional news release (www.virtualthirst.com/pressrelease.html)

Download: PDF file, traditional news release (www.virtualthirst. com/VirtualThirst_PressRelease.pdf)

Launch event photos: www.flickr.com/search/ ?q=virtualthirst&m=tags&z=t

- Related links

del.icio.us page for more information: http://del.icio.us/ virtualthirst

Subscribe to del.icio.us Virtual Thirst RSS feed for ongoing cov- erage, industry news, and reaction: http://del.icio.us/rss/ virtualthirst

Add news release to your del.icio.us account: http://del.icio.us/ post?http://www.virtualthirst.com/pressrelease.html

Digg the news release: http://digg.com/business_finance/ VirtualThirst_com_Best_example_yet_of_a_Social_Media_ News_Release

Technorati tags: Virtual Thirst virtualthirst Coca-Cola Coke Second Life experience

Defren covered the campaign on his PR Squared blog. His post had several interesting comments on the use of Coke's SMR.

Have A Coke, Play With Crayons

By Todd Defren

Coca-Cola, in association with the social media stars at crayon, recently launched an integrated Social Media campaign titled, "Virtual Thirst." It's a design competition that asks folks to submit ideas about a virtual vending machine — one which dispenses online "experiences" vs. carbonated sugar water. The winner gets a trip to San Francisco, to observe the SL development wizards at MillionsOfUs implement the chosen design.

Below is my unasked-for critique... But first, please note that everything below comes from a place of deep respect for crayon, for Coca-Cola (Pepsi? Yuck.), and, from a keen desire to help improve such campaigns in the future.

Please also note that where I offer critical assessments, it's likely because I've screwed up on similar issues. We are *all* still learning.

What I like:

I like it that a big brand like Coke is trying something of this magnitude in the Social Media space. I like seeing an integrated, multi-platform 2.0 effort (SL, del.icio.us, SMNR, YouTube, Flickr, MySpace).

I like it that they tapped smart folks at crayon, instead of stumbling through this on their own.

I like it that they used a Social Media News Release. Yay! (Please report back on how this was received.)

I like that this contest is standing on its own, without air-cover from advertisements or a hardcore PR push to the mainstream media.

I like the premise ... creating a vending machine that dispenses "experiences," i.e., a truly fantastical "machine" that can fully exploit multimedia. (Not sure how they'd pull off anything *truly* amazing without 3D Virtual-Reality surround-sound MP3 sunglasses and a full-body force-feedback suit, but hey, we can wish 'em luck!)

What I think could have been done better:

The prize is kinda lame. No disrespect intended to MoU but if Coke/crayon really wanted to drive entries, they'd have come up with a more scintillating award. Many entrants will probably already live in the Bay Area — and likely work in high-tech. For them the prize = fight traffic to get into the City, to watch some folks coding for a dozen hours. Anyway, forget about the Bay Area issue. My 14-year old son might have been excited by the contest concept, but I can tell you he'd yawn over the prize. Multiply that less-than-ideal response by the X millions of 13 thru 30-somethings on MySpace, SL and YouTube. This is COKE, folks: could we think bigger? (Note: Steve Coulson of crayon answers this complaint at Greg Verdino's blog, but not satisfactorily, IMHO.)

What, no blog? Did I miss something? How about a "purpose-built" blog that allows the judges to transparently judge some of the entries? Throw some ideas out there to stir up some creative juices? Agonize over whether it's too late to juice up the prize? Disclose some of the internal debates that went on during the development cycle? Coke wants us to give up some of our creativity — this sounds cool on the surface but also requires us to spend a lot of our personal time, and to be a li'l bit vulnerable; how about giving us a peek at some of Coke/crayon's own feelings of vulnerability?

The del.icio.us page misses the mark. Mere bookmarks do nothing for anyone: the *value* comes from the bookmarker's associated comments on each entry. WHY should I click on these links?

There are elements missing from the SMNR, even something as basic as the Coke exec's headshot. ("Coming soon." That comes across as kinda' bush league.) More interestingly, this release was not posted to Coca-Cola's main website. So, the SMNR only "exists" on the Virtual Thirst website. Why?? And, forget about "why" for a sec: wherever it lives, the SMNR can and likely *should* be treated as if it were a blog post, i.e., let's see trackbacks to the SMNR, and allow for (moderated) comments, right there within the release's dedicated webpage/post.

There are also elements to the campaign that **I don't understand:** why is there a headshot of crayon's Joseph Jaffe in the release? Why is crayonville such a big component to the program? Couldn't a gajillion-dollar company like Coke afford its own patch of virtual real estate? Am I thinking too 1.0 to suggest that the PR/marketing guys be more behind-the-scenes? There's no T'rati tag for "crayon" in the release, after all....

One of the most important statements in Defren's blog post was that "we are *all* still learning." No one really expects, at this stage, that you create the "perfect" SMR. Even the largest companies are still trying to figure this one out. However, you need to take the initial steps, even if you don't get it completely right the first time. Defren applauded Coke for its efforts to use the SMR as a part of the Virtual Thirst campaign, but also gave helpful criticism on how it could have been a better communications tool.

A Final Word on SMRs

Our personal "secret" about SMRs is to create a fully dressed-up social release under a private, nonindexed URL to share with key contacts in advance of the announcement. This gives bloggers and journalists everything they need to create an online story while minimizing the need for them to conduct additional research. After the news is public, the SMR goes live with links to the traditional and SEO releases and company blog posts, and each also links back to the SMR. Also, to create a seamless conversation bridge, wherever the social content is hosted (for example, YouTube, Flickr, Scribd, Utterz) should link to the SMR.

The Brand New World of New Releases

For all the releases previously discussed, we add a note of caution: *The same tools that help you expand your visibility can also set you up for failure.* Wire services edit only for typos, not for content. This means that you can publish a release riddled with hyperbole, spin, buzzwords, and hype that will only confuse and dissuade your customers from doing business with you—it will send them to your competition.

The news release has evolved during the past 100 years and, similar to PR, it is enjoying a renaissance. Although in many cases it might still take its traditional form and be search engine-optimized, it has also morphed into a tool that facilitates direct conversions and great storytelling to benefit many different people through text and multimedia.

Today bloggers, journalists, consumers, and just about any stakeholder of a company can gather, share, and communicate information easily and with more content and resources than any release template previously provided. The fact that you now understand the evolution of the news release and are (we hope) willing to change and use the SMR appropriately means that you have clearly turned the page to begin a new chapter in PR. If so, you are helping to facilitate more effective conversations, and you are also joining in a powerful movement to reinvent an industry.

Millions of people still enjoy receiving information in a one-to-one format. But at the end of the day, nothing beats relationships. Now you just need to genuinely engage, and SMRs enable you to reach the right people in a one-to-one and one-to-many approach. Branching beyond the traditional news release enables communication to truly incite; it's what you see in Web communities today—the many-to-many conversations that will impact a brand's bottom line. The moral of the story is to be the person you want to reach, regardless of the technology you use to get there.

Chapter 9

Video News Release (VNR) 2.0

As you're becoming more familiar with the evolving array of traditional and New Media news releases available today, Social Media is also ushering in an emerging era of multimedia storytelling. Dubbed the Video News Release (VNR) redux, or VNR 2.0, PR professionals can now tell stories through video much easier than ever. Ready or not, it might be a good idea to start brushing up on your Web video capturing, editing, and uploading to social networks.

Traditional VNRs

As broadcast TV gained in popularity, Public Relations adopted the use of video production and satellite distribution to create and send B-Roll (Broadcast Roll) and VNRs, to help news studios package and present breaking stories or trends easily, without having to send crews around the country or the world. The VNR continues to be recognized as a great visual communications tool in broadcast television programming, whether it's used to launch a new product, document trends or shifts in consumer behavior, or tell a compelling visual story. The VNR truly revolutionized the way we created and disseminated news releases for the television market.

Although you might not have direct experience with VNRs, they are related to many of the stories that you see on traditional broadcast news networks. When you're watching the evening news and you're introduced to the latest new gadget or you're swept off to a popular new hotspot on an island far away, chances are they're using footage sourced from a VNR. Although VNRs are effective, they are also incredibly expensive. Production segments, B-Roll, satellite transmission, and the legwork associated with calling attention to the distribution time of transmitting the feed can easily cost $20,000 for one story. Previously, only the elite or Fortune 500 companies had access to video production and the ability to mass-broadcast.

VNRs and Social Media

With the dawn of video social networks, VNRs are again earning a place in a communicator's portfolio of tools. Online video is the next frontier for Public Relations professionals, adding a new layer of engagement to any existing PR, marketing, and Web initiative. In our opinion, Social Media has reinvented the VNR, putting the power of creation and distribution in the hands of those with a video or Web camera, a PC, and a broadband connection. If you add in a little marketing and word-of-mouth savvy, knowledge of capturing visually stimulating or creative footage, and an understanding of the pains and needs of the people you're trying to reach, you have the formula for a potentially valuable two-way, media-rich communications tool.

Every day, more companies are building networks and the tools that enable you to broadcast video either live or as episodes (Webisodes), reaching audiences online and through mobile appliances such as iPods and cell phones. Online video is modernizing and expanding the way we create and utilize VNRs, and how we tell stories in general. Don't get us wrong—traditional VNRs are still highly effective and valuable for broadcast PR. The Web and the proliferation of video social networks (such as YouTube, BlipTV, Metacafe, Veoh, Viddler, Revver, Flickr, Magnify.net, and many others) are providing an easy and extensive distribution network to connect stories with people and, in turn, people back to the content creators. You're now able to foster relationships through video and also the ensuing interactions. The Web represents what could be constituted as the new broadcast channel, in addition to television.

A key point here is that online VNRs (visual storytelling) represent only one tool in a shed that houses many other solutions for reaching each of your respective communities. You must consider where the people you want to reach go for information and where they go to share content.

Through research, you can determine specific channels, networks, strategies, methodologies, and digital bridges to participate in a valuable, mutually beneficial way—to build relationships.

A redux of the VNR and a move to integrate video-based initiatives into your marketing communications (marcom) programs is important not just because it's easier to create and distribute online video. It's driven mostly by the surging consumption of video by today's Internet population. Amazing statistics are being released about consumer video behavior on the Web, and it's incredibly motivating. A report filed on January 9, 2008, by the Pew Internet and American Life Project revealed the following:

- Nearly half of all Internet users frequent a video-sharing Web site.

- Daily traffic to video-based sites has doubled since the previous year.

- By 2011, it's estimated that more than 60 percent of consumers will regularly watch at least one video per month.

- Nearly 14 percent of companies plan on using Web video over the next year as a part of their marketing plan, a number that's expected to increase dramatically over the next few years.

Just to give you a quick snapshot, Comscore Inc. reported in March 2008 that U.S. Internet users viewed 11.48 billion online videos on video Web sites, up 64 percent from a year ago. The numbers continue to dramatically ramp. With the technology barriers of entry so low (in terms of expertise required and cost of equipment and production), there's never been a better time to experiment with video. Although traditional VNRs are costly, many businesses are spending only a few hundred or a few thousand dollars to create and share videos that reach a global audience.

However, similar to all forms of Social Media, VNRs require a level of understanding, ethics, and transparency that is possible only with hands-on experience—not necessarily as a marketer, but as a participant in all forms of Social Media. Although many professionals embracing the

PR 2.0 approach are in the tech sector, the entire concept of Social Media VNRs can benefit and provide value to any business of any size. At the very least, social video enables companies to demonstrate their product in a way that is consumable, shareable, and more interesting than just reading text-based collateral materials.

When it comes to creating a formal video strategy, it's less about production quality and theatrics, and more about participating and contributing genuinely and authentically. Online videos range from funny and witty shorts and series, to product demos, tutorials, and screencasts, to executive interviews and customer success stories.

Blendtec is one company that has blazed the trail for social video while tying together Public Relations, branding, and sales—becoming a cult classic in the process. This Salt Lake City company mainly manufactures high-performance kitchen appliances—specifically, blenders that seemingly grind up anything and everything. George Wright, marketing director at Blendtec, and Tom Dickson, company founder and CEO, came up with the idea for a clever series titled "Will It Blend?" that has become a viral marketing sensation. (Some consider viral marketing as word-of-mouth with enhanced reach by the effects of the Internet.) The series features Dickson, wearing a white lab coat and goggles, asking a simple question before feeding various items—everything from outdoor rakes and glow sticks to iPhones and video cameras—to a Blendtec blender: "Will it blend?"

Originally funded with an unbelievably low budget of $50, the videos have proved so incredibly popular and viral that visits to some of the videos have hit 46 million views on YouTube and 71 million on Revver. They have also earned Tom Dickson appearances on *The Today Show* and *The Tonight Show;* stories in the *Wall Street Journal, Business Week,* and *Forbes;* and a dedicated episode on the *Discovery Channel.* The videos have also delivered a 500 percent increase in sales. And more than 100,000 people have subscribed to the company RSS feed for future videos. It's important to note that all this was accomplished with nothing more than an idea, creativity, a small budget, a video camera, and the ability to get that video on the Web. They've shown us that anything is possible in online video.

Blendtec's marketing now serves as a profit center for the company: The videos not only have generated sales, but also have earned more than $50,000 in ad revenue from online video host Revver. This is only one example of a company that has created its own recipe for a successful online video franchise. Let's take a look at some of the tips and tricks that will also help you as you venture into the new world of online video.

Robert Scoble, one of the world's most famous bloggers, recently ventured into Web video for FastCompany TV. He encourages PR and corporate marketing to worry less about trying to have broadcast-quality production and to instead focus more on the uniqueness of a product when pursuing campaigns through online video. Scoble's blog post, "This Is Why I Love the Tech Industry," clearly reveals his passion for video and points out why it's critical to capture the story in the moment.

This Is Why I Love the Tech Industry...

BY ROBERT SCOBLE

Sometimes I get caught up in all the bubble and ego talk. You know, all that stuff that the industry insiders care about and what keeps tech blogging sometimes feeling like a high school (who has the bigger ego? The bigger puppet? Who is going to start a snit on Gillmor Gang? Etc. Etc.)

That stuff is all fun for the insiders as they create drama so that we'll get you to pay attention and comment on our blogs.

But then, once in a while, something will happen that'll snap you out of the World Wide High School and remind you that this industry does, indeed, create cool stuff that makes our lives more productive and interesting. Well, actually, for me, that happens very often because I have a front-row-seat on this industry and get to see tons of interesting stuff.

But this is one of those times when what you're seeing and who you're talking with is much more interesting than usual. And the response from people who participate (this was filmed live, with a live audience) tells me that I'm not alone in recognizing this was a special moment for my camera.

So, that was a long way of saying, don't miss this conversation with Microsoft Researcher Andy Wilson. He's the guy behind the "Surface" technology that you use your hands on. Thursday at Microsoft's Silicon Valley offices he was showing off his latest version of that technology and taking questions from some interesting people themselves (my producer, Rocky Barbanica, who was a software developer for two decades before going back to film school, as well as someone from Symantec's CTO Office were part of the conversation, along with people who dropped by my Qik channel while I was filming these).

It's split into a few pieces because the cell phone connection died a couple of times, but you'll see why I started up the phone again.

...

This stuff is just so cool. If you agree, can you link to this from your Twitter account, your blog, or vote for this on Digg or Reddit? This conversation deserves a far wider distribution than my usual stuff because it could inspire kids to see how just one developer can change what we think of the tech industry. Thanks to Andy Wilson for the inspiring conversation and thanks to Microsoft Research for hiring him and helping this conversation to happen!

Scoble's blog post teaches you that, in an instant, you can grab an interesting piece of knowledge and history in the making. The ability to pull out a camera to videotape researcher Andy Wilson happens only once, and his work can inspire many. Scoble knows that you can't re-create the moment. Even if you are using a cellphone to capture footage, it's not the quality, but instead the participation and the ability to share with hundreds, if not thousands, of people the critical footage you take. Examples such as this make us think that the PR people of tomorrow should all walk around with the ability to create video news as they see it.

Jeremiah Owyang, an analyst covering social computing for Forrester Research, discussed the value of humanizing the company story through video and how to get started in a great post, "Why Online Video Is Good for Your Corporate Executives and How to Deploy."

Why Online Video Is Good for Your Corporate Executives and How to Deploy

By Jeremiah Owyang

Here's some of the reasons why I listed why Online Video is good for your CEO. (or any other executive)

It makes sense I share this info not only with that client I emailed but with the rest of the good folks that are deploying Social Media. Having evangelized and built a program at Hitachi Data Systems, I know what it's like.

Who am I writing for?

This knowledge is best suited for your CEO, other Executives, Corporate Communications, PR, Multi Media, Interactive Marketing, Integrated Marketing, Web Marketing, and Executive Communications, please forward this to the appropriate person.

Why Online Video is good for your Corporate Executives and Strategies to Deploy:

1) Time Efficient

For many CEOs, committing and writing a blog is not going to happen. This was evident in this video where Michael Dell is asked point blank "why don't you blog?" Video is a happy middle point as it takes about double the time (prep time and recording time) to get recorded.

2) Talk directly to the 'people'

Frankly, I'm sick of press releases talking about CEOs in the third person, or corporate bios talking about an executive. With online video the executive comes to the 'edge' of the company to have a real conversation with the marketplace. It's real, with real emotion, nuances, and body language that can't be expressed over text.

3) Take advantage of the Network Effects

The term Network can be interchanged with "Viral." By placing your video online, it should be put into viral players that encourage bloggers, and other website manager to embed the video and sharing it with others. Google Video, YouTube, Blip, and if you create content with PodTech you'll have the benefits needed to share.

4) Reuse Opportunities

These videos can be displayed on your corporate website, the extranet, intranet, embedded or linked to from a press release, email newsletter, sent to investors, and encouraged to spread on other websites. For those in Integrated Marketing, you'll love this.

5) Speaking in person to the whole world across time

Since the web is global (and the top medium in the workplace in North America) it can be easily found and shared across distances and is saved in the internet for access over time. Some theories suggest that the content over the long term is more effective than big media buys. How many people does your CEO reach by giving a speech? 10? 100? 1000? On the web it can reach mass audiences.

Owyang's blog post at www.web-strategist.com goes into more detail about online video and includes a breakdown of what online video conversation is and is not. He also gives great tips on how to build your own internal video team and the best way to evaluate an online video show (in case you were planning to create one).

Integrate with Other Social Media Strategies

Before working with Forrester Research, Owyang worked at Podtech with Scoble. As New Media journalists, they captured company stories, executive interviews, and news through online video programming. Both Scoble and Owyang have shared many posts detailing how and why companies should create and share their own content in addition to pursuing traditional and New Media publicity. It can only help in building communities, relationships, and telling the company story from a very human perspective—instead of the usual faceless broadcast process of churning and distributing news releases.

Another example is Michael Arrington, publisher of TechCrunch, the world's most linked-to and visited blog, and another strong supporter of the *use* of corporate marketing through video. Arrington has recommended that companies seeking coverage on the Web 2.0 network develop short, creative, and informative demo video clips when pitching him. It helps him grasp the value quickly and usually compels him and his staff to write about the company and also include the video in the story. He's on record saying, "I love start-up videos," and has repeatedly asked for companies to create and present videos.

Online videos help tell your stories to people who enjoy visual media, regardless of their industry. Videos apply to all industries—consumer lifestyle products, science and green initiatives, agriculture, big business, and just about everything you can think of. As long as you have a story to tell, adding a video dimension to your platform can help your story reach those you wouldn't normally connect with through other tools.

However, the use of video is not just about getting the attention of bloggers and traditional media. It's also an effective way of reaching markets and, more important, the people who can benefit from the story. That's the beauty of a viral social network. Because we are talking about different groups of people (they're no longer lumped into groups formerly known as "one" audience), you must consider several ingredients when developing a video or screencast. The choices you make for implementation will determine the success or failure of the campaign.

What Does All This Mean?

Let's take a look at the tech, jargon, networks, tools, and classifications of video campaigns to better understand how, when, and where to engage in online video.

We're sure you're familiar with YouTube (or have at least heard of it), the largest, most visited social network for uploading and viewing online videos. YouTube, and the many other online video networks, enables you to create a social profile where you can upload your individual videos for all to see (or you can mark them as private, which sort of defeats the purpose of our discussion). You can create a corporate or individual channel and tag each video with keywords to help others find it based on relevant searches. Most importantly, however, these networks provide a unique "embed" code that enables viewers to share your video on their blog, social network, Web site, and so on. And the more compelling your videos are, the more likely they are to be embedded elsewhere (creating an exponential viral success story).

Videos can be treated as a single episode, such as a product demonstration, or as a series, such as the "Will It Blend?" franchise. Other forms of online video include livecasting and mobilecasting. Livecasting is the ability to live-broadcast video for people to watch in real time, combined with an integrated chat forum, creating an immersive and engaging environment for companies and customers to connect. Companies such as Veodia and Ustream enable livecasting anywhere, anytime. Companies such as kyte, Mogulus, and BlogTV facilitate episodic broadcasting. For business, these tools are ideal (whether live or not) for Webcasting training sessions, HR and executive announcements, product reviews, marketing events, lectures, conferences, speeches, panels, and so on.

Mobilecasting is the livestreaming of online video from a mobile, Internet-enabled device such as the new Nokia video-enabled smart phone devices. Services include Qik and Kyte.tv. Many companies are using these services to host customer Q&A, communicate product and service updates, showcase events, highlight behind-the-scenes footage, and host impromptu discussions to maintain a consistent dialogue with their communities and continue to build relationships with them.

Screencast is another term you'll hear when discussing online video. Similar to video, screencasts are also viral and effective. Wikipedia provides a simple definition of the screencast: "Just as a screenshot is a picture of a user's screen, a screencast is essentially a movie of what a user sees on their monitor."

Strategies for Creating Successful Video Programs

Review these helpful tips to get you started or perfect your video or screencast:

1. Be genuine and use video as a way to inform visually. This isn't just another opportunity for PR to spam the world.

2. Know your targets, their pain points, and why your product will help them. And please don't use the word *audience*. As discussed in Chapter 6, "The Language of New PR," viewers today are considered the people formally known as the audience. This ensures that we engage by conversing with, not marketing to, people. As mentioned earlier, this is Jay Rosen's philosophy, which many Social Media purists hold sacred when discussing how to participate through Social Media.

3. Keep it focused on what's unique, interesting, and compelling.

4. Take the time to experiment. Don't just stop at one—keep the line of communication open through video similar to how you would with blogs, marketing collateral, newsletters, and news releases.

5. Consider the placement of videos on your company's site and offer RSS feeds for them.

6. Ensure that the videos are placed in the social networks where the people you want to reach search for new and interesting content.

7. Remember that placing videos online isn't enough. Just because you place a video in social networks doesn't mean it will be viewed and shared. You have to do "PR" for it through the folksonomy of strategic tagging, linking, and having others point to it and republish it to spark the viral potential of your content.

8. Be creative and think outside of the box.

9. Worry less about polish and more about content.

10. Keep it short—usually about three to five minutes, definitely less than ten.

11. Listen carefully to all feedback and use it as an opportunity to create an even more compelling video next time.

Although social video represents a new opportunity for marketing and PR programs, we can't emphasize enough the importance of maintaining traditional programs and fostering relationships with analysts, reporters, bloggers, and customers. VNRs with Social Media can only enhance a proactive and all-encompassing marketing and PR campaign. Remember that, in any adoption cycle, new solutions move from the left to the right of the bell curve, earning mass acceptance along the way. Social Media is indeed breathing new life into VNRs, and that's why VNR 2.0, as a communications tool, helps reinvent PR for the new Web—helping us communicate visually and enabling us to become more effective storytellers.

Lights, camera, action.

Chapter 10
Corporate Blogging

Blogging is nothing new, but it is still highly underrated and misunderstood by a majority of businesses, from small businesses to corporate America. The information we provide in this chapter about corporate blogging might not be anything new to the rapidly expanding pool of Social Media-savvy professionals. Instead, it's intended as a discussion to benefit communicators who are looking for the appropriate ways to participate and to get buy-in from decision makers.

Many people use their blogs as a part-time platform to express their insight, opinions, and observations online (or, as we call it, in the blogosphere). Other bloggers and "blogerati" have become incredibly influential (with many blogging full time), more so than many of their traditional media counterparts, regardless of industry and journalistic background. Their intelligence, words of wisdom, and associated niches attract legions of loyal readers. Blogging is inspiring millions of people to expand from content consumers into content producers. As we noted previously, there are more than 112 million blogs and counting that are active in the world. Some of the most successful blogs are run by big businesses, such as Whole Foods, Dell, Sun, General Motors, SouthWest, and Google, among many others.

Capability vs. Competence

Web platforms available today make it incredibly easy for writers to jump in and publish, link, feed, and market globally—without requiring any technical expertise. Many have even left their "day jobs" and have jumped head first into the ocean of full-time blogging, receiving financial support from advertising revenue and, in some cases, investments from strategic partners to help nurture and reach a specific community. For many bloggers, it's equivalent to winning the lottery—at varying levels, whether it's money, influence, networking, career advancement, or something else. Many blogs that are generating income offer direct advertising, by which Company X can purchase real estate on the blog page or post. And although many blogs are run as full-fledged media properties, earning millions per year, most are run as independent shops or small businesses. The primary focus for most bloggers is creating the content that defines their brand—not on selling. However, blog networks and advertising syndications are helping bloggers monetize their sites by selling and channeling advertising and, in turn, sharing the revenue based on traffic. Many bloggers also embed a Google Adsense widget on their blogs as a way of generating additional income. (Adsense is a keyword-based window that analyzes the content on the page and serves link-based ads from a Google library that match the existing topics.)

Although many of the same tools and strategies that make blogging so popular and influential are beginning to force new channels of business-to-business communications, most corporations either are slow to respond, thinking blogging is more of a toy than a tool, or treat blogging as another form of content marketing. At the opposite end of the adoption cycle, some corporate bloggers jump in too quickly and neglect to focus on what truly makes a good blog: being a resource for customers and peers, enabling valuable conversations, and creating and maintaining relationships.

Jeremiah Owyang discusses how to get the most out of business blogging (from "Web Strategy: How to Be a Corporate Blog Evangelist," January 2007):

> Now that you've been reading about blogs, and have been blogging yourself, start immersing in the art of business blogging. Read business blogging books, attend blogging conferences, join blogging user groups, keep on blogging yourself. Learn some PR skills, writing skills, be able to articulate the difference between casual conversations from corporate communications....

Owyang clearly defines how corporate blogging needs to shape up. Bloggers need to first define the purpose of their blogs. Owyang also provides several helpful hints about strategic blog deployment:

1. Delight your customers (you'd better say yes).

2. Demonstrate corporate openness.

3. Express goodwill.

4. Provide thought leadership.

5. Mitigate PR damage risks.

6. Control the conversation in your market.

7. Develop a product with customers in real time.

8. Harness a rapid-response tool.

9. Casually release products and get feedback.

10. Create word-of-mouth marketing.

11. Amplify a strategic message.

12. Use your blog as a competitive positioning tool to create visibility and differentiation.

Then there's the completely opposite type of blog post that whole-heartedly mocks self-centered and useless business blogs, and instructs you how to continue with your less-than-adequate posts. We were amused by Ian Lurie's blog post "How to Write a Really Crappy Business Blog," as we think you will be, too.

How to Write a Really Crappy Business Blog

By Ian Lurie

There are sooo many awful business blogs out there, I figure folks must really want to create them. So, in 13 easy steps, here's how you write a terrible business blog, torpedo your internet marketing strategy, and gain the scorn of your customer base at the same time:

1. Talk about yourself. Ooooh, this is a winner every time. Blather on about your latest product, how great you are, why readers should buy your stuff. Link to your own site a lot. Bore the heck out of 'em. I guarantee blog suckage within a week.

2. Go negative. Tell everyone why your competitor/fellow bloggers are total idiots. Don't be funny about it! People might misunderstand and think you're starting a debate! Make sure they know You Are Smart and They Are Dumb. You'll shed readers like Gore Tex sheds water.

3. Plagiarize. Cut-and-paste from other sites! It's so easy! Best part is that when you get caught (and you will) you'll be disgraced, and no one will ever darken your virtual door again.

4. Use lots of small, unreadable type. Tiny type gives everyone a headache. No one wants a headache. So they'll leave.

5. Spam the world. Send out unsolicited e-mails begging for links, clicks, attention and such. Use really bad grammar, too. The recipients will never come back. You're now that much closer to crapdom.

6. Use unreadable colors. Put gray text on a dark gray background. Your readers' eyes will cross so fast they'll switch sockets. Once their vision is permanently damaged, they'll have to stop reading. Craptacular.

7. Create really unclear links. Make folks *think* they're going to get something useful when they click, but send them to the page for the worst-selling product you have. Not only will your blog suck, your sales will too! Bonus!

8. Write badly. Remember, you can't build a crappy blog with good grammar and complete sentences. Insted use lots of misspelings and stuff. If you look too smart you'll attract readers, which are the anti-crap.

9. Write too much. Verbal diarrhea will drive away your audience. The stench alone can kill.

10. Digg every post you write. Yah, no one's every thought of that one. Go for it.

11. Stumble every post you write. See above.

12. Never post anything. The easiest way to have a blog that's crappy: Set up the blog, post once, and then never. post. again. This tip's great because it involves no work on your part. It's like you never created a blog at all. Which might have been better...

13. Don't care. Whatever you do, don't care about what you write. If your audience detects sincerity they'll stick around, and you'll have to keep writing. Ugh.

Remember: Some of us are struggling to write decent business blogs. We don't need the competition. So please, keep writing your crappy one.

Those are some of the best corporate blogging tips and some of the worst. If you searched further, you'd find hundreds of posts dedicated to how to blog and why executives should or should not blog. We believe that companies that blog should do so with the intention of speaking directly to their customers; the blog also should be transparent, genuine, and not a vehicle for repurposing marketing content and messages. Transparency is the key to participating in Social Media in general, with blogs and social networks leading the way.

Believe it or not, many company blogs today aren't actually written by the names associated with the posts. Instead, executives are allowing junior, PR, or marketing personnel to write these seemingly genuine words that are no more real than the quotes in company news releases, as discussed in Chapter 8, "Social Media Releases (SMRs)." You've heard the saying that "content is king," which defined Web 1.0. However, in Web 2.0, "conversation is king." Blogs are considered the most direct source for reaching people and hosting direct conversations with them in an informational and helpful public forum.

John Cass, a marketer who writes about corporate blogging, discussed how PR people should refrain from being the ghostwriters on blogs in his post "Are You a Sanctimonious PR 2.0 Professional?"

Are You a Sanctimonious PR 2.0 Professional?

BY JOHN CASS

It appears from Sterling Hager's recent post he thinks that the panel members of the PRSA Boston social media event a week ago are a bunch of sanctimonious 2.0 people; at least that's how I read his post. I assume I am included in the list.

Mr. Hager described on his blog how he disagreed with the advice PRSA panel members gave an audience member who had asked a question at the event, the panel had advised that corporate employees should write all their own material on a blog. He went onto to suggest that the panelists need to get a clue, and that a PR person would be a lousy public relations professional if they are not aware of the details of their client's company, such as product, competitive facts, R&D, finance, channels, positioning and differentiation and therefore if the public relations professional is not aware of the inner workings of their client the professional should not blog on a client's behalf. Also, that if only client corporate staffers have the ability to write a blog it will only be a matter of time before clients decide they do not need an outside PR consultant to talk for them.

He went on to say, "What the anointed should be saying is that if a senior corporate executive has the time, the talent, and the interest, the blog he or she authors will without question be better than anything a PR stand-in could produce. But a PR professional worth his or her salt and who can write can do a good job of it and readers, quite frankly, don't give a darn who writes the copy as long as it is real, useful, entertaining, varied, insightful, consistent, regular, and important."

I am wondering if Sterling Hagar thinks that the purpose of blogging is to solely conduct public relations? I may be wrong about this, but the reason I ask this question is that Mr. Hager appears to be saying that most clients don't have the time to write or the ability to write good blog posts. And so it is a good idea for public relations consultants to write their blog posts for them. What about product managers or senior scientists? Would it really make sense for public relations professionals to talk about engineering issues with customers, or to try to solve customer support issues? Mr. Hager if you are suggesting that the sole reason for blogging is PR I am afraid I must disagree with you. Blogs can be used for many things, though in the process of answering a customer support question you can certainly gain a boost to the perception of your brand.

Agency people and public relations professionals can choose to offer their services and blog on behalf of their clients, and even act as ghostwriters for them on a blog. However is it a good idea to do that? I think that in the perception of the reader blogging is more like talking with someone on a telephone or even in the same room. You would not expect an actor to take the place of the individual to whom you are chatting with on the other end of a telephone line, well it is just the same with blogging, when someone puts their name to a blog post the expectation on the part of the reader is that the person who wrote a blog post is the person whose name appears on the masthead.

As a follow-up to this post (and in response to Sterling Hager), Kari Hanson discussed the subject of whether to ghost post on her blog, First Person PR. Hanson's goal as a blogger is to chronicle her experience as she transitioned from an agency to an internal PR role, and to present a first-person case study of what works as she experimented with new Social Media technologies. Her blog is immersed with her thoughts on PR, Web 2.0, and Social Media. Hanson, who facilitated dozens of briefings on behalf of her clients, had a slightly different opinion than Cass.

To Ghost Post, or Not...

By Kari Hanson

John Cass recently responded to Sterling Hager's somewhat spirited attack, called Sanctimonious 2.0, on a recent PRSA panel. (I didn't attend the social media panel, but I did read Dan Katz's great recap. It sounds like the panel, which featured PR 2.0 evangelists Todd Defran and Todd van Hoosear, certainly took a "purist" slant to social media—everything must be transparent, press releases must have all the latest Web 2.0 widgets, etc. They're pushing a new, cutting edge approach to PR, and so understandably are a bit extremist in their opinions. But, they're also encouraging PR people to experiment with these new technologies, share successes and failures, and then debate how relevant each is, which is to be commended.)

Back to Sterling's rant. Apparently at one point during the panel discussion, someone dared to ask whether a PR person can/should ghost write a blog (I'm sure there were gasps in the room). The panelists all said no, that's better left to corporate employees. Sterling Hager disagreed, and thus began his somewhat humorous online rant. I hate to admit it, but I agree with a lot of what he says. As he points out, we've always written speeches, quotes for releases, and even bylines. Given the right circumstance, a blog is no different. When I was at LP&P, I often wrote blog postings for one of my clients. I knew his hot buttons from the dozens of briefings I facilitated, I obviously knew the message we were trying to convey, and often I was more on top of industry news than he was. So while he was traveling across the country, it made sense for me to feed him content—that's what we do.

At the same time, I think the panelists have a good point—blogs are often designed to create an online dialogue. Just as we run executive opinion pieces by the "authors" and ask them to personalize them, we can't expect to always craft perfect blog posts for clients and executives. But, we can certainly provide a foundation to help feed that online conversation and prevent a blog being abandoned.

False Assumptions

One of the most common fears or reasons for resisting blog implementation is the concern about inviting and hosting negative commentary. If you open up comments, which we believe you should, the reality is that not everyone will agree with your point of view or commentary. However, it's a bit unrealistic to assume that these types of comments or exchanges aren't occurring elsewhere if you're not blogging.

If a conversation about your company takes place online and you're not there to see it, does that mean it didn't happen? Of course not. Inviting comments helps unearth feedback that you might not have otherwise learned. Every negative comment is an opportunity to grow and also shape perception. We highly recommend implementing moderated comments, which enable you to approve or deny comments before they actually appear on the site. The important thing to remember is that as your community grows, the culture for dialogue also takes shape.

Another false assumption is that people will automatically appear if you start a blog. Blogging is an art and a science that combines thought leadership, dedication, passion, empathy, and some publicity and promotion of the content and the ideas embedded in them. Unfortunately, as with all things in Social Media, if you build it, it doesn't necessarily mean they'll come. We have to get the word out through sharing, commenting, linking to other sites, and doing good old-fashioned PR. But over time, it works.

Leveraging Blogging in B2B and B2C

True corporate blogging represents a tremendous opportunity for any business-to-business (B2B) and business-to-consumer (B2C) company to

- Have a voice.

- Communicate with customers.

- Use a nontraditional platform for conversations.

- Unmask predispositions.

- Help mold perceptions.

Geoffrey Moore's books *Crossing the Chasm* and *Inside the Tornado* inspired a generation of innovative marketing strategies. In 2000, *The Cluetrain Manifesto* predicted a shift in how companies would ultimately engage with customers—the phenomenon known as Social Media and the notion that markets are conversations and participation is marketing. Put more simply, you can't market *to* customers; you must engage *with* them.

Blogging is considered one form of Social Media, and it has become a viable, respected, and tremendously influential channel for corporate communications and customer relations. Effective blogs have measurable impact on customer service, product development, marketing, PR, sales, and corporate policies. Many businesses are learning to use executive and corporate blogs as a means to tap into this rich and evolving vein of customer relationship management (CRM), and they are experiencing mushrooming support and increased customer loyalty. They're leveraging the power of Social Media and the prospect of sparking new conversations within markets.

However, many businesses are not capitalizing on this tremendous opportunity, and some are just "dropping the ball" by treating blogging like any other marketing communications program—which it isn't. Unfortunately, many company blogs fall into the category of online newsletters, sales pitches, and repositories for repurposed news releases. These are age-old examples of one-way communication, where companies push their messages at audiences as a way of attempting to control perception. But this isn't about using the Web as a one-way medium. Blogs integrate several basic principles of the read/write Web—the introduction of a more dynamic Web where people can also share their voices. To truly leverage the impact of Social Media, the conversation must be two-way. Making the conversation interactive—enabling visitors to read, communicate, and share with company executives and peers—makes corporate blogging effective and very compelling. It also humanizes the company, allowing people to interact with each other, instead of pushing brands to the masses.

It's Not about Selling, It's about Dialogue

Companies truly concerned with their customers (and influencers) on an emotional level will strive to build a bridge to increase traffic and, ultimately, their sales and brand loyalty. One way to facilitate this bridge is to dedicate a portion of the company Web site to invite people to hosted conversations. The "people" we refer to include customers, employees, peers, channel partners, decision makers, and competitors. It's important to address each of them, acknowledging that crossover exists.

Remember, people blog, not companies. To blog, you must participate first as an individual and a peer. You need to make sure that you start real conversations and have something to bring to the table that is valuable to the party on the receiving end. In addition, it's important to designate frequent posts to each of the influencer groups. You need to create content that speaks to the different stakeholders that you're hoping to connect with.

Consider this high-level formula when creating a corporate blogging program and pipeline:

$$\text{Frequency} + \text{Quality} + \text{Responsiveness} + \text{Focus} \times \text{Stakeholders}$$
$$= \text{Community Building}$$

Consistent posting frequency will ultimately help you build your community. Therefore, corporate blogs should strive for at least one post per week that speaks to each of their target stakeholders. Individual posts should share helpful content, information, facts, insight, trends, and relevant initiatives, and those posts should spark conversations through open and inviting dialogue. Responsiveness is also important (and should be considered a required prologue to creating and publishing your content). You need to respond to blog comments. Comment across other blogs and link back to your blog. Extend the value and expertise you possess from your community to other communities. This is how we network in Social Media.

The key to blogging and participating in Social Media is not to propagate or pontificate. Instead of using the corporate blog as an arm of marketing, identify customer pain points and deliver the painkiller in a direct, personal, and believable fashion. Address critical points in each stakeholder group, and do so consistently. Try to segment information across each market to make the interaction more personal and believable. We call this opening up the corporate kimono—exposing the soul and personality of the company to facilitate genuine communication. One of our favorite resources on corporate blogging is *Naked Conversations,* by Robert Scoble and Shel Israel. The book explicitly spells out why and how to leverage a corporate blog to cultivate target markets at national and global levels, and its associated return on investment.

Scoble was formerly with NEC and was a blogger who frequently criticized Microsoft. Microsoft, in turn, hired him and encouraged him to continue blogging without censor. Many credit his blogs, along with Lenn Pryor and others, with the humanization of Microsoft among business partners and customers, helping to shift views away from the evil empire façade. According to the *Economist,* "Impressively, he has also succeeded where small armies of more conventional public-relations types have been failing abjectly for years: He has made Microsoft, with its history of monopolistic bullying, appear marginally but noticeably less evil to the outside world, and especially to the independent software developers that are his core audience. Bosses and PR people at other companies are taking note."

Another must-read is Debbie Weil's *The Corporate Blogging Book,* which demonstrates how companies can use their blogs as a meaningful channel to reach their customers, and how your customers can become your best advocates through blogging. Blogs such as ProBlogger.net and BloggingTips.com actively share tips and techniques on how to write more effective blog posts and advice about how to increase their reach, exposure, and "shareability." You can take advantage of many other corporate blogging resources to help you understand the power and art of blogging and how to leverage this incredible social channel to foster relationships, convey thought leadership, and earn customer loyalty. You can easily begin your search just by entering "blog tips" into your search engine.

Defining the Path

As you explore and define your path to blogging, you must think about how to maximize Social Media, blogging strategies, and the associated opportunities. It's a good idea to first sit down with the executive and communications team, including business development, marketing, Public Relations, and Web managers. Chart out an official plan, identify prospective participants and writers, establish goals, and dedicate time to making it happen. It's also imperative to develop blog guidelines and work with legal or internal corporate communications to have these procedures in place before the very first blog is published. Also collaborate with sales and customer service to learn the real pain points and needs of the market. Our best advice is this: *Capture it, distill it, and publish often.* Most important, read the comments and interact with the people who want to converse with you. It can only help—after all, it's a two-way street.

At the end of the day, any company that reaches business customers should take the time to understand how its products and services can help those customers succeed. Blogging is about embracing unique technology, and strategically and carefully opening windows to expose the corporate culture. By doing so, the corporate culture will evolve, and a company can quickly prove through open and transparent communication that it possesses important traits (such as leadership skills, years of experience, and customer respect and loyalty). Most of all, communicating through blogs and engaging in dialogue will demonstrate that your company has its customers' objectives in mind.

Finally, remember this: *Learn by reading other blogs and from the successes of others.*

PART **III**

Participating in
Social Media

Chapter 11
Technology Does Not Override the Social Sciences

As you delve into socialized PR, one of the most immediate realizations you'll experience is that the social tools used and discussed within relevant communities will quickly and consistently overwhelm you. There's always a shiny new object. There's always migration from network to network. Remember that these are merely tools to communicate with others; they're not representative of the strategies and methodologies for observing and communicating with people. These are merely the tools communities use to share, discover, and discuss what's important to them. The tools will change, but people and their behavior remain constant.

Social Media is changing the PR outreach paradigm from pitching to personalized and genuine engagement. PR must now influence the new influencers as well as traditional media and analysts—and to do so, much work must be done before conversations ever start.

The reality is, conversations are taking place online right now, usually without you. If you're not part of the conversation, answers, questions, suggestions, complaints, observations, and eventually incorrect perceptions will go unmanaged, unresolved, and unchallenged. Even worse, competition or uninformed peers will step in and engage communities in your absence.

Don't be afraid of online conversations and your participation in them. Yes, you will encounter negative comments. Yes, you'll invite unsolicited feedback. Yes, people will question your intentions. But negativity will not go away simply because you opt out of participating. Negative commentary, at the very least, is truly an opportunity to change a perception (which you might have known or not known existed).

Modern Communications

Today's communication strategies can benefit from social sciences such as sociology and anthropology. The study of society and human relationships and the communities people create and participate in is instrumental in any communication program. Of course, it requires integration into every proactive marketing strategy, well before these are planned and executed. When socialized media is applied to the communications program, it gives you a foundation that unites awareness, proper engagement, and technological applications to increase unobtrusive human interaction—and this leads to meaningful relationships. These applications, powered by social platforms and the people who use them, offer the channels for people to converse, create communities for interaction, and ultimately influence behavior. However, technology is just that: technology. *Social Media is about people and how we can approach them as informed and helpful peers.*

You've seen the tools change and the networks evolve over the years. It might seem archaic to mention this, but not that long ago, the fax machine was a critical pillar for day-to-day business. The point is that the mediums for distributing, sharing, and discovering content will also continue to grow and evolve. These tools will become more sophisticated, while also providing simpler ways for humans to initiate and cultivate relationships with each other. Remember, however, that tools tend to change more quickly than the people who use them. (Old habits die hard.)

On the other hand, with every new tool or service that's introduced, our attention shifts to the latest and greatest innovation. Should we focus on Twitter? But wait, now there's Plurk. Oh, and now Identi.ca is the latest micromedia tool to surface; we'd better jump over there, too.

The speed at which new technology and platforms for communicating are introduced is almost mind numbing. It's contributing to the possibility of a great attention crash and social network fatigue. However, the opportunity for engaging existing and potential stakeholders is unprecedented. Before you overwhelm yourself with all the potential tools and networks to leverage on behalf of your brand or your clients, it is crucial that you step back and realize that you're the communication bridge between your company and the people you ultimately want to reach.

So how do you keep up—and how do you even start? Everything begins with observation (a.k.a. listening). Social Media is rooted in conversations, relationships, exchanges, shared ideas, and common, interests, similar to societies and communities in the real world. Therefore, identifying the online communities where your constituents are congregating and collaborating is the first step in determining—well, everything.

Social Media helps you uncover all the relevant online communities that warrant observation. The most important lesson in Social Media is that, before engaging anyone, you must first observe and understand the cultures, behavior, and immersion necessary to genuinely participate in the communities where you don't already reside. People now enjoy amplified voices in the world of Social Media, which carries into the real world, and now represent a powerful channel of peer-to-peer influence (for better or for worse). However, marketing at them or broadcasting messages in these online communities is about as welcome as the telemarketers who constantly call your home every day.

You cannot afford to ignore this reality. New marketing necessarily integrates traditional and social tools, and builds upon successful, ongoing relationships with the media, influencers, and people. That's right: It's about relationships, and it's about people. Relationships serve as the foundation for every interaction, whether with traditional media, New Media, or just everyday people. And remember, you're now reaching individuals, not *audiences*. Focusing on this fact will keep you on the path to relevance.

The tools you use will change over time (evolve, multiply, and even condense). Some tools will win over others, some will thrive, and others will fly under the radar (but perhaps still remain relevant). It is imperative, however, that you not let the tools overwhelm you. But don't underestimate them, either (especially soon after their introduction).

Don't Fear Change

We often hear these laments: "With so many tools out there, I don't even know where to begin," and "I don't know why any of this matters—maybe I'm just too old." These "whines" represent the classic generation gap regarding how we communicate. First, just admit that new tools will continue to be introduced. Nonadopters (bystanders) might find the onslaught of new technology overwhelming. Younger generations, however, are already communicating with each other through social networks and social tools (and, once properly guided, have an advantage for joining and leading more strategic conversations online). However, hope is not lost for the other generations. These groups just have extra work to do to catch up (perhaps even a complete overhaul on how they currently do things).

Social Media is forcing changes that should have happened a long time ago in everything related to business, from PR and sales to customer service, to product development, and also to corporate management. Whether or not you jump on board, these changes will continue to occur. And, to be honest, not every current PR professional will survive the transition: The fittest and those most willing and able to adapt will be the survivors. The PR industry ultimately will benefit from these changes and the winnowing of its ranks, and will thus be propelled into the forefront of marketing communications. The PR professionals of tomorrow should all be engaged in meaningful conversations using the Social and New Media applications that enable forward-moving dialogue. In fact, every department of every business will soon find itself embracing social strategies.

Social Networks Are Not Legos

Social networks and their associated cultures are defined by the people who participate in them. In turn, each network flourishes as its own island. Over time, a somewhat impenetrable culture emerges (which helps to ensure a more meaningful and commercial-free experience among its residents). Of course, networks need to sustain themselves through revenue, and many sell advertising. But advertising differs from direct marketing, especially from conversational marketing. In fact, making the network flourish with a strong sense of community and culture isn't marketing at all, in the truest sense. Transparent and genuine participation is now an effective form of marketing, without the "marketing" or the snake oil. The bottom line is that you have to understand the sociology and the dynamics of human interaction within particular social networks before you can either write them off as useless or participate within them in the hopes of becoming a resource and building meaningful relationships. You must also understand that technology supports the sociology of the network—it doesn't replace it. Marketing departments of tomorrow will require their savvy communicators to take the time and develop the right approach to understand the various networks.

You will most likely agree that customers and their peers are critical to your success. After all, their emotions, experiences, state of mind, and resulting influence within their community are imperative to the perception of the brands you represent. Broadcasting controlled messages is no way to earn trust and relationships. We must earn them (and, thus, their business, loyalty, and referrals). Social Media gives us a first-ever opportunity to overhear relevant conversations that, in recent times, would have transpired without our knowledge. And we can join in before they build and landslide into something that catches us off guard and potentially lunges us into a reactive crisis communications emergency.

Essentially, Social Media empowers customers to effectively sell and represent your brand as a powerful and influential surrogate sales force. Similarly, Social Media can negatively affect your brand if it is left to open interpretation and dissemination freely without input or guidance. Therefore, Social Media is driven by sociology and the study of human behavior and online cultures. You must begin to effectively identify relevant online community cultures and listen to and respond directly to the people within them.

Other professionals agree with us, including Jason Preston, a professional blogger from the Parnassus Group, who discussed how to avoid the snake oil in his blog post "[Brian] Solis Is Right: Avoid Classic Marketing Like the Plague in Social Media."

Solis Is Right: Avoid Classic Marketing Like the Plague in Social Media

BY JASON PRESTON

Social networks are often *more* tightly knit than blogging niches, and more easily offended by blundering, well-intentioned but poorly-informed marketers. I mean, there are Facebook groups (like this one) dedicated to hating on "internet marketers" in Facebook.

The fact of the matter is that poking around Facebook as an individual is a fun and often rewarding experience, even if you don't know what you're doing. As people, I encourage you all to sign up, and friend us (sidebar!).

As a business, it can be a much less welcoming experience. I've spoken to a number of people, including several of my college friends who are on Facebook, about "advertising" on Facebook. Almost universally, they consider advertising, or blatant product-shilling, to be a no-no (makes sense).

In fact, I think the best thing to do is to remember that quote I threw in at the top of this post. I'll type it again:

> Transparent and genuine participation is now a very effective form of marketing, without the snake oil.

The general idea is to avoid the snake-oil. People are overly suspicious of slimy things on the internet, and there's no juicier, viral blog post than getting to call out some sneaky, hidden marketing campaign.

So, you decide to jump in. Great, but slow down and think about what we've discussed so far. Underestimating social networks is dangerous. We've already witnessed too many companies attempting to spark conversations by "marketing" to "audiences" through "messages" within social networks. This is traditional marketing, and it's insulting to everyone on the receiving end. If you follow this approach, it can have disastrous consequences for you and the brand you represent. The conversations that drive and define Social Media require a genuine and participatory approach. Just because you have the latest tools to reach people, or have played around with them, doesn't mean you can throw the same old marketing at them. We continue to stress a very important point (in every chapter): Having access to the social tools doesn't make you an anthropologist or a sociologist.

Social networks are no place for real-time experimentation. You'll find that the communities and the people within them are unforgiving in their tolerance of sales or marketing pitches. Businesses who are leading the way can learn much by listening and observing before establishing contact.

Many companies are participating in social networks as a form of proactive outbound customer service with a twist of social marketing, including the following:

- Zappos
- JetBlue
- Home Depot
- *USAToday*
- Southwest Airlines

- H&R Block
- Dell
- Wine Library
- FreshBooks

They're engaging customers on their turf, using their channels of communication, to help customers (and potential customers) solve problems and find information, or simply to engage them in valuable dialogue.

Margaret Mead is known for championing a style of anthropological research called participant observation. When she studied in the field, she set out to both observe people and participate in the life of the community. Mead believed that this was the only way to more fully understand a culture. Participant-observation fieldwork is the foundation of contemporary anthropology. In Social Media, communities take the form of social networks inhabited and governed by the people within them. People establish associations, friendships, and allegiances around content, objects, products, services, and ideas. How they communicate is subject to the tools and networks that people adopt based on the influence of their social graph (and the culture within). It's important to note that cultures are unique to each social network and require a dedicated ear and observant pair of eyes to objectively learn and ultimately adapt to each.

Through social sciences, we can now see the very people we want to reach, along with their shared content, thoughts, perceptions, and predispositions. By doing so, we're reminded that we need to humanize our story and the process of storytelling. The process of observing and listening gives us insight and instills empathy to more realistically enter each online society as a citizen of each respective community in which we hope to participate. By listening, reading, and participating, brand marketers have an opportunity to make their brands more approachable and shareable than ever before. This is how you humanize brands, create loyalty, and earn your customers' business. Yes, there are many networks. Yes, they're thinning our attention. And, yes, this is the new form of media and influence, and it is transforming corporate communications, traditional media, and how people communicate with each other.

The Proof Is in the Politics

The 2008 U.S. election year represents a good example of the sociology of New Media in Web communities. Before we even discuss 2008 and the presidential campaign, however, we want to trace the roots of Web sociology back to 2004 and the well-recognized campaign executed by Howard Dean. Dean's campaign was way ahead of its time and led the election participants into a new realm of communication through social networking. In many of Dean's early campaign speeches, you may have heard him say, "You don't know me, but you will." Many feel that Dean meant what he said. For Dean, his platform spread quickly via the Internet. A few key players and their forward-thinking strategies propelled Dean's run for office. Joe Trippi, Dean's campaign manager, brought the experience of six presidential campaigns and knowledge from a former career in computer software. The campaign soared to heightened awareness from Trippi's expertise in technology and managerial skills. Dean also had two Web experts, Matthew Gross and Zephyr Teachout, who were the brains behind what people described as Dean's "Web sensation."

Dean's Web site used a blog and various forums that helped to spread the word quickly. Best of all, a strong community formed on the Dean Web site—it was the community that built the Dean campaign, which, in turn, built a one-of-a-kind run for office. Other collaborative strategies involved meetup.com, the Web site used to organize events for different groups. The Dean for America campaign was able to gather hundreds of people from cities across the country through the meetup.com strategy. Although Dean did not win the Democratic nomination, his campaign achieved noteworthy success: He garnered more than 140,000 supporters before he even announced his candidacy.

Dissident Voice: Remembering Howard Dean's 2004 Campaign

BY JOSHUA FRANK

The Dean campaign was truly an example of how technology played a tremendous role on the campaign trail. The technology enabled people to congregate around his platform and rally together for a cause. The Dean organization formed a bonded community. However according to the blog post by Bill Ives in May 2008, the Dean campaign only understood the technology, yet failed with the sociology. On the other hand, the Obama campaign in 2008 is a campaign where you can see sociology at work much more so than in 2004. Obama's campaign is a good example of the strength that sociology plays to create communities and bonds.

It's the Sociology, Not the Technology: How to Be Effective on the Web—Lessons from the Obama Campaign

BY BILL IVES

Last year I was on a panel at the Enterprise 2.0 conference titled: 90% People, 10% Technology. The premise being that many people say as they go to implement a new technology, Well, It's really 90% People, 10% Technology." Then they invest in the opposite ratio. My good friend, Valdis Krebs makes a similar point in his recent post, It's the networks stupid, about how the Obama campaign is using the web. In the context of linking to an excellent NYT OpEd, The Obama Connection, he writes:

"...the Dean campaign thought they understood the internet in 2004, but they really did not get "social networks". They made some breakthroughs in technology, but screwed up the sociology, and lost in a big way. Obama seems to be focusing first on the sociology of building networks and then supporting those social networks with technology—the correct sequence of attention. The Obama campaign is successful because they know that sociology & technology properly mixed give a better result than either of them alone, or improperly mixed."

I have found it always makes sense to figure out the business problem and then apply the technology. This works whether it is the business of business or the business of political campaigns. I have already written a bit about Obama's use of the web on this blog. In one post, How Barack Obama is Using Web and Enterprise 2.0 in the US Primary Campaign Through Central Desktop, I quoted commenter Rob Patterson (from the Fast version) who said, "Others say -"He has no experience" But isn't the organization of his campaign a model for effectiveness and does it not show a brilliant insight into his understanding of the new reality? Imagine a Fortune 500 CEO with this approach and what they could do."

Here is a model for viral marketing for any web startup. There [are] lessons to be learned for any business that wants to make better use of the web. The NYT piece seems to agree as it mentioned, "More than any other factor, it has been Barack Obama's grasp of the central place of Internet-driven social networking that has propelled his campaign for the Democratic nomination into a seemingly unassailable lead."

We agree that the Obama campaign is a good case study of how sociology plays an important role during an election year. It's about the people and their issues, causes, and concerns (and an understanding of the technology to support and drive the campaign causes). A *New York Times* editorial opinion by Roger Cohen published on May 26, 2008, and mentioned by Ives pointed out that Obama's people understand the importance of networks and how to open up the Internet to make great dialogue as opposed to war; through the dialogue, people are able to change what he calls the "centerpiece of policy."

The Obama campaign truly sought to identify the people they wanted to engage, and then engaged those people within their own communities on their own terms (in the process, giving those people the tools and content to empower them to become surrogate evangelists). Obama's Democratic nomination campaign will forever be a hallmark for future campaigns. The 2012 election, and every election thereafter, will be driven by Social Media, social tools, and the people who populate influential social networks.

The sociology of Internet communities is a fascinating topic that will continue to be an area of focus and study as more people embrace and define the Social Web. In looking at how Internet cultures have emerged over the years, there's a huge shift in the way people are making connections, building relationships, and forming distinct cultures in the Long and Short Tail. Even more important, human interaction in PR, or any form of peer-to-peer marketing, has been and always will be the cornerstone of the best relationships.

Today, with a shift in how media is democratized, people favor the movement toward user-generated content and such related practices; they comment on blogs, review and rate content, make friends in Web communities, use mashups, and build their own groups on social networks. Whether it's an election that inspires younger and older generations alike or it's U.S. corporations learning that people want to interact with the human voices behind the companies, sociology play a tremendous role in educating professionals on how to better observe, listen, learn, and participate with the people who will mean the most to their causes or concerns and who will take a desired action.

The Web is a dynamic and complex environment laden with pride and passion from the people who drive the communication. It's an environment for sociologists and communications professionals to study, as it continues to present the greatest potential to foster and deepen the strongest relationships between people and between people and their brands. It starts with a combination of social and traditional tools to discover, listen, learn, and engage directly with customers. This early research enables you to find where the relevant conversations are taking place, with your underlying goal being to help people make decisions and accomplish things because of your participation. It's about gathering intelligence. This process also removes the tendency to "market" *at* people and naturally shapes a more honest, meaningful, and informative approach.

You probably didn't realize that part of your job is to become a Social Media sociologist and participant observer. In fact, your job now is to get to work—study online societies, their culture, and how they interact, and thus build meaningful relationships that will contribute to the company's brand equity, resonance, and overall bottom line.

Chapter **12**

Social Networks: The Online Hub for Your Brand

As a part of the New Media regime, strategically participating in Social Media is not only critical to the evolution of PR, but it's also necessary to effectively communicate with the people who can help you extend the conversations that impact your business. It's important to know where to start and to recognize the best way to jump into the dialogue—understanding that listening and actions speak louder than words.

It begins with listening and observing. Eventually, participation becomes clear. What we do with the information that we learn counts for almost everything. As they say, it's FTW (for the win). We will do our part to help you identify the networks and strategies necessary to embrace Social Media in a way that makes you more successful as a communications professional.

Everything you do online today, whether it's personal or on behalf of a company you represent, contributes to public perception and overall brand resonance. Your profile, your feeds, the groups you belong to, the events you attend, the pictures you upload, the comments you leave, the posts you write, and the friends you share all say something about you.

Social Media can work for or against you. Just because you engage, you're not necessarily contributing to the advancement or expansion of the brand you represent. This chapter helps you take a proactive role in defining and shaping who you are and what you stand for. It also explains why what you represent matters to those you're trying to reach. Social networks will come and go, but it's your job to observe, listen, and participate within those communities that will most benefit from your story.

The Rise of Social Networks

Facebook evolved into the social network *de jour* for business professionals who didn't understand or missed out on the MySpace phenomenon, or who didn't understand how to creatively leverage their LinkedIn contacts.

Since Facebook opened its network, the user base has grown exponentially. Its growth can also be directly attributed to the attention Facebook received during the 2007 F8 Facebook developer conference in San Francisco, where CEO and founder Mark Zuckerberg opened its application programming interface (API) to third parties to build applications that run on the network. Personally, our contacts have skyrocketed along with new requests from "friends" (including people we might not know) pouring in on a daily basis.

It's not just Facebook, however; networks such as LinkedIn and Plaxo are connecting business professionals while also promoting a packaged brand—the experiences, positions, and contributions we have made throughout our career. Our profiles on social networks say a lot about who we are and why people should connect with us.

What you invest in social networks—from your profiles, applications, and aggregated feeds to your relationships—is exactly what you will get out of them. Your network strategy defines your experience. It's not a nightclub, buffet breakfast, picnic, or spectator sport. It's a place for you to build and maintain relations with key contacts and friends, and it's also the most effective way to package and present your online business persona, your accomplishments, and your expertise.

We've talked about three popular social networks for professionals: Facebook, Plaxo, and LinkedIn. And that's just the beginning. New networks will come and go, especially those in the niche market segments where many of us specialize. In our case, we live in the world of marketing with many relevant social networks for us to join to learn and promote our own online brands. For example, networks such as MarcomProfessional. com, Junta42, Gooruze, SocialMediaToday.com, and dozens of others housed at ning.com are potentially valuable networks for anyone in the marketing world to showcase thought leadership.

Although many cringe at the thought of having to set up yet another profile with every new network that is introduced, you have to focus on building your relationships and sharing your capabilities and vision within the networks that foster the visibility critical to your real world. As communications professionals, it's your job to stay on top of all the new applications and networks where the people you need to reach are participating and communicating.

Participation and Visibility

Social networks are becoming primary mechanisms for connecting with people, ideas, brands, news, and information. However, thinking of social networks as just personal playgrounds will come back to haunt you and any company you work with in the future. Yes, beware of the things you share online because they're indexed in search engines and live on the Web for a very long time. Yes, your activity appears in search engines such as Yahoo! and Google. And your blog posts, Flickr photos, comments, Twitter updates, and so on, show up in Google Alerts and also in Technorati. You need to think about online participation in an entirely different and more useful and productive way.

You are the brand. Use the power of search and Social Media to your advantage.

This is about leveraging your personal social graph and Social Media tools and channels to more effectively cultivate online relationships and, at the same time, leverage the network to increase visibility for your expertise, reputation, and activity. As a marketer, your collective "brand" can also impact and bolster the brands you might represent. The one thing that connects everything is *you*. You are on the frontlines for everything related not only to you, but also to everything you represent, now and in the future.

You are the hub of your online activity. With every comment, new profile, update, post, image, or video uploaded, you are intentionally or inadvertently constructing an online persona that, at the very least, contributes to and ultimately creates a personality that is open to perception and interpretation—with or without your implicit direction. Why leave pieces for people to find across the Web through searches and the various platforms you choose to engage in? Reel it in, package it, and present it in a compelling way.

It's not just about the ability to connect with people. It's about creating, cultivating, and promoting a strategic online presence and personal brand. Remember, participation is marketing. This is your online identity and your online brand. It's yours to create, cultivate, define, and manage.

Think about it. Whether you're an entrepreneur, part of a company, or a student, remember that your Web activity is an open book that remains open for all to read for years to come. Those who are strategic about how they participate online will elevate above the masses that choose to experiment and learn the hard way.

The bottom line is this: Whether you're applying for a job, pitching a business prospect, or representing a bigger brand in Social Media engagement, you *will* be Googled for reference. That's just the way it is. Besides, you know you Google yourself, too. It's one of our guilty little pleasures.

We've maintained profiles on Facebook and LinkedIn for a few years and still do. LinkedIn was sort of Web 1.0's version of a social network that attracted business professionals and connected them with each other (and introduced them to their extended contacts).

As PR professionals, LinkedIn will serve you well, enabling you to manage a virtual Rolodex, cultivate relationships, find people you need to know, promote your business and areas of expertise, ask questions to crowd-source qualified responses, and help valuable contacts to find you. LinkedIn's core benefits are valuable as an online static resumé, combined with links and a list of contacts ripe for networking and pilfering. However, the personal network depends on connections and introductions to flourish.

In contrast, Plaxo started as an online address book and calendar that synched with all popular contact-management tools, not just for your own database, but for your contacts, too. It has evolved into a social network and also presents a feed that collects updates from the other social tools you might use outside of the service. For example, if you use Flickr or YouTube, write a blog, or send tweets on Twitter, Plaxo can receive those updates and present them on your profile so that connections can view them in one place. Facebook also offers this capability in the MiniFeed feature.

We can't leave MySpace out of the discussion, as it is based almost on the same business model as Facebook but is executed differently and targeted at a pop-culture demographic. MySpace is the one of the most popular and successful social networks online, but Facebook is quickly becoming a dominant force in its own right.

With MySpace, profiles are completely over the top with animation, music, video, and atrocious template designs. But with Facebook, users can customize their profile with specific content, applications, and correspondence that further enhance their online aggregated presence. Facebook offers customization, scalability, elegance, and cohesion, collectively representing the tools, services, people, and activity that are important to you.

In terms of profile aggregation, many third-party applications can help you centralize your disparate online profiles and activity, and integrate RSS feeds for services you use that don't yet have a Facebook application available—microblogs, blogs, pictures, videos, bookmarks, and so forth. Not only does this channel your activity, but it also promotes your brand in your own way and showcases your ideas and expertise. Think about it: You can cleanly package everything you do online into one strategically crafted profile for all to enjoy. It's also a way of promoting your expertise and staying in contact with peers and other influential people.

Dedicated services are focused social content networks that aggregate all your online activity so that subscribers can tap into everything you (and others) do—all in one constantly updated and easy-to-read feed. These services include Tumblr, Jaiku, FriendFeed, Strands, Lifestream.fm, and SocialThing, to name a few. FriendFeed is becoming immensely popular because not only can people see everything that you do as it hits the Web, but they can also comment in the stream for you and others to see and reply. These feeds are called lifestreams or brandstreams because they channel all activity into one easy-to-view channel (or stream).

Again, social networks enable you to aggregate and promote your online brand while nurturing and managing important relationships.

We focus on Facebook because it's one of the easiest and most versatile social networks for professionals today. Facebook is a profile and presence aggregator, channeling all your online activity through one main hub and combining almost every online social tool that can be used. And as a communications professional, especially in this social economy, it's your job to monitor online conversations and the networks in which they take place. Although some say it's the ultimate marketing tool, we believe it is the closest thing we have to navigating through our first life instead of contemplating starting a "second life."

Facebook Is a Template, Not a News Release

The core capabilities of Facebook enable you to e-mail, instant message, and comment on each other's wall, leaving comments, links, and strategic propaganda on each other's home pages. Robert Scoble recently asked whether the Facebook Wall would be the new press release. In this example, it's your personal brand that represents the starting point for any outreach. He started this discussion on his blog.

Hmmm, Facebook: A New Kind of Press Release

PR people pay attention.

I don't answer email anymore. Too much of it.

But there's one thing that gets passed to my Nokia phone: Facebook wall messages.

Anyone around me knows that occasionally my phone goes "beep, beep." That's Facebook (I only pass wall messages onto my phone via SMS).

Today we were walking around Babies R Us in Colma (buying baby stuff) and my phone went "beep, beep." It was a Facebook message from Frank Roche. If you're on my Facebook profile you can see it.

It says *"Cool new iPhone app: Mock Dock http://mockdock.com."*

I quickly turn to Patrick, say "try this out." He tried it out and says "it's cool." I took a picture of Patrick using it and it, indeed, is cool. It'll be the first thing I put on my iPhone when I get my own.

It's a Web page that adds a ton of cool Web apps to your iPhone.

And now we have a new way for PR people to let me know about their apps. Write it on the wall please. Facebook: the new press release.

Oh, and you now know how to get my phone to go "beep, beep" too.

UPDATE: It's 10:16 p.m., my phone just beeped so I headed over to Facebook to see what was just posted. Well, Otto Radke just posted on my Facebook wall: *"if you liked mockdock.com checkout mojits.com. I prefer that over mockdock.com."*

I'm already starting to be trained like a pavlovian dog. Beep beep brings good stuff. Mojits rocks.

In response to Scoble's blog post about Facebook being the new press release, Brian answered the question and continued the discussion with his blog post.

Robert Scoble Asks, "Is Facebook the New Press Release?"

Robert Scoble recently asked whether or not Facebook may represent a new kind of press release.

Let me answer this for you.

No. Facebook is not the next template for press releases, no more than Pownce, Twitter, and Jaiku collectively represent the replacement for traditional wire services.

I know he wasn't serious about it becoming the next template for a press release, but what he is saying is loud and clear, and you should pay attention. Reading between the lines, "I get too many emails. I cannot respond to most of them. Find a way to stand out. Be creative and reach me in a way that appeals to me. Oh, and give me another reason to love my iPhone."

For those who have yet to join Facebook, it is a social network. And, in my opinion, it is the most prominent social network out there today. It's everything Myspace could never be and it is important, significant, and only beginning its reign of economic influence. The difference is the caliber of people in the network and the tools they use to communicate with each other inside and outside the network.

On each profile in Facebook, there is a "wall" for people to leave comments, questions, recommendations, and also share media with each member, which is not unlike the comments section in Myspace. Each addition is visible to anyone and everyone.

With a little imagination, you can envision how the new generation of social presence applications and social networks appeal to marketers and PR. If you can read it above, there are two quick pitches made on Robert's wall. If not, click here for a larger view.

This is why I write about social media, networks, and social applications in the first place. They represent the ability to spark conversations with people directly, as well as those that influence them, in new and unique ways. And, they're forcing PR to evolve and step out from behind its cloak of anonymity.

Now that Facebook is open to everyone, as well as all of the latest social applications, it's very easy to join and find the people that matter to you and your company, wherever they may congregate.

While they represent new opportunities to reach people however, they are also indicative of why today's PR practice will fail miserably in the realm of social media, unless a new approach is embraced. And, it's not easy. A deep philosophical examination of the PR practice today and its ills, is critical and necessary in order to even THINK about participating.

The first problem is that we as PR people (generally speaking), don't understand what it is we represent and why it is important and also unique to specific people. The second problem is that we speak in messages and assume that one message covers all the bases. The next issue is that we view journalists and customers as an audience speaking "at" them and ignoring (or forgetting) that audiences are comprised of different groups of people from a variety of horizontal and vertical groups. Finally, we use antiquated tools that broadcast the aforementioned problems to the masses with little regard for the recipient's wants and needs.

I wholeheartedly believe that leaving a traditional pitch on the wall of Facebook for all too see is fundamentally a bad idea.

It's the difference between spam and information - and it's a fine line.

Whether participating in social media is a good or bad idea, the answer lies in our ability to understand the culture of any community and why we should be there. We must analyze why other people are there, who they are, how they participate, while understanding the differences between journalists, bloggers, and everyday people.

The price of admission is respect, listening, and transparency. This is about relationships. And remember, this isn't the one and only time you may need to reach certain people. So take the time to do this the right way.

What if we as PR, took the time to analyze what it would take to be compelling to each person as it relates to the culture of the community we're evaluating? What if we reverse-engineered where people went for their information and in turn, truly understood how to use the same tools they use to communicate. What if after thinking through these challenges you developed something that looked nothing like a pitch, but ultimately effective? Well, we'd end up creating a new breed of PR professionals that will survive the impending collision between old and new PR.

We developed our top ten list of how to target people through Social Media or traditional media:

1. Determine your value proposition and the most likely markets that will benefit from your news.

2. Humanize and personalize the story. One version no longer cuts it.

3. Identify the people you want to reach and how they prefer to see information.

4. Read and watch their work.

5. Participate in their communities and use their tools of choice (but as a person first, not as a PR spammer). Don't start pitching right out of the gate.

6. Monitor the vibe and how people share information within their communities. Learn the dynamics and the rules of engagement. Listen. Learn. Respect.

7. Don't pitch. Stand out. Be compelling.

8. Use a variety of approaches but without spamming.

9. Don't forget the traditional tools that work. Make sure that you cultivate relationships across the board.

10. Repeat the previous steps as you move across the disparate groups of people you need to reach. This is how to do PR across the bell curve of customer adoption and in the Long Tail.

Facebook might not be the next news release, but it's certainly a place that can get someone's attention. It doesn't matter if it's Facebook, Twitter, MySpace, LinkedIn, FriendFeed, or some other tool. It all begins with you, your brand, and your expertise. The work you do and the attention you pay to the cultivation of your online persona will speak volumes about your credibility.

Avoid the Clutter and Build Relationships

You can use many ways to communicate and gather information using Facebook. Another point of interest on Facebook is the Newsfeed that is on every profile page. It is a powerful and insightful glimpse of your, and your contacts', recent activity. It summarizes recent applications that are added or deleted; new friendships that are made; groups that are formed, joined, or abandoned; upcoming events and RSVPs; and so on. It gives you everything you need to determine what groups to join, which events to attend, which new apps you should evaluate, and who you should know. And now with the newly announced Facebook Connect service, supporting communities, blogs, and social services can also feed back to your Facebook feed as you participate outside the network.

You can embed many other interesting applications in Facebook, such as these:

- A social calendar, to enable others to see where you are or where you are going

- Flickr photos

- Apprate (www.apprate.com), an online community of reviews for all Facebook apps

- Upcoming.org, to stay connected with friends and coordinate activities and events

- Top Friends, to create a shortcut to your inner circle

- A comprehensive social network panel that visually displays links to all the other communities where you might maintain profiles

One of the main reasons we favor Facebook is that everything we need is in one place. It's similar to a broadcast center where you can communicate with individuals or groups while also reading what your contacts are doing.

For example, aside from updating your status simultaneously across several outside platforms, you can manage your calendar to see what other events are coming up and where your contacts will be going. You can also join groups dedicated to a variety of topics and organizations that you support and follow, enabling you to communicate directly with other members without having to manage dozens of outside groups and links just to stay in touch. And if you need anything to help you accomplish a task, you can search the Facebook application directory and find the right tool for the job. You can communicate with everyone in one place, using a variety of embeddable tools that reach people in the manner they prefer.

Remember, this is about getting away from clutter, overflowing inboxes, contact spam, and unannounced phone calls. This is about building and maintaining personalized relationships. It's also about a new take on marketing, enabling you to reach individuals and very targeted groups with specific information that is of value to them.

This is participation. This is personal branding. This is marketing redux. Note, listen, and watch before you begin any marketing campaigns within the network. We've said this a lot throughout this book, but as with all Social Media, you first need to think about who you're trying to reach, how to reach them, and why your story matters to them. This is no place for spam or traditional marketing.

Your job is to not only promote your expertise, but also engage in conversations and discussions that matter to you and to your business. Facebook is one of many social networks that require your attention. To truly engage in Social Media, you need to be wherever the people who matter to you congregate, even if it requires your participation across many different locations. However, this isn't a pass for you to start marketing blindly. Research, observe, and listen before even thinking about jumping in. Absorb the culture of the community and participate as a person, never as a marketer. Social Media requires respect and intelligence.

It's about demonstrating expertise and reinforcing good ideas with mistakes and lessons learned. This is how you consistently build and support an online brand. It's about what you share and how you participate. It defines not only your brand, but also the brands you represent. The rest is just the tools that facilitate the exchange of information and dialogue.

Chapter 13

Micromedia

Micromedia dates back to 2000, but it really didn't take shape, or garner momentum, until 2005 and 2006, with the rise of popular social networks and the emerging need to focus conversations. Social Media analyst Jeremiah Owyang, who frequently discusses this topic, describes it this way:

> Quick audio or video messages published to a trusted social community. May be created and consumed using mobile technology, and often distributed using other Social Media tools.

We offer an alternative definition:

> Any form of concentrated content created using social tools that broadcast voice, video, images, or text to friends and followers within dedicated Web and mobile communities.

Micromedia represents a significant change in how we create and share content online, and it continues to rapidly evolve. The catalyst propelling exponential adoption is the ability to quickly create and consume conversation-inducing, highly focused bursts of content. For example, with Twitter, Identi.ca, Plurk, and other micro-communities, posts are usually maxed at 140 characters or less. Micromedia is transforming the dynamics and rules of engagement for PR, marketing, and customer service. It's also challenging PR professionals with a type of communication that is different from any other channel (whether traditional or Social Media) in how and when we communicate with people.

Micromedia, and the emerging market for what some call "media snacking," is usually served as "byte"-sized snacks instead of a full meal of information.

Media Snackers

The inflection point for this topic occurred in late 2007 when Jeremiah Owyang publicly asked whether enthusiasts respected media snackers. He then tagged several Social Media experts—Francine Hardaway, Chris Brogan, Shel Israel, Connie Benson, and Bill Claxton, among others—to continue the conversation. Ultimately, co-author Brian Solis was pinged by Todd Defren. To ascertain its value and potential, Brian thought it might be more helpful to examine what it is and why it exists instead of discussing whether he *respected* media snacking.

Media snackers are content creators or consumers who read small bits of information, data, or entertainment when, where, and how they want. Many relate this specifically to the Millennials (a.k.a. Generation Y—those born between 1980 and 1991) because, in a sense, they grew up more "connected" than the generations before them. However, it's not just about the younger generations. Instead, it's about media in general and how it is carving new channels and creating new vehicles to facilitate conversations, relationships, and sharing by, and for, the people—across every generation and market demographic. The content curators, creators, consumers, and thought leaders who are defining the new social economy, and are building social capital for themselves in the process, are driving micromedia.

Media Fatigue

Many edglings and early adopters are already starting to show signs of Social Media fatigue, with so many networks, content-publishing tools, and voices vying for, and thinning, their interest and attention. Their RSS readers are overflowing with blog posts. Tools such as Twitter, Jaiku, Plurk, Tumblr, Identi.ca, and other microblogs push content at a rapid-fire pace. Social networks are addictive and immersive—their respective communities are constantly calling for attention, participation, and updates.

But don't think that micromedia will fade into obscurity just because people become overwhelmed with choices and content. We believe it's how we all will eventually communicate with one another, and the right micromedia tools will usurp the daily services and solutions you use today (e-mail, instant messaging, text messaging, and even phone calls). Micromedia provides a new platform for microsized discussions.

A Closer Look

Let's further define micromedia as applications and usage, which requires additional exploration and explanation. Micromedia is similar to blogging, in that you proactively share updates. However, the updates aren't blog posts. They're similar to public updates (for example, what you're doing, reading, thinking, observing, contemplating, learning, or sharing). And most important, you share these updates in a public timeline, which is similar to the MiniFeed in Facebook or newsfeeds in your feedreader. A public timeline enables your followers or community to see and reply to your updates, and people can proactively subscribe to your updates so that what you share appears in their stream of updates.

On one end of the spectrum, these updates are shared in 140-character (or fewer) bursts (Twitter). Other services, such as Tumblr, enable you to share more than 140 characters, but using additional characters or words is highly discouraged. After all, it's about brevity and value—saying more with less. You can also share files, pictures, links, audio, and video (and include short captions).

Micromedia is actually creating a new paradigm for conversations and the dynamics in which people communicate with each other. It facilitates the opportunity to share the puzzle pieces, bit by bit, and to ultimately represent the bigger picture of who you are and why someone should follow you.

Perhaps one of the most compelling attributes of micromedia is the ability to listen to conversations relevant to specific brands. Instead of searching "brand name" in Google, Yahoo!, Ask.com, or blog search engines, micromedia channel searches reveal real-time conversations taking place in a variety of contexts across popular communities related to your brand.

These conversations mean everything. They represent not only a reflection of the current perception, but also an opportunity to contribute to the evolution of that perception. Perhaps one of the greatest value propositions of listening to and engaging in micromedia-based conversations is the ability to learn from those experiences; observe new perspectives, insight, and feedback; and assess the dialogue to shape future participation. In the business world, these lessons spotlight public sentiment and educate us on the very things that we can feed back into our product development, customer service, and marketing processes to make the next iteration more relevant and poignant.

In fact, many top brands are using tools such as Twitter as an outbound customer service channel to engage and help people with questions, negative opinions, information, or direction. New tools, networks, or services are continually introduced, and edglings flock to each of them, test them, and then share their experiences. Their reports and opinions determine whether the rest of the herd follows.

Twitter took off as micromedia's early leader, but the overall landscape for new communications tools and communities is really in its infancy. At the time of this writing, we can't declare clear winners. People are always on the hunt for new information, and they will go to great lengths to find and reach like-minded people. Of course, as in every market, people naturally follow guides and trendsetters, and with enough momentum, the crowds increase (because no one wants to get left behind). People naturally go where their peers, friends, and family go. However, with every new, exciting service that gains momentum, individuals—whether early adopters or mainstream users—are forced to create and maintain new and existing profiles across multiple networks simply to communicate with their contacts and maintain their relationships.

As mentioned previously, micromedia represents a shift in how people are talking to each other. You're probably wondering how you will keep up with all these different tools and networks that currently exist—and those not yet introduced. People are pulled in so many directions, and many just don't have the time or desire to read and watch everything that's pushed to them. But this conversation is not about those who don't use these tools; it's about those who do. And millions are already experimenting with micro tools and associated communities.

Micromedia tools inspire a completely new culture of online behavior that is dedicated to staying connected through the active art of updates, participation, and discovery. Tools such as Twitter, Jaiku, Utterz, Tumblr, Seesmic, and even Facebook are becoming more popular, and they are widely recognized and utilized as primary forms of casual and even professional communications. Users praise micromedia services as a step in the right direction for enhancing our media consumption and production, increasing our participation within dedicated communities, and transforming those who would rather watch and listen to the discussions than contribute to their outcome. For example, some bloggers have stated that micromedia is the ideal solution for when they don't want to write a regular blog post, but they still want to be connected. Short snippets of information on Twitter, Identi.ca, or Plurk might not always be relevant or fit into the regular content of your blog, but they still enable you to interact with your community and share information in real time. Perhaps one more sentence will help explain the phenomenon of micromedia. It's not just the ability to publish updates whenever and wherever; it's the flourishing dynamics of receiving immediate responses and responding to those within the community. Micromedia is the newest form of online "conversation," and it is viral, global, and inspiring.

Micromedia Marketing

One of the most compelling trends that we can't ignore is that scores of people are discovering and sharing information. As a marketing professional, therefore, you should pay attention. With every new channel that gains momentum, you can build a connection between you, your peers, and your customers to foster healthy and dynamic communities based on conversations and relationships.

And it's not just about the many early adopters who blaze the trail by experimenting, documenting, and sharing their experiences with shiny new objects. It's about the people dictating their preference for creating, receiving, and sharing information in specific ways. Steve Rubel, a leading authority on New Media and PR, and senior VP at Edelman, wrote earlier this year that micromedia enabled him to do more with less. It freed him from the pressures of having to write daily posts, forcing him to focus on sharing shorter, more frequent thoughts and discoveries across myriad dedicated social networks, including his blog, microblog, and lifestream.

In micromedia, however, sometimes less isn't more; it's just less. We participate in almost all forms of macro and micromedia production and consumption. Plenty of garbage is out there. Just because we can produce things easily these days doesn't necessarily make them good. But you choose what to share and what to watch, read, and listen to (just as everyone determines when, where, and what they consume).

As a content producer, don't contribute to the irrelevance of the communities in which you participate. Earn followers because you are sharing updates and information that spark responses and stimulate bigger and more relevant conversations.

Micromedia-Inspired Macro Influence

To reach these increasingly discerning groups of people, you need to understand their culture and the communities in which they participate, search, and share. You must then reverse-engineer the process from a position of sincerity and empathy. Again, it all starts with listening and observing. In the world of business communications, companies can actively monitor the use of their brand, or the brands of their competitors, to tap into real-world, real-time perception. Those who proactively monitor these bustling communities will learn everything they need to know not only to address individual conversations, but also to design targeted communications programs for imminent use.

For example, H&R Block used Twitter to respond to people who had questions about taxes during the last tax season. The company used Twitter search tools, such as Search.Twitter and Tweetscan.com, to monitor the conversations taking place and were quick to respond with information and answers.

JetBlue and Southwest Airlines are actively engaging fliers on all forms of micromedia; they're communicating with fliers who have questions, those who want to share experiences, and those who are just seeking advice. Among others, Tony Hsieh (CEO of online shoe e-tailer Zappos) and Dell are actively answering customer questions, solving problems, and promoting specials. Comcast, which currently has a PR and customer service challenge, is using Twitter to actively address customer issues, and the approach is working.

These examples represent just a few of the growing number of companies that are online daily, listening and engaging via micromedia. All these businesses are contributing to and cultivating dedicated and loyal communities of brand ambassadors across all popular and niche micromedia networks.

Lifestreams and Brand Aggregation

Lifestreams and brandstreams are the inevitable derivative by-products of distributed conversations and scattered online presences.

For example, as a marketing professional or a brand officer, the results generated from actively listening and observing around the Social Web might have prompted you to create accounts on every relevant micromedia, social network, and content network.

Not only can micromedia tools provide a forum for reading and sharing short bursts of relevant information, but some can also aggregate your updates from various networks into one easy-to-follow data stream.

Streams funnel social information by receiving RSS feeds produced from each service, collecting the updates, and automatically presenting them in one elegant river of focused activity. Followers of lifestreams can easily view and, in some cases, comment directly within the stream. Aggregators are true micromedia channels, in that they share only a fixed amount of content so that the updates are "short and sweet."

Services such as FriendFeed not only aggregate and publish online updates from the Social Web, but they also offer a community around streams. It's similar to Twitter, but imagine if every tweet (Twitter update) were representative of everything you created, regardless of the point of origin. Now imagine a timeline in which the content not only reflects what you create and share, but also includes the activity produced from those you also follow. And it enables everyone to comment directly in the flow, which actually fuses distributed conversations.

Distributed conversations are becoming as pervasive as micromedia, and streaming applications channel responses away from the point of origin. As each distinct and niche community attains traction, conversations can take place in multiple networks around the same content, just in different places (wherever it's broadcast). Therefore, it is increasingly difficult to monitor and participate in relevant conversations. But tools such as FriendFeed and other aggregation solutions help organize conversations so that you can participate easily and without restrictions.

Brands can also leverage micromedia to engage customers and cultivate communities. Instead of looking at it as a lifestream, companies can create brandstreams that tie together all the company's social assets into one feed. Brandstreams give people choices of whether they want to subscribe to one feed, such as the company blog or micromedia account through Twitter, or the entire stream through something such as FriendFeed or Swurl. People choose the format that works for them, similar to how they can choose which social networks in which to cultivate friendships.

Micromedia represents a new paradigm for information to reach people and an opportunity for brands to monitor conversations related to their business. Micromedia and aggregated streams will continue to evolve into legitimate rivers that reach people, however and wherever they find and share their information. Even if you don't subscribe to the "less is more" philosophy, many people do. People have choices, so ignoring them will only ensure that we're not included in their diet of relevant media snacks. As mentioned throughout this book, the best listeners make the best conversationalists. Micromedia provides an active hub for listening and perception management, and it represents another avenue by which to become a resource and cultivate valuable communities.

When enough individual voices pool together, the whisper becomes a roar—transforming micromedia into macro influence.

Micromedia Tools and Services

Many micromedia tools are available today. Which ones you use will depend on a variety of factors, specific to your ultimate communication goals. The following subsections list some of the most popular micromedia tools and services currently available. Remember, however, that this list is current as of this writing. As mentioned earlier, this is a rapidly evolving phenomenon, so we can expect continual development, release, and use of "new and improved" micromedia tools and services.

Text and File Sharing

- **Jaiku**—Brings people together by enabling them to share activity streams and also comment directly in each update.

- **Twitter**—Answers a simple question: "What are you doing?" It also shares the answers among family, friends, coworkers, and those who choose to "follow" your updates.

- **Identi.ca**—Built on open source, Identi.ca enables users to send text-based posts of up to 140 characters, but it is more suited for experts to customize and for specific applications in host-customized micromedia communities.

- **Tumblr**—Users can post text, links, music, video, and more, to express themselves in shorter bursts compared to traditional blogs.

- **Twitxr**—Enables you to share pictures and updates from your mobile phone.

- **Plurk**—The "social journal" for your life that you can share easily with family and friends—and earn "karma points" in the process.

Video/Audio

- **Seesmic**—The Twitter of video—a microblogging video Web application.

- **12Seconds**—Similar to Seesmic, it creates a community around short video updates that extends to other outside networks. The community places a cap of 12 seconds for each video.

- **Utterz**—Enables you to instantly share and discuss text, video, and still images through your mobile phone within the Utterz community and via broadcasting to Twitter.

- **Eyejot Kyte.tv**—Enables you to send videos to family and friends through your computer's Webcam.

Aggregators/Lifestreams

- **Jaiku**—Although it's a micromedia solution, as noted previously, it's also an aggregator. It can receive updates from a variety of social communities and feed them directly into your Jaiku stream.

- **Swurl**—Brings your Web life together by supporting your existing blog, pictures, video, and so on.

- **FriendFeed**—Enables you to create a customized feed to capture your friends' conversations on other collaborative sites.

- **Facebook**—Enables you to network with family, friends, and associates, to stay connected with your social graph and share in each other's activities and updates.

Mobile Phones

- **Jott**—Offers voice-to-text services through your phone that enable you to capture thoughts, send e-mail, and set reminders.

- **Kwiry**—Lets you send text messages to an online repository, which you can also share with friends in the Kwiry community.

- **Pinger**—Provides instant voice messaging from your phone so that you can send your messages without ringing or lengthy prompts.

Chapter 14

New "Marketing" Roles

In the era of the "new" Social Web, the field of communications is actually devolving back to its origins of communicating *with* people, not *at* them. It might seem implied, but communications doesn't usually embody two-way discussions. Unfortunately, communications has evolved into a one-way distribution channel that broadcasts messages at target audiences. In the process, communications stopped being about communication, and people stopped listening. The focus became the marketing aspects of top-down message push and control. We now commonly refer to this as marketing communications (marcom). Marcom embodies traditional and new marketing branches, including advertising, PR, Web or interactive, and events, among many other disciplines (depending on the organization).

Socialize to Survive

With the soaring popularity and adoption of Social Media, companies are realizing that, in addition to marcom, listening and engagement is quickly becoming pervasive and necessary to compete for precious yet thinned and distributed attention. The days of focusing solely on Web stickiness, eyeballs, and click-throughs are waning. These are the days of immersion, conversations, engagement, relationships, referrals, and action.

We mark this important time in history and note the transformation. Some call it Social Media marketing, others refer to it as conversational marketing, and other thought leaders simply classify it as the socialization of media and marketing in general. In the world of marcom, we're placing the *communication* back in *communications*. It's the transformation of monologue to dialogue, and it's breaking down those walls and barriers that separate people from brands. With so many choices and a simple click taking customers to a competitor's product or service, brands cannot afford to have communication obstacles in this market.

The problem with Social Media marketing and conversational marketing as classifiers is that both still include the word *marketing*. It doesn't imply authenticity and the two-way process of listening, internalizing, and responding. Each is complementary to traditional marketing, but their intent, practice, and metrics differ. And the socialization of communications is also unique.

Social Media marketing is using Social Media tools to participate online in distinct people-powered communities. Conversational marketing involves understanding that markets are conversations. In marketing, the term *market* describes the group of consumers or organizations that might be interested in a product, have the resources to purchase the product, and be permitted by law and other regulations to acquire the product (see www.netmba.com/marketing/market/definition/).

The observation that markets are conversations was originally published in the now iconic book *The Cluetrain Manifesto:*

> These markets are conversations. Their members communicate in language that is natural, open, honest, direct, funny and often shocking. Whether explaining or complaining, joking or serious, the human voice is unmistakably genuine. It can't be faked. Most corporations, on the other hand, only know how to talk in the soothing, humorless monotone of the mission statement, marketing brochure, and your-call-is-important-to-us busy signal. Same old tone, same old lies. No wonder networked markets have no respect for companies unable or unwilling to speak as they do. But learning to speak in a human voice is not some trick, nor will corporations convince us they are human with lip service about "listening to customers." They will only sound human when they empower real human beings to speak on their behalf.

The traditional definition of a market refers to an open place where buyers and sellers meet for the sale of products and services. However, today's markets include online communities that create dynamic conversations between brands and their customers, resulting in purchases. These very conversations create and affect purchasing behavior. A brand cannot thrive in the market if it doesn't engage in these conversations; therefore, we can now also conclude that, in Social Media, conversations are also markets. Conversations economically impact content and also commerce related to brands, products, and services.

The tools, channels, and approaches differ in today's market, and actually span across advertising, marketing, SEO, widget marketing, and word-of-mouth marketing (WOMM), among others. In the world of PR, Social Media marketing primarily concentrates on blogger relations and comment strategies—working with bloggers to retell your story, and sharing feedback and insight within comments that link back to something helpful to the community, while also benefiting the company you're representing. Again, the difference in each of these disciplines is the intent, execution, and results of any program.

What's occurring now is so different and revolutionary that this new genre of PR and marketing clearly deserves its own classification. By recognizing this new genre, we will inspire adherents and advance these concepts within organizations, affecting the soul and personality of outward-facing brands and dictating an entirely new and proactive role within society. For the first time in years, we might need to adapt Lasswell's much-studied communications theory to describe the field of marketing in a New Media world.

In 1949, American political scientist and sociologist Harold Lasswell introduced an important communications model:

Who

Says what

In which channel

To whom

To what effect

Dissecting Lasswell's model, we can conclude the following:

- *Who* is the origin.

- *Says what* implies that you have a message to distribute.

- *In which channel* represents the places where people find information.

- *To whom* refers to the people within our target markets.

- *To what effect* documents the results of the distribution of a message.

Because we now live in an economy driven by the socialization and democratization of content and the empowerment of a new class of citizen influencers, Lasswell's model could evolve into something that more accurately reflects New Media:

Who

Says what

In which channel

To whom

To what effect

Then who

Hears what

Who shares what

With what intent

To what effect

The definitions and results will radically vary depending on how you use those variables and which marketing or media discipline you represent. The difference is that Lasswell's model had an implied beginning and a conclusion. Social Media is pervasive and regenerates thoughts and ideas through a cyclical process of listening, discovering, sharing, and contributing personal or professional perspective:

- The new *who* refers to the community.

- *Hears what* reflects those who actively listen to relevant conversations online.

- *Who shares what* refers to the group of people compelled to distribute content to their social graph with or without additional coloring, perspective, and commentary.

- *With what intent* looks at how that information is shared and, in turn, interpreted and processed. The tone and sentiment will determine the type of response it might incite.

Social Media is forcing the evolution of all marketing and Public Relations. It's now the art and science of socializing _____ (fill in the blank).

We refer to this era as our "industrial revolution." Brian discussed the topic in a recent landmark post on his blog: PR 2.0.

Towards the end of the 1990s, the Web, and its architects, forged the tools that would spark a renaissance of influence and empowerment. These tools would inspire people to build new interconnected platforms for content that would collectively and ultimately ignite a social revolution and usher a new exchange for information that has all the signs and economic potential of a modern day Industrial Revolution.

The socialization of media and information is our Industrial Revolution. For the first time in history, media technology and the tools and channels for broadcasting information has been disrupted and open for true global collaboration, while also effectively changing how people interact with each other.

The Social Revolution is the catalyst for the democratization of content and exchange of information, but we're still experimenting and wrestling with the true impact of this change and how exactly these new models, on every side of the equation, will ultimately settle.

Integrating Social Roles

We need to consider that if we're in the throes of a social revolution, does the act of socializing outbound communications require a new division within an organization?

We think so, at least for now (even though Social Media is a stage in the overall evolution of marketing and media, and it will give way to something new and different). In the meantime, what do we name this new division or discipline, and is it just an extension of the existing marketing department that already encompasses advertising, PR, marketing, the Web, and New Media? A rapidly growing list of organizations are hiring experts to lead the integration, with some earning titles of Social Media officer and complementing existing chief marketing officers.

No shortage of genuine and purported Social Media experts and Social Media gurus exists. But what does it mean to be an expert, and, more important, who's truly qualified to socialize real-world marketing departments with real-world business demands, dependencies, infrastructure, opportunities, and responsibilities? The answer is this: those with the experience and the understanding of business and service dynamics and how the socialization of communications, development, and support impacts and benefits people and their peers. It's that simple. And it's not the level of experience that one earns from talking about Social Media or just participating in the newest networks.

It takes more than the ability to listen to people and then engage. It definitely encompasses more than the skill to create profiles on every popular social platform and befriend everyone across the networks. It's the ability to identify meaningful conversations, comprehend them, determine those valuable enough to participate, and then feed that collective insight back into the organization (marketing, service, product development, and so on) for positive change. It also requires the knowledge to uncover opportunities and crises to "trendcast" into proactive initiatives that prevent reactionary and defensive responses.

Proactive = Relevancy

Reactive = Damage control

Web and social tech expert Louis Gray calls Social Media experts the "new" Webmasters. Social tools developer Greg Narain compares the current state of Social Media to the *e* in the old *e-conomy*. Early on, we predicted that we would eventually see Social Media officers as the new chief marketing officers. We were correct. These views share the belief that these classifiers emerged to document important shifts, migrations, and growth stages of new media, and the roles that further solidified them as catalysts for maturation. Obviously, we need a new, important stepping-stone to escalate to the next phase in influencer and customer interaction.

Brian Morrissey wrote in a recent article for *Adweek* (July 14, 2008) that brands need a new kind of leader, claiming, "As conversations with customer[s] matter more, brands seek social-media evangelists." So which division within an organization is ready to fund this experimentation? Perhaps it's not just one division, but instead an amalgamation of several departments.

Experience has shown that it's different depending on the company and the champions within it:

- Peter Kim, formerly an analyst for Forrester Research, recently joined a start-up to help large companies engage in Social Media. The company was funded with $50 million from Austin Ventures and was created by Razorfish founder Jeff Dachis.

- Deborah Schultz, a social software and marketing strategist, was tasked with creating a lab to explore new business and marketing models for consumer powerhouse Procter & Gamble.

- Scott Monty, a marketing expert, was recently hired to socialize the Ford brand.

- Shel Holtz, a PR pro, is helping Coca-Cola and other consumer brands expand into social worlds.

- Connie Bensen, a community relations expert, is the community manager for Network Solutions.

- Chris Heuer, a Web and New Media visionary, is currently guiding Intel Corporation on best practices and new opportunities for social strategies. The company also tapped several social activists, including Brian Solis, to advise the company on Social Media.

- Marshall Kirkpatrick, a thought-leading blogger in the Web 2.0 landscape, actively publishes stories related to how companies can benefit from community managers—those charged with listening to conversations that are driving relevant social networks and coordinating necessary responses and change (outbound and internally).

We, too, have recently received calls from various brands (major beverage and food companies, auto, aerospace, power, and entertainment) asking advice and seeking referrals for an internal social champion and expert (all within the same week of writing this chapter).

The list goes on. These stories represent only a few of the bigger shifts within existing marketing departments as they attempt to socialize their brands.

These are the times when the social revolution is redefining not only how you communicate with the representatives in your communities, but also how, as a collective organization of people, you process the information, intelligence, and insight garnered from external conversations to more effectively and genuinely participate.

But Social Media isn't limited to marketing or outbound activity. Social Media benefits and develops every department within an organization. Therefore, the future of Social Media and its effectiveness depends on the champions, participants, analysts, and opportunists who are actively involved.

The intelligence collected while listening and observing affects everything. You can improve your products and services based on the real-world input and feedback from a true, vested public focus group. You can improve and tailor your story specifically to the assemblies of people you're hoping to reach in a way that's convincing and accurate. You can enhance your inbound customer service practices to transform cost centers into customer investments. In the process, you're humanizing your brands and transforming customers into evangelists, people into storytellers, and brands into resource centers.

The goal is to connect brands, and the people representing them, to new groups of important people in the places where they discover and share new content and, in turn, interact with each other. This is the latest incarnation of digital communications, and for the moment, it takes us back to the foundation of relationships that started everything. This time, however, it's not only the tools that have changed, but also the realization that people matter to everything you do.

This is the socialization of

- Communications

- Advertising

- PR

- Customer service

- Product development

- Interactive

- Sales

Whatever discipline you represent, you are the champion for the socialization of that branch, as it relates to the greater good of the company, the brand, and all stakeholders. Only you can specifically understand how social strategies affect and complement the daily campaigns already working well for your organization.

Ultimately, each department will independently implement and deploy social initiatives, working with a social coordinator such as a community manager, in conjunction with a chief marketing officer, vice president of marketing, or even chief social officer. Everything depends on the existing infrastructure and social savvy of the organization. However, social initiatives won't always be rooted just in social strategies. As the communications landscape evolves, new and interactive media will continue to influence business. The landscape of communications and the tools used to connect people and stories will continue to evolve. Remember, this is about the sociology of Social Media. Technology changes; people don't.

Wait until you see how semantic platforms, which many hail as the next iteration of the Web, will change the dynamics of information discovery, creation, and connectivity. In the meantime, the future of your business depends on champions emerging who will implement and justify your company's socialization—its ability to listen, empathize, respond, advise, and evolve based on the online discussions currently occurring with or without you.

PART **IV**

PR 2.0:
A Promising Future

Chapter 15

Community Managers and Customer Service 2.0

The Social Web levels the playing field, giving both businesses and everyday people access to powerful tools and services to share their voices, opinions, and experiences with their peers. It also enables them to shape perceptions and decisions, and build long-term relationships. In the new world of PR, communications professionals must listen to and observe (and sometimes engage) today's world of new influencers. By *new influencers*, we're referring to people just like you and me. They could be customers, peers, employees, partners, enthusiasts, influential bloggers, reporters, or analysts. This dynamic of listening to and engaging in everyday dialogue is often referred to as *the conversation.*

With new and meaningful conversations proliferating the blogosphere every day, an important question arises. We're thinking seriously about this question because the answer affects the future of the PR industry. Who actually owns the conversations, and is it possible that ownership and responsibility belong to more than one person or department in an organization? Thought leaders are currently discussing who should own the responsibility of conversing with stakeholders. Some argue that PR, marcom, or advertising should take the lead because these areas in a company are the watchful eye and monitor the brand messages. In contrast, others are demonstrating that new hybrids of traditional customer service teams can manage the responsibility. With Social Media and the ability to publish an opinion almost instantly, traditional customer service might not be equipped to handle an extreme influx of inquiries, especially during a situation that requires immediate damage control. For example, when Apple launched its iPhone at a price point of $600 and then two months later significantly lowered the price, the blogosphere was filled with angry Apple customers blasting the company. The news spread via the Social Media highway with every new blog post, link, tweet, and podcast. This example tells us that the easy answer to the question is that every facet of a business is responsible for its channel of social monitoring and interaction. However, depending on the organization, the answer lies directly within each department.

Although Social Media is starting to attract the attention of business and marketing executives, much of the tactical execution associated with socialized marketing is still new and foreign to many. In addition, the task of socializing the existing infrastructure is daunting when viewed from ground zero. However, people within an organization can take on this role; we call them champions, and they can reside in one department and be the catalyst for change and evolution interdepartmentally (as well as organizationally). Either way, the socialization of the corporate marketing infrastructure isn't a matter of *if* it should happen, but instead *when* it will happen. We realize this is always easier said than done. The larger the organization, the harder it is to change the organizational structure (often because of bureaucratic red tape and levels of management that would have to buy in to a change of this magnitude).

Connecting People to the Human Beings Who Define Corporate Brands and Culture

You've heard our humble opinions and the opinions of many Social Media thought leaders that brands don't engage with people—people engage with people. The idea of empowering your customers or stakeholders so that they become an extension of your marketing isn't new. Even in Web 1.0, you were using more interactive features on your Web sites and viral marketing to spread the word. Transforming people into an additional sales team is ideal for any service organization. However, the landscape has shifted in such a way that to excel in the marketplace, good customer service is no longer the minimum effort to stay in the game—you must do more to have a winning chance.

We mentioned previously that the Social Web is this great combination of Public Relations, marcom, advertising, and customer service. It's crucial that all these areas work together to become a holistic inbound and outbound campaign, one of listening to and engaging with customers. We believe that this approach will rewrite the rules of the game, and escalate the corporate brand and loyalty in the process. We believe that these game-changing rules will advance our industry and make PR, once again, a crucial part of an organization. And most important, the lessons learned in the field will be fed into the marketing department to create and run more intelligent, experienced, and real-world initiatives across all forms of marketing, PR, sales, and advertising.

During the past two years, Social Media has intrigued and even inspired companies to engage in the communities in which their brands and products—and those of competitors—are actively discussed by the very people they want to reach (a.k.a. the new influencers). At this point, companies should not be questioning their participation—it's no longer an option. Social Media isn't a spectator sport. We cannot stress enough that these conversations are taking place with or without you, so ignoring them just eliminates you from the conversation and the radar screens of your customers. Companies should be inquiring about the best way to strategically plan their participation and what goals they want to reach by engaging in conversations.

Participation looks less like marketing and more like customer service, whether you're in advertising, PR, or marcom. Marketing-savvy corporate executives are working with PR, advertising, and marcom teams to explore options and strategies on how to participate in relevant online conversations. This concept represents a shift in outbound marketing as it creates a direct channel between companies and customers, and ultimately people. For example, take a look at how Dell and Comcast are embracing Social Media.

Richard Binhammer, also known as @RichardatDell, is responsible for improving the Dell brand from being among the lowest-ranked service organizations to the opposite end of the spectrum, and improving the overall public perception of the company. Dell began an active campaign of listening and engagement. Binhammer and his team learn and discover opportunities to help people by listening first and then fixing problems, answering questions, and improving customer service. This process ultimately leads to future product development. Under Binhammer's guidance, the company is actively monitoring conversations in blogs, in social networks, and also on Twitter—all in an effort to identify and solve problems, and cultivate a sense of community by genuinely and transparently participating in long-term relationships (a sincere investment).

Comcast, along with Dell, has not enjoyed the highest level of customer satisfaction in the past. Their customers have been extremely vocal through Social Media channels. As a result, Comcast has created a community-management team to begin the slow but genuine process of improving its service infrastructure. The company tasked Frank Eliason with creating and leading the new @ComcastCares program; the role was featured in the *New York Times*.

Similar to Dell, Eliason uses various social tools to listen to relevant online conversations (on blogs, Twitter, and discussions forums). He listens to people as they actively voice problems and challenges they experience with Comcast. Eliason identifies activities that require an immediate response from Comcast, which is then followed by a hands-on process of building relationships, one by one, to show that Comcast does listen and care. Since the start of the program, Eliason has successfully reached out to more than 1,000 customers online. His quote in the *New York Times* article said it all: "When you're having a two-way conversation, you really get to clear the air."

PR Evolves into a Service Center

Many of us dreamed of the day that PR would be so important—an indispensable function that becomes the responsibility of the entire organization. Our dream has come true and then some. But it's much bigger than just boxing it into the existing PR paradigm. As we alluded to earlier, Social Media impacts every department. In many cases, PR will eventually coalign with outbound customer service as a new form of *unmarketing*. The marketing hats come off, and your listening skills kick into gear. And because communities are, at the very least, opportunities to engage, these opportunities are presented as questions, complaints, observations, or general conversations. PR and customer service can work together to position the company as an industry resource.

Social Media is rooted in conversations between online peers, regardless of the technology that facilitates the conversation, and every day these conversations take place across blogs, networks, forums, micromedia, and online groups. And each day, with the creation of every new community and social tool that is introduced, brands, products, and services are actively discussed, supported, and sometimes disputed and disassembled. Some companies are listening, whereas many others aren't even paying attention.

We want you to take away from this book the idea that you're empowered to start the process of listening and observing. By doing so, you are actively pursuing New PR and your organization will reap the benefits. Don't wait for someone to assign those tasks to you, another person in your department, or elsewhere within (or external to) the organization. You can be the champion, even if you have to monitor related discussions outside of work to demonstrate the pervasiveness and prominence of related dialogue. We work with many companies whose employees are so overloaded with expanded job responsibilities that they cannot pursue "lower-priority" or "noncritical" objectives for the company. *We believe that you should make this one of your critical objectives, even if it's on your own time.*

Whether the online conversations are positive, neutral, or negative, the insight garnered from listening and observing will reveal opportunities not just for engagement, but also for gathering real-world intelligence— the type of information that is "ear to the street" and that you can feed back into your organization to improve the existing service, product, and management infrastructure. Then your organization will be able to effectively compete for the future.

Online customer-focused communities are playing host to conversations between prospects, decision makers, and customers regarding products and services. These communities include Ning, Yahoo! and Google Groups, and Facebook. Emerging services such as GetSatisfaction promote problem solving and relationship building between people and companies. ThisNext is also a place where people can get great product recommendations and rave about the products they like. And although they don't invite marketing, they do seek helpful information, advice, feedback, and direction.

These discussions take the shape of any dialogue actively discoverable and potentially influential online. They populate forums; they're driving and amplifying blog posts; and they inspire new podcasts, videos, articles, tweets, and micro comments (and thus extend the entire cycle of conversations). We also believe they are driving topics published by traditional media.

Social Media represents an entirely new way to reach customers and connect with them directly. It adds an outbound channel that complements inbound customer service, traditional PR, direct marketing, and advertising, placing companies and their customers on a level playing field to discuss topics as peers. At this point, you are wearing a different hat. Although your marketing hat is close by, you are, first and foremost, a peer—always listening and offering relevant information to help people make decisions. Most important, your new role transcends the process of just broadcasting messages and reactively answering questions to investing in and building a brand-centric community of enthusiasts and evangelists.

Developing a Complementary Inbound and Outbound Communications Program

Years ago, it was logical to think that if customers were unhappy with a product or level of service, they would either make a telephone call or write a letter. Then the Internet enabled companies to receive customer service inquiries and complaints online, 24/7. Companies, for the most part, relied on these channels to hear when their customers had questions, comments, or concerns. And as customers become more Internet savvy, more companies are relying on a 24/7 inbound customer service approach. However, if a situation escalates today, the complaints will no longer just be inbound; those customers will quickly take their dissatisfaction to the Web to discuss their comments, concerns, and discontent in online communities.

Today you can bet that for every inbound customer inquiry, a significant number of existing and potential customers are actively discussing the same topic with the same (if not greater) level of conviction out in the open. When customers don't get the response or immediate action they desire, they look elsewhere for guidance, feedback, acknowledgment, and information. These discussions usually transpire quickly and without company participation, leaving people to resolve issues and questions on their own.

Brands should not leave the door open for unknowledgeable individuals (or even worse, their competition) to jump into the conversation. Doing so presents an open invitation to steer away your once-loyal customers. Companies must engage; otherwise, they place themselves on the long road to inevitable obsolescence. Remember the old adage: Out of sight, out of mind. Quite simply, you must engage or die. A few mantras circulating among thought leaders were inspired by the corporate-culture-changing book that started it all, *The Cluetrain Manifesto.* You might have heard these mantras before. They are truly simple yet powerful in their meaning. *Participation is marketing.* We believe that if you are engaged and involved, the marketing is happening whether you are aware or not. Markets are conversations, meaning you no longer broadcast and talk to the market. The markets talk and you listen, and in doing so, you can earn the right to also participate.

Before we go too far down this path, we need to clarify the term *marketing* because we're not referring to the traditional marketing that typically *speaks* at audiences through *messages.* If you recall in Chapter 6, "The Language of New PR," the pitch is history and messages for audiences no longer exist in the traditional sense. In the social world, this is about dialogue—two-way discussions that bring people together to discover and share information. However, joining the conversation isn't as simple as jumping in. Think of it this way: You would never jump into a body of water without knowing the temperature, how deep it is, or whether sharks are present. Not knowing simple, valuable information is very dangerous. If you apply our analogy to a Web community, we recommend the same thing: Companies must first listen to accurately analyze where, when, and how to participate.

Companies need to formalize outbound communications and community participation, creating a dedicated team to ensure that customers and influencers are not overlooked but are instead embraced and integrated into the entire service organization. Social Media forces companies to look outward to proactively find the conversations that are important to brand building and to monetize business relationships. And it's not just the responsibility of PR or customer service. It requires the participation by multiple disciplines across the organization to genuinely provide meaningful support and information.

Again, we're not talking about messaging or sales propositions. If you stop to think about it, we're talking about fusing marketing, PR, community relations, product marketing, and customer service in an entirely new, socially aware role. We believe this is a natural role for the PR or communications professional, who, even in the days of traditional PR, was responsible for building strong relationships (after listening to and learning from the needs of customers).

A New Role for a New Generation of Communications

You might already be seeing companies either dividing outbound responsibilities among existing teams or dedicating roles to full-time listening, participating, responding, and commenting across all forms of Social Media. But this isn't limited to a select few businesses. This is a role that will become a recognized standard in companies around the globe—from small- and medium-size businesses to enterprise organizations— and will likely scale from one person to teams of people globally.

This is more than prioritizing enhanced customer service to bloggers or people who are familiar with social networking forums. You shouldn't aim your fire hoses at fires that have only public attention. You need to focus on customers who take the time to contribute to and participate in social networks while just seeking information (even if it is delivered in the form of a rant). Nor can you just rely on inbound service. You must analyze inbound activity, tracking its numbers and severity, to find related conversations among those who decide to take the conversation outside of the traditional service process.

In addition to PR and marcom, these new roles are combining a variety of marketing disciplines (including communications, customer support, and product management), and are called several titles:

- Community advocate

- Community manager

- Brand ambassador

- Social Media specialist

- Social Media evangelist

- Vice president of Social Media

- Chief social officer

- Community relations manager

- Community builder

Connie Bensen, a highly regarded and renowned community manager, defined the role of a community manager this way:

A community manager is the voice of the company externally and the voice of the customers internally. The value lies in the community manager serving as a hub and having the ability to personally connect with the customers (humanize the company), and providing feedback to many departments internally (development, PR, marketing, customer service, tech support, etc).

Forrester social computing analyst Jeremiah Owyang shared his four tenets for budding community managers to embrace to be successful in their new roles.

The Four Tenets of the Community Manager

By Jeremiah Owyang

In the following, I'm not going to list out all my findings, but it was clear there were 4 Tenets, or beliefs that each role holds. In nearly all the job descriptions, the following beliefs were spelled out as requirements for the role.

1) A Community Advocate

As a community advocate, the community managers' primary role is to represent the customer. This includes listening, which results in monitoring, and being active in understanding what customers are saying in both the corporate community as well as external websites. Secondly, they engage customers by responding to their requests and needs or just conversations, both in private and in public.

2) Brand Evangelist

In this evangelistic role (it goes both ways) the community manager will promote events, products and upgrades to customers by using traditional marketing tactics and conversational discussions. As proven as a trusted member of the community (tenet 1) the individual has a higher degree of trust and will offer good products.

3) Savvy Communication Skills, Shapes Editorial

This tenet, which is both editorial planning and mediation, serves the individual well. The community manager should first be very familiar with the tools of communication, from forums, to blogs, to podcasts, to twitter, and then understand the language and jargon that is used in the community. This individual is also responsible for mediating disputes within the community, and will lean on advocates, and embrace detractors —and sometimes removing them completely. Importantly, the role is responsible for the editorial strategy and planning within the community, and will work with many internal stakeholders to identify content, plan, publish, and follow up.

4) Gathers Community Input for Future Product and Services

Perhaps the most strategic of all tenets, community managers are responsible for gathering the requirements of the community in a responsible way and presenting it to product teams. This may involve formal product requirements methods from surveys to focus groups, to facilitating the relationships between product teams and customers. The opportunity to build better products and services through this real-time live focus group are ripe, in many cases, customer communities have been waiting for a chance to give feedback.

The role of community manager, or whatever title your organization assigns, is invaluable and instrumental in bridging traditional corporate communications and outbound service with the overall act of listening, internalizing, and improving business infrastructures and methodologies. Perhaps most notably, it facilitates the act of investing in relationships that are priceless to today's businesses.

Public Relations (and, to some extent, marketing and sales) has long suffered from the ramifications of a few bad apples (well, perhaps more than a few) who represent companies, products, and services without a deep understanding of the benefits and value proposition to the very people they are trying to compel to action. It's the difference between earning a living, skating by, cashing in, and being a resource for your community.

Things have changed since the days of Web 1.0, and we believe it's for the better. In the "old days" of Web 1.0 (circa the 90s), online community relations existed through topic-driven discussion groups, user forums, and other online communities such as DejaNews, Yahoo!, and Groups. During Web 1.0, it wasn't about Social Media, and those participants didn't try to BS the people who were seeking advice and answers. This is important because you need to recognize not only the details of your products, services, reputation, strengths, weaknesses, and benefits, but also how you compete in the market, where you stand against the competition, and how you're different. You can do this only by truly listening and being proactive to market conversations.

Today in the world of Web 2.0, the venues for influential interaction span an extremely wide social canvas. In most cases, community management now requires the attention of more than one full-time person dedicated to monitoring, listening, observing, and then trafficking the necessary action to the appropriate teams. In fact, because the Social Media landscape is rapidly growing, this might require several internal people to listen and participate every day across blog posts, blog comments, forums, groups, social networks, micromedia, and so on. Companies are also investing in proprietary software that tracks the conversations in the blogosphere to reveal not only keywords, but also whether the dialogue is positive or negative (so that they can ultimately determine what action the brand needs to take).

Contract Community Managers

Even as you read this book, the idea of listening and participating in the Social Web on behalf of a company is catching on in the business world. In fact, companies that are ready to experiment might encounter difficulty hiring for this role. It's just a simple case of supply and demand. And with more opportunities arising than people learning the art of community management, a new category of contractors is emerging.

Contract community managers are commanding a premium, and they're forming a new breed of consultancies and agencies dedicated to the outsourced process of listening, engaging, and routing the necessary action within the organizations they represent.

In some cases, the process of listening is outsourced to overseas companies—where the hourly rate is extremely low compared to in the United States, but the level of Web sophistication is on par with (if not superior to) the junior-level people who would be tasked with tracking conversations in the United States. However, we don't believe that practice is sustainable. The positions are outsourced while companies rethink and rebuild their infrastructure to accommodate for the position of the community manager and community participants. We believe that contract Social Media experts and community managers are enjoying a small window of opportunity, similar to how Webmasters enjoyed incredible premiums in the days of Web 1.0 before many organizations brought Web-savvy programmers and designers in-house.

In some cases, community managers and Social Media experts are banding together to offer more robust services in addition to monitoring, participating in, and facilitating conversations. In many cases, they're offering a series of social services such as online video shooting and uploading, comment marketing, event marketing, and blogger relations.

As an executive charged with building out a new outbound engagement strategy, you now have full-time and contract options to help you achieve your goals.

The Humanization of Marketing Communications

Although anarchy might appear to reign on the Social Web (perhaps because best practices and governing rules are only now starting to emerge), Social Media and community cultivation and relationship building are not a free-for-all and should not be taken lightly. Not just anyone can jump in and solve problems or become a resource for a community. Companies need to create an internal strategy that officially assigns specific, versed, and highly knowledgeable people to help customers—nothing less. Every company has a planned inbound customer service approach. The outbound customer service approach should be given the same level of importance.

The amount of listening you do in active communities will dictate your level of participation. The conversations and reactions stemming from your participation will reveal immediate metrics. Any company can rely on reactive community relations; that's easy. But at that point, it's a little too late because you're embarking on a control-and-repair program instead of a proactive campaign of nurturing and empowerment. Companies must learn from listening to and talking with customers to create specific content that addresses the wants and needs of customers and distribute that content within their communities. Doing so will enable you to translate the lessons learned from one-on-one conversations for the greater good of the company (and of the masses).

Outbound customer and community relations are among the most important campaigns any company can integrate into its immediate and future initiatives. Doing so not only helps PR and customer service, but it also builds relationships, creates enthusiasts, and ultimately instills customer loyalty. Proactive, not reactive, people forge and cultivate relationships. People have choices. By actively investing in relevant and meaningful conversations, you can continually gain priceless insight and improve processes, products, and services. This also enables you to build active and enthusiastic communities, as well as inspire loyalty among them.

Chapter 16

Socialization of Communication and Service

In Chapter 15, "Community Managers and Customer Service 2.0," we explained that the era of Social Media requires more than just traditional marketing, Public Relations, and customer service infrastructure to compete for attention (today and especially in the future). Now it's about people and engaging stakeholders, customers, and peers on their level; it's no longer about connecting faceless companies to anonymous audiences. Putting the *public* back into Public Relations is humanizing the entire process of communications and service—not just keeping customers happy, but also cultivating loyalty and engendering enthusiasts along the way.

The evolving landscape of social tools and technologies is socializing the very infrastructure of business and transforming everyday people into new influencers—including PR people. We're learning how to adapt to the changes that are forcing the social evolution of the marketing, communications, and service industries that have remained relatively unchanged for more than 100 years. It's not easy because many companies don't yet understand the need for change in their service structure. Other, more socially aware businesses are publicly experimenting with new proactive procedures of listening and adapting to engage customers, influencers, and constituents (without documenting a formal return on investment). Many people need to be educated, and you can be a part of it. Change is never easy. It usually requires understanding and time to internalize the change, embrace it, and pursue it. However, we don't have the luxury of time; the people in Web communities don't stop sharing information, bloggers don't stop publishing their opinions, and customers are seeking solutions, insight, and answers *right now.*

The Social Web requires that we exercise more human, genuine, sincere, and personalized traits to forge and nurture relationships. But this Social Media era is not the last time we'll have to change and adapt. Every era of technology has an impact on the PR profession. As technology continues to forge ahead, innovative tools will inevitably introduce new dynamics into relationship marketing and management.

Understanding the social sciences is only the first step. The true value lies in our ability to also become experts in the markets, products, and services we represent. This expertise creates a stronger foundation to grow into the role of a community resource. Web 1.0 rang the alarm, but Web 2.0 really woke us up. The Social Web is demonstrating a clear lack of tolerance or reward for complacency and outdated processes. The new Web and relationship-centric PR is inspiring us and driving us (via higher standards) to improve the models for service and communications—and the bottom line for businesses.

Customer service, product marketing, and marcom professionals who commit themselves to both inbound and outbound initiatives no longer rely on just answering questions when they come in (which has been the practice for decades). Now we must be diligent and identify concerns and questions in the various forums and media through which customers or other stakeholders seek insight from their peers and other experts who help them make decisions. The only way to do this is to use both traditional and "social" tools to discover, listen, learn, and engage directly with our customers—not as marketers, but as purveyors of solutions. We must still exercise care and empathy in the process: We don't want to market *at* our targets or broadcast our messages *to* them. Instead, we want to help stakeholders make more informed decisions and to introduce previously unrecognized (or previously impossible) solutions on an individual basis.

Communications professionals must now do more than just listen, participate, and help. This isn't a top-down process of telling people what to think and how to respond. Every day, people are bombarded with 3,000 to 5,000 messages (through all the various media and people they are exposed to). Therefore, perception management must now be a key focus, too. We must also learn from our engagement and from the experiences of our customers and influencers.

Organizations don't do enough "learning"—even if insight is coming through inbound service phone calls and e-mail. It's expanding into online societies and spurring reactions, actions, and discussions in the real world, too. For every negative comment or experience, we can take what we learn in the field to improve processes, methodologies, services, and products. In turn, businesses will run more human, informed, and experienced dialogue-based campaigns and programs that improve all forms of marketing, PR, sales, customer service, and advertising.

The trick is to know when customers just want you to listen instead of taking an immediate response or reaction. We believe communications professionals must determine whether they're facing this scenario on a case-by-case basis. In many conversations, customers just want to be heard—although they often appreciate when feedback shows up in the form of a better product or customer service focus. However, immediate action and response are sometimes required (the iPhone incident, "ComcastSucks," and "Dell Hell" are examples discussed in other chapters within this book). These examples also show how interaction can produce a new level of appreciation and understanding that inspires the necessary changes to fix and improve what's not working well and to ultimately restore positive perception.

Lobbying for Change

Getting started is a step in the right direction, but how should you proceed? As we discussed in Chapter 15, the answer is simple: *The whole process starts with you and a new mindset.* Every organization is different, so a cookie-cutter approach is not feasible. However, some factors are universal. For example, a champion must lobby for change, including new ways (and mindsets) to reach customers and influencers (perhaps in ways not even possible within existing infrastructures).

Lobbyists (or champions) could exist in the C-Suite (corporate level) in marketing communications, customer service, Public Relations, advertising, or interactive product marketing—any department where external dialogue either is a job requirement or could benefit through interaction and feedback. A champion is key to jump-starting this new and important outbound service-minded approach.

As discussed in the preceding chapter, thought leaders are currently debating this very subject. We suggest that you don't wait. To advance your own career and keep the business you represent from falling off the radar of its existing and potential customers and fading into obscurity, take the time to investigate how socializing your role and your department will inspire champions (and perhaps even inspire change just based on your actions alone). You might even want to take this issue to your own Web communities and discuss it among peers. Start a forum or a group to determine what other people consider the best approach from a PR perspective.

Again, this is no longer an inbound-only process. As discussed previously, Social Media is *not* something you can engage in from the sidelines. Those who remain spectators will inevitably remove themselves as an option for their customers, enabling their competitors to make them obsolete.

Any good PR person must research and analyze. Compare your position to that of your competitors. Monitor conversations. Document answers (or the lack of them). Measure the frequency of relevant conversations across each social network and in the blogosphere, charting it from month to month. If you do your homework, you will quickly see the opportunities and be able to chart and demonstrate potential rewards.

Then speak up. Present the conclusions of your research (along with supporting data). Make it your goal to pull your company into online conversations to help influencers, customers, and prospects gather the information they need. Also empower people to help each other. By engaging influencers directly, you strengthen the integrity of "the grapevine," as stories and benefits are passed across the Social Web. A beneficial side effect is that you are investing in your knowledge and experience—and in your career prospects and future. You will immediately become a more valuable asset to any organization you choose to represent. The PR industry has fought hard to be understood as a valuable company resource. Your participation in an outbound customer service approach will demonstrate that value to "the suits" even more.

After completing all your homework, you are ready to create a listening and response strategy. Your strategy should assign the listening and responding responsibilities to the most appropriate persons, which could be within your organization or external (champions in the field). As discussed in the preceding chapter, businesses are hiring "community managers" to keep the company's "ear to the ground." These managers act as the hub for coordinating all outbound conversations. The community manager usually works directly with PR, product marketing, customer service, sales, and the executive team to coordinate the most relevant and effective person or response based on each discussion. Community managers are also responsible for directly answering questions, when appropriate.

An easy and cost-effective way to start is by setting up Google Alerts and by monitoring http://search.twitter.com for your company, products, key personnel, and competitors. Every time you receive an alert or uncover an interesting conversation in a Web community (such as a rumor, unpleasant experiences, simple questions, or a hostile "share of voice" takeover of a brand), you have an "almost" real-time opportunity to engage.

Social Tools for Social Service and Communications

It's also important to evaluate and utilize services that track conversations and relevant topics (services such as Technorati, Blogpulse, Twitter, FriendFeed, or Google Blog Search). Then you can assess which of these tools enables you to proactively monitor memes and individual instances that determine your level of engagement. Your participation also sets the stage for perception management and reduces the risk of negative discussions publicly snowballing.

Social Media isn't limited to blogs and communities. In the new world of PR, marketing, and service, we must find and participate in the relevant and potentially influential conversations taking place across the Social Web. In fact, Social Media is fueling social networks (which are springing up everywhere as niche communities based on different topics) and enabling us to find and host conversations related to brands and products. For example, we can create Facebook groups and Fan Pages. We can find or build dedicated networks for our brands or services on social networks such as Ning. We can create and monitor a dedicated product page on GetSatisfaction. We can also search other related networks. We have incredible opportunities to converse with real people who hunger for content, information, and community (and, in the process, perhaps influence groups of like-minded people).

Ning

Ning is a do-it-yourself (DIY) social network. Basically, it's a 2.0 version of Google or Yahoo! Groups, and it's definitely a place where people congregate to share and learn, among other things.

GetSatisfaction

GetSatisfaction is a company- or customer-created forum to discuss problems or other experiences and to ask questions and provide answers in one centralized location.

Corporate and employee-driven blogs also help stakeholders and customers find information relevant to their objectives. Companies can also host an integrated social network or discussion forum (such as those provided by Leverage Software and KickApps). These companies facilitate hosted networks and conversations directly on the company site as a way of embracing customers and encouraging peer-to-peer interaction (thus building and strengthening their community). This level of customization and integration requires high-level buy-in and participation from the chief marketing officer and the Web marketing team.

Micromedia is also critical, such as creating a presence on Twitter, Kwippy, Plurk, or Identi.ca (among others).

The Twitter Paradox

Even Twitter faces complaints about its own services and receives negative feedback almost daily: "Twitter is stressing" or "Twitter is overloaded again and I can't tweet."

Twitter's own service challenges have given birth to the "Fail Whale" phenomenon—the now ubiquitous metaphor for underperforming products and services. The Fail Whale represents a system-wide, crippling hiccup (and is the screen shot that greets visitors when Twitter is down).

Micromedia helps you and the companies you represent to find, listen to, and respond to relevant discussions. These microformat tools can help companies track discussions related to their brand in real time. Try it. Go to search.twitter.com and type in your company or product brand name. You'll see that these conversations are taking place, right now, without your support, advice, or insight. And although you're probably in more places than you thought, that presence alone is probably not enough. PR is expanding to include more than media, analyst, and blogger relations. PR is aligning with outbound service to embrace a new opportunity for hypeless and spin-free influence.

For example, companies can create a corporate or user-driven account from which they can proactively update their customers (a.k.a. followers) with new updates, answers, and so on. Cisco does this on Twitter through @CiscoIT, @CiscoNews, and @CiscoRSS; Zappos through @Zappos; JetBlue through @JetBlue; H&R Block through @hrblock; Dell through @richardatdell or @lionelatdell; and Comcast through @comcastcares. Customers can also contact them through "direct" messaging or public @companyname posts. Keywords such as #hashtags are a growing trend within the service. These enable users to call out specific topics such as #nike or #comcast for others to locate through a dedicated search tool such as twemes.com or hashtags.org. If you use services such as tweetscan or search.twitter.com, you can find these keywords without a hashtag.

Hashtags

Hashtags are a community-driven convention for adding context and metadata to tweets (updates on Twitter). See www.p2pfoundation.net/Hashtags for more information.

However, even though these new technologies and associated opportunities are impressive, we can't overlook an important Web 1.0 component: User groups and forums, such as Yahoo! and Google Groups, Amazon reviews, and e-pinions, haven't gone away. You need to figure out which communities host conversations that are important to your business, and determine which communities are critical to maintaining customer service and to instilling satisfaction and fostering enthusiasm among your brand enthusiasts.

With all the communities and tools we have mentioned, you're probably wondering which ones to use. The best way to begin is by surveying the landscape and then starting the process of listening. The results will tell you where to engage and how. Monitoring the culture of each community and the sociology of the interactions will guide you in how to participate. *Just remember to take the time to think about what you're doing and why.*

Be helpful, sincere, and transparent, and definitely be prepared to answer the same questions and concerns over and over again. Know what you're talking about and how your story benefits a wide variety of specific communities.

You Are the Customer

In some ways, we relinquish a portion of our message control in Social Media. Although we can't retain 100% control of what we say, what others hear, and what others share, we can help steer perception. Instead of speaking in buzzwords and hyperbole, we need to ensure that our solutions and benefits are clearly understood by all the different users (demographics) who populate our markets. *Feel the pain and deliver the painkiller.*

When we're not representing companies, we are also customers. We share with others our appreciation of products and services that deliver value, and we react as other customers to an oversell, hype, or spin situation.

Remember that customers need to hear things differently across each market segment, demographic, and psychographic—people need to hear things front-loaded with the benefits and painkillers that will compel them. Reaching the masses is still important, so casting a wide net doesn't necessarily go away, but focusing on specific niche markets is also critical to creating groundswell. Those customer groups respond to only unique and dedicated storylines. The requirement of engagement is that you participate according to the rules and terms of the community (just like everyone else) and as defined by the group's culture across each network, forum, blog, and so on.

Social networks aren't thriving because their citizens are eager for marketing. Remember that, in the real world, we are all customers. We buy products and purchase services, complain about the ones we don't like, and recommend those that we love (our trusted brands). A satisfied customer tells many, but an unsatisfied customer tells many more. We need to bring our real-world experiences to the table in order to provide a genuine and empathetic perspective.

Companies today must be aware that unsatisfied customers can reach millions of people via Social Media tools. The lesson is that we have to "be" a customer to think like one and legitimately approach a customer. As communications professionals, we must embrace Social Media and understand the technology so that we can be an immersed customer, similar to so many of the people with whom we want to converse. Connecting with them any other way isn't truly genuine, it extinguishes any chance for an honest relationship, it eliminates the possibility for a solid foundation on which to build trust, and it just might push customers away and fuel resentment. If we can think, communicate, and act like our customers, then we will truly be the people we want to help.

One of the most compelling ways to showcase solutions and benefits is to prepare a portfolio of customer experiences across multiple-use cases. Customer success stories can only benefit PR and marketing programs (not just in a traditional sense, but also in Social Media). These stories foster peer-to-peer connections based on real-world experiences. Showcase them on your blog. Have them in the form of quotes or even Web video endorsements on YouTube, or create a branded channel on Magnify.net. Record podcasts about them. Invite satisfied customers to events. Partner with them to be proactive voices to help rally other customers. After all, satisfied and enthusiastic customers keep you in business. Show them that you know this by reaching out to them, not just waiting for them to come to you. If you wait, they could easily become someone else's customers.

Augmenting Message Broadcasting with Market Value Propositions

The process of influence is shifting from a top-down message-broadcasting system to include a multifaceted, direct, less-is-more approach—focusing on the more valuable and influential people across all market segments that are important to our business. We now want to include storytelling rich with benefits and solution delivery based on strategic market influencer relations. All this requires individuals within marketing, sales, or service departments to visit each camp of representative and potential constituents to increase the visibility of the company's value proposition and explain how it helps and matters to each segment. Traditionally, PR professionals have written news releases and fabricated quotes for executives; that's largely still true today. Some even laugh about how horrible the quotes really are. They inject adjectives and irrelevant positioning statements. Then they identify potentially interested journalists and bloggers (usually through a database instead of targeting or qualifying them), and queue up the release for wire distribution. They contact those with whom they have established relationships, and then they send the news release to everyone else on that list. This is why PR often seems to be synonymous with spam.

You can now augment your activity with human and individualized market solutions to include a more street-level approach that connects you directly with the very people you're trying to reach. In addition to the top-down approach, your process of storytelling is now reverse-engineered through three easy steps:

1. Determine the groups of people who might benefit from your story, where they seek information, where they communicate, and how they communicate.

2. Listen and observe the exchanges and conversations that serve as the undercurrent for the respective online communities and cultures where they collaborate.

3. Adapt your story to the individual groups that are seeking information.

In addition, you'll garner incredible insight throughout the process of research, listening, and observing. In this way, you can also identify the new influencers (who can then reach new groups of people).

As you can tell, we are huge proponents of the social sciences. Therefore, we believe that these processes invoke new techniques and principles—all are available online (and in this book) to help you learn. If you either skipped or slept through those courses in school, brush up on those subjects. (Chapter 11, "Technology Does Not Override the Social Sciences," explains their importance in more detail.) To be a true member of the online community, you must humanize your intent and story, and learn how, where, and why to participate. By doing so, you reset the dynamic for engagement from top-down to one-on-one interaction.

This is probably one of the most important tips of the book, and it's critical that you understand that PR is no longer rooted in broadcast methodologies and the single-focused, general messages that drive them. PR needs to follow the authoritative dialogue, wherever it takes place. Without you, who will answer questions, clarify confusion, defend the brand, or develop relationships for the long term?

Message broadcasting is usually ineffective in New Media, especially as it relates to influencer relations. Traditionally, PR has focused on the right half of the infamous bell curve of product adoption. For those who might be unfamiliar with it, the bell curve features segmented portions that reflect the stages of market adoption, going from left to right. In Figure 16.1, innovators represent 2.5% of the market opportunity, early adopters represent 13.5%, early majority represent 34%, late majority also represent 34%, and laggards are at 16%. When we say that PR has concentrated its efforts on reaching the masses, they're usually lobbing news releases, messages, and pitches to the right side. Social Media unlocks and reveals the thriving communities and corresponding influencers that reach and stimulate the left side of the bell curve.

This is an important distinction and a new opportunity for general PR. Historically, adoption of new trends, as well as information in general has moved from left to right, as each group is influenced and motivated by the segment before it. By using the bell curve, we know that by reaching customers who are innovators, early adopters, and early majority, we can spark enthusiasm and support to help carry our story to the late majority and the laggards, which represent the other 50 percent of our market opportunity. However, speaking to and potentially befriending highly sophisticated customers requires an entirely new approach than what most PR people have learned. They're usually not swayed by our usual tools of relationship-marketing techniques. They want to hear and see things specifically, and know how a new approach will earn them the distinct and regarded position of trying something new without wasting their time.

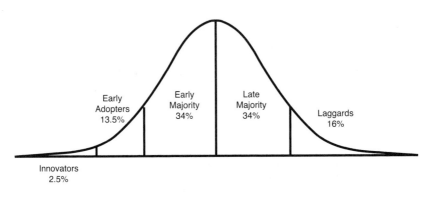

Figure 16.1   Categories of innovativeness

Reaching Tastemakers

In addition to our top-tier reporters, analysts, and A-list and magic middle bloggers, a collective of powerful influencers are present in each unique group you're trying to reach: They are the tastemakers. However, they don't usually appear in any marketing database to which communications or marcom typically subscribes.

Tastemakers are customers and consumers who reside higher on the ladder of influence than the rest of those who define the market. Similar to traditional journalists, analysts, and now A-list bloggers, tastemakers are a beacon for trends and activity, and their decisions and publicly shared opinions (through blogs, tweets, Facebook messages, and so forth) spark and affect adoption.

Tastemakers have typically been recognized as determining or strongly influencing trends or styles in fashion or the arts. But they are increasingly visible and active in almost every market and industry. The tastemaker category isn't new; neither is the desire to reach them. The Social Web makes this category even more interesting. The same tools that have democratized content and amplified our voices beyond their previous realm of influence have created a broader and more extensive network of tastemakers and new influencers who might not realize they possess this powerful ability to help people make decisions.

Social Media tools now make it possible to more easily identify and reach tastemakers. It all starts by listening and tracking conversations related to your brand and identifying those individuals who continually emerge as pundits, focusing on those with extensive social contacts (a.k.a. the social graph—usually the number of friends and followers they have in a network). This is a new and relatively undeveloped practice for PR, and, quite honestly, it changes the approach and dynamics of communications. This is an elusive group of incredibly sought-after innovators, and they do not respond to spam, pitches, or general contact. Reaching this group requires an intelligent, well-researched plan that provides and delivers benefits to both sides of the equation.

Introducing Psychographics to Traditional Demographic Profiling

Whereas marketing might have previously focused on demographics and target markets, socially aware organizations are now also balancing profiles with psychographics. This change in focus represents the difference between categorizing people by gender, class, and age, versus grouping them by interests and behavior.

A demographic is a representation of a grouping or market segment, usually aggregated by age group. For example, a marketer might want to create a campaign that reaches females, middle class, age 18–24. Psychographics, also referred to as IAO variables (for interests, attitudes, and opinions), is the observance and classification of attributes relating to personality, values, attitudes, interests, or lifestyles.

When classifying target groups and markets, researchers first determine which segments exist so that they can paint a clear and divisible picture that represents and segments the characteristics of a typical member of each group. After these profiles have been identified and documented, we can use them to develop a marketing strategy and plan.

For Example: The Ramp

When BMW recently (and semi-anonymously) released an online video to promote its new 1-Series, it used psychographic marketing techniques (in the hopes of making the video viral) instead of targeting demographics. Titled "The Ramp," BMW created a mockumentary (a fake documentary) that depicted the fictional small Bavarian town of Oberpfaffelbachen. The community was struggling through a recession and had devised a plan to reinvigorate the local economy. The plan was to launch a high-powered 1-Series BMW over the Atlantic into the United States with the help of an enormous ramp. A supposed U.S. documentary filmmaker, Jeff Schultz, was traveling through Germany via train when he noticed a gigantic ramp in the middle of nowhere and decided to uncover the rationale, aspirations, and madness behind the huge manmade structure.

Rampenfest (www.rampenfest.com) was viewed and shared by millions. BMW marketing, which later revealed that it officially created the video, had a surefire hit on its hands. The company's guerilla marketing and promotional strategies demonstrated how, instead of targeting age groups and genders, BMW could reach and compel people who shared interests in cars, speed, fun, online video, and, potentially, mockumentaries to further spur virality. The social experience was complete, surrounded by an Oberpfaffelbachen Web site, a Facebook profile, a Friendster town council, and a portable and embeddable series of widgets (among many other social tools).

In the increasingly Social Web, brands, and those who represent them, are learning that demographics might limit the full potential for reaching those people who share common interests—whether they're 8 or 80. People are making connections with each other because they share interests and passions. This creates and forges social graphs that expand the potential for reaching a larger, potentially captive series of audiences.

Aside from demographics versus psychographics, let's take a look at a few more examples of companies that are embracing a more outbound, socially focused service infrastructure.

Social-Service Case Study: FreshBooks

FreshBooks is a really good example of a company that understands the importance of customer service inbound and outbound in the Social Web. The company spends a great deal of time investing resources into customer service and mandates that everyone, at every level, engage with customers to stay connected with them. In doing so, all functions from sales to marketing to product development stay on track, focusing on what their customers really need and want.

FreshBooks participates in the Social Web in a number of ways:

- Comments on its blogs
- Google Alerts
- An active hosted forum
- People answering phones (no automated attendant)
- Twitter
- Customer dinners
- Conferences (where its customers go)

According to Michael McDerment of FreshBooks, "Since day one of FreshBooks' operation, there has been a mandate to overserve FreshBooks customers. A customer service department was formed before even a marketing team. That original mandate has carried on today with all the same principles."

This company believes in the following principles:

- **Real support and staying tapped in**—Every member of the FreshBooks team, from the CEO to the developers to the marketing department, also doubles as a member of the support team. The process of hearing, empathizing, finding solutions, and solving problems pervades everything they do and sets the guiding principles for the company's mission.

■ **Real-world relationships**—FreshBooks communicates with customers through its blog, forums, Twitter, and a newsletter called the "FreshBooks Supper Club." (The newsletter is basically an adjunct of the actual FreshBooks Supper Club. Anytime someone from FreshBooks travels, that person takes a group of customers out to dinner, for no reason other than to hang out and get to know them.)

FreshBooks also makes customers part of the PR process. It features them regularly on the company blog and in other promotional materials. The company also uses an interesting approach for its own employees, which it refers to as the "treat people the way you want to be treated" philosophy. FreshBooks believes that if the people are happy inside its walls, they will convey that happiness and excitement to their customers. In turn, customers will share that positive experience with others.

FreshBooks sometimes takes customer service on the road, too. For example, the company rented an RV in February 2007 to drive from Miami to Texas, and regularly booked stops to eat breakfast, lunch, and dinner with customers along the route. The idea came to fruition when FreshBooks planned to attend two conferences just one week apart (Future of Web Apps and South by Southwest). Instead of flying, FreshBooks conference attendees decided to drive and make key stops along the way to meet customers in their own cities, host BBQs, and generally just show the customers that they're important. (FreshBooks had reached an unbelievable 99 percent referral rate in its annual customer survey process in 2007.)

Case Study: ACDSee

ACDSee has long strived to deliver quality software for digital photographers. This case study shows how Social Media was used to provide excellent customer service and how ACDSee engaged a completely new market. This niche market continues to expand and thrive as customers tell others.

Listening Initially

ACDSee established a community manager position long before it was in vogue, and Connie Bensen, an early thought leader in community management, was hired to lead the charge. While monitoring online conversations, ACDSee became aware that customers were using its software in unconventional ways. This discovery initiated a dialogue with customers as the company sought to better understand how its software was being used.

Engaging the New Market

Engaging the new market required identifying the evangelists first. After ACDSee accomplished this, the company trained and encouraged the evangelists to use Social Media tools, including Google Alerts, SEO, and, of course, word of mouth. Next, ACDSee created a site with a wide range of resources (tutorials in various languages, videos, FAQs, tips on product use, blogs, and weekly newsletters). ACDSee also participated in blogs, online forums, and real-time chats on Web sites.

Evangelists Provide Personalized Customer Support at a Community-Centric Site

The ACDSee evangelists provided tech support by IM with Hello. They also created resources, including FAQs, to encourage customers to take advantage of self-service customer service. As a result, both noncustomers and customers directed others to these pertinent resources. ACDSee was able to gather useful product tips from customers and then consolidate these ideas into resources.

Listening and Providing for the Community's Needs

ACDSee knew the importance of feedback that was gathered on desired features. New features that were specific to the community were integrated into the product. The evangelists were able to maintain continual conversations with relevant communities. The communities were often offered promotional items created specifically for them. ACDSee integrated Social Media with traditional marketing, PR, and affiliate marketing efforts to meet the needs of its customer communities.

Expanding on Success

ACDSee was able to recruit additional evangelists to continue the level of support the community came to expect. By offering a public beta version of new products, ACDSee facilitated community input. Because this integrated approach was so successful, ACDSee plans to apply the model to other user segments.

Chapter **17**

The Rules for Breaking News

B reaking news used to be easy: You would write a news release and organize a national media tour. The tour would usually occur a couple of months in advance, to brief the monthly print publications and industry analysts. You'd hit weekly print media outlets about two weeks before the official launch day, and then you'd go after online sources a few days before the event. Of course, everyone would have to respect and abide by the same embargo date. At the time of the embargoed announcement, the news release would cross a wire service with the support of outbound call downs, outreach, and mass e-mail blasts. You would then hope that the efforts paid off in the form of news coverage, both print and online, appearing on or near the embargo date. But everything old isn't necessarily new again.

Public attention is thinning as new information sources emerge, and the traditional news cycle is a luxury of the past. Visibility (which is required to compete) depends entirely on frequency, and that frequency has radically shortened the time span between communicating news. As a result, the business of news targeting and distribution is favoring newspapers, weeklies, broadcast media, and online venues (all short-lead outlets). This change started with Web 1.0 and continues today, with new rules now applying.

Influence: Mainstream and Otherwise

Blogging has gone mainstream, with certain bloggers becoming well-known, highly sought-after personalities. They have earned a right of influence and recognition that rivals some of the journalists from top-tier traditional news outlets. Many of these individuals are referred to as the A-list. Their right of influence and clout has inspired new rules for breaking news. The right approach to breaking news has always been a hot topic for PR professionals. When done right, an appropriate release can result in tremendous impact and serve as the groundswell for future coverage in the blogosphere and in traditional media.

Robert Scoble is one of the most recognized names in the blogosphere. He frequently discusses the subject of blogger relations; embargoes; and news, product, and company launches in tech PR (and the tech landscape in general). PR professionals from myriad industries reach out to Scoble because he is an influencer. Therefore, Scoble has seen his fair share of both great and horrible pitches (and he openly discusses what he likes and dislikes about PR people, and how they approach him). Because of the sheer number of pitches he receives, and his desire to analyze what does and doesn't work, Scoble is quickly becoming an expert in the inner workings and best practices of PR, especially the more effective approach for breaking news.

The art of influence is changing. Although Scoble comes from a tech and photography background, his opinions influence multiple industries. Scoble takes the time to observe trends in PR and then openly discusses them in the blogosphere. This practice represents an important shift in news distribution. He and many other influential A-list bloggers, across every vertical and mainstream market, actively comment and share their opinions when it comes to PR.

We wish that we could report that these influencers' comments and information give PR professionals the stellar reputation they deserve. Unfortunately, most of the discussion about PR people, pitching, and their approach is negative. Collectively, the influencers' opinions border on resentment. (We shared many of these less-than-favorable opinions in earlier chapters of this book.)

It's a scary proposition that someone as influential as Scoble can go on the record and suggest that companies can survive without a PR firm or representative: "Believe me, we all will hear about your product if it really does rock. There's no reason to go crazy with a PR firm if you build something that people want." Scoble's quote is certainly not one that we want spreading like wildfire through the blogosphere. After all, we believe that our industry has the potential to help companies build effective, long-term and valuable relationships because we understand the nuances, needs, expectations, and predispositions of both parties in order to seamlessly connect them.

As mentioned in Chapter 6, "The Language of New PR," Gina Trapani, editor of Lifehacker, a popular blog dedicated to sharing productivity-centric "lifehacks," created a blacklist. She created her list in the spirit of Chris Anderson's infamous posting that banned PR people. Trapani and Anderson both shared the same sentiment that PR people were nothing more than spammers: "The only way bloggers can stop constant press releases is to simply filter messages based on a company's domain name."

Another well-known and respected thought leader in New PR, Micropersuasion blogger Steve Rubel, wonders whether bloggers even need PR assistance. He implied that they're more than capable of finding the best products on their own. He also had this to say:

> Does the thrill of the chase make PR obsolete? It's our view that increasingly, bloggers (and maybe journalists too) simply don't want our help. Many bloggers—particularly those who cover tech—love to discover new things and experience them on their own.... We know that when we write about news...I mostly do so if I discovered it on my own.

Too many influencers are asking questions and making statements that are damaging to the PR industry and the reputations of its practitioners. Another influencer, Marshall Kirkpatrick, who is one of the tech sector's most thorough and insightful bloggers and thinkers, constantly asks, "Does good tech need PR?" Marshall could have asked, "Does any good product or company need PR?" He might not have come out and said that, but you can relate his comment to any company or product. His thorough discussion concluded that yes, good products still require good PR. Although these examples involve technology and Web industries, the reactions are global and scalable. Is this merely a preview of what's to come, regardless of the industry? Let's work toward a different outcome. As PR professionals, we must rethink our approach. It's time the influencers support, discuss, and reinforce in their conversations the very value that we provide to so many different markets. To do so, however, we must prove our worth and value through actions, not words.

We believe one of the key components to rising above the negative commentary and opinions is to evaluate the business of news distribution to improve the dissemination and connection of poignant and relevant information to the right people. From a "smart" PR perspective, the distribution of news is evolving out of necessity. Savvy practitioners are dictating new processes for distribution that accommodate how influencers want to receive information. However, we believe you must uncover and expose the mechanics of the New Media machine to reach this goal, which will ultimately lead to improving the entire PR industry.

Blogs Are on the Scene

Blogger influence continues to grow exponentially, with many bloggers receiving millions of page views per month. For example, the Huffington Post claims to reach nearly two million unique monthly visitors. Famed entertainment-gossip blogger Perez Hilton has reported 1.3 million readers on a monthly basis.

Other top blogs include the following:

- TechCrunch (3.2 million monthly unique visitors)

- ARSTechnica (1.1 million)

- Drudge Report (1.1 million)

- Mashable (735,000)

To put that in perspective, the country's largest newspaper, *USAToday*, boasts just more than 2.2 million subscribers. The *Wall Street Journal* reports close to 2.1 million subscribers. The *New York Times* has almost 1.1 million paid subscribers.

PR people want to know how to best engage bloggers, launch products, and broadcast news. Many communications professionals are in a frenzy over the amount of influence bloggers have today and how blogging has changed what was previously a more constant process of launching products and distributing news. Those who are still questioning whether blogs matter to a company's strategic communication program run the risk of obsolescence. Ignoring the inevitable will only lead to an aggressive and extensive crisis-response program when company executives finally realize that they're losing customer attention and loyalty to their more perceptive and proactive competitors.

The race for public attention is underway, with the volume and intensity varying across markets and demographics. Consumers and peers on the left side of the bell curve (innovators and early adopters) are already advanced in their daily routine of finding and sharing information in Web communities. The majority of their activity is occurring online. In mainstream industries, where the brand and sales volume are synonymous with mass movement and the associated tools and practices that stimulate the process, the business of news might seem trivial and inconsequential.

However, a well-focused and exceptionally orchestrated news program that combines traditional and New Media influencers can and will cast a spotlight that illuminates your entire industry. And although New Media has altered who you target and how you bridge information to your contacts, the fundamental principles of Public Relations remain intact. You still need to do your homework: Understand what you represent, why it matters, to whom you're speaking, and what voices will carry your story to others. We still need to tailor the news and story for the specific people we're trying to reach, and package it based on their preferences. We still need to build direct and mutually beneficial relationships with media and vocal customers.

The new, more socially aware processes that we develop will inspire action and build communities across the entire bell curve, over time, and will affect every industry. We're defining and refining new processes and strategies, and bringing them from the edge back to the center. So when bloggers emerged as a necessary ingredient of the mix, we found ourselves rethinking (scrambling, in some cases) how to incorporate bloggers into this process without upsetting traditional relationships and established internal methodologies.

Scoble observed the activity of a few tech-savvy PR practitioners who realized the value of condensing the long cycle of prebriefings into a few days of focused, embargoed blogger relations for their news releases:

> I've noticed that PR types are getting very astute with dealing with bloggers lately.... First they'll call Mike Arrington [of TechCrunch]. Make sure he's briefed first (Mike doesn't like to talk about news that someone else broke first, so they'll make sure he is always in the first group to get to share something with you all). Then they'll brief "second-tier" bloggers

like me, Om Malik [of GigaOM], Dan Farber [of Cnet], Read/Write Web, and a variety of others. Embargo us all so we can't publish before Mike does.

Look closely at what Scoble states in his quote. We believe he is only partly correct. A process definitely exists, and we know it's rooted in respect, admiration, and cultivating relationships (at least, for the more effective communicators). However, even if you're not in tech PR, the names Scoble provided could be swapped out for any top blogger in his or her respective industry.

We can simplify the process this way:

1. Identify targets.

2. Determine traditional and new voices that influence those groups.

3. Rank those individuals based on their willingness to be part of an embargoed news launch and their news-related authority (A-, B-, or C-list, for example). Less is more here, so focus on a tighter set of those who popularize your A group. Don't forget to include your A-list of traditional newsmakers, as well.

4. Draft the release and news summary, and organize (or create) supporting artwork, video, and examples.

5. Determine the embargo date and time.

6. Reach out in advance to new and traditional contacts to begin discussions about embargoed news. Request their participation, and gauge their interest. *Do not* send embargoed materials without consent.

7. Follow up with all supporting materials.

8. Coordinate the release of news at the specific day and time.

9. Issue search engine–optimized (SEO) releases over the wire.

10. Reach out to other relevant contacts to share the news with them, based on their preferences for contact (from the left to the right of the bell curve).

11. Listen, observe, participate (with appropriate reactions), and answer questions across the Social Web.

12. Build a bigger story to take to more prominent business reporters; leverage the Google "juice" that's now bolstering your story courtesy of the barrage of simultaneous online coverage.

13. Identify midtier bloggers who write about your industry, competitors, and products. Find a way to keep them involved in a more dedicated relationship program driven by news and one-off stories.

By providing bloggers with early access to news and information, we're effectively making bloggers a new "wire" service. Suddenly your relationships with bloggers enable your news to bubble up to a point where it gains credibility and momentum. Finally, it attracts attention from traditional journalists and analysts who monitor trends. The conversations in the blogosphere feed the media, which helps them to report their stories.

Although we're making a bold statement that bloggers are the new wire service, that doesn't mean that traditional wire services don't have tremendous value. Wire services are important for sharing financial information and meeting disclosure requirements. They also have integrated capabilities with search engines, to enable news releases to reach people directly when they search for related items online.

The Beta Test

The beta test is a new and important step that's been added at the beginning of the news process in the tech world. Tech and Web companies initiate private or public "beta" launches because they want feedback directly from those inclined to "jump in" early and provide honest feedback. We're seeing the equivalent of "beta" in many industries outside of tech. The ability to package and share news on products, services, events, models, and so on before they're fully baked or ready for public consumption is highly effective in creating a new stage of news distribution and thus a strategic groundswell. These beta testers will share their experiences with their friends and associates long before the product or service is released to the general public. Traditional media was slow to recognize the importance of this beta phase. However, many journalists now realize that they are competing with bloggers, so they are covering beta releases. In fact, many news reporters at mainstream magazines, newspapers, and broadcast stations are now required to blog (in addition to their usual reporting method), to compete directly against bloggers.

As discussed throughout this book, we believe that it's vital to listen and read before you create any marketing strategy. Working with bloggers not only adds a new step to the communications process, but it also affects product marketing. It requires the team to factor in time and energy for a private or public focus group to build awareness and garner feedback. However, the time and resources it takes to listen prelaunch is well worth the investment. As we mentioned, other industries besides tech can now release a beta version of a product or information. Doing so adds a public component to the beginning of a modified process. Through this new methodology, you can spark conversations, elicit feedback, and generate significant awareness. Then when you are ready to announce the official availability of a new product or service, you have a captive group of people prepared to react.

New Influencers vs. Traditional Journalists

A distinct difference between new influencers and traditional journalists is that bloggers want early information (even in the testing and preproduction phases), whereas traditional media just want to hear about groundbreaking changes, or products or services that have already gained significant popularity (although this is changing). After your early or beta news gains momentum and enough people discuss it favorably, traditional media will notice.

This question arises: How do you share news with bloggers and journalists? Much of "how" you share news depends on your relationships. Currently, different industries approach the process of sharing news in various ways; there's no exact science yet. However, most bloggers and New Media personalities require a more personal, careful, and delicate approach because they're not trained in classic journalism. Blogger relations is a good reminder for communications professionals that everything needs to be reset to a one-on-one approach. And remember that certain bloggers have more clout than others (so do your homework).

Through blogger and media relations, the business of news has advanced to the point of this public component, adding a new layer into the equation. Of course, a thriving news business still exists within traditional media. However, early information, prototypes, previews, dress rehearsals, leaks, and R&D all give bloggers their edge these days. And if executed properly, they escalate the brand and the anticipation for new things among traditional press and, ultimately, customers.

But going to bloggers and top journalists isn't as easy as you might think. You can't play favorites and expect to make all your new influencers happy. Favoring one over the other can cost you credibility and relationships. For example, if you reach out to more than ten bloggers, you run an increased risk of someone breaking the news early. Borrowing a page from the traditional PR and journalism playbook, bloggers have embraced embargoes to maintain the privilege of receiving early information.

We can tell you from personal experience that bloggers do occasionally break embargoes. These breaks can prove costly if you don't have backup plans in place. When one blogger runs with a story, most other bloggers will probably pass on the opportunity to write about your "story" (as in the traditional world of PR). We have also witnessed the wrath that can result if one blogger goes before everyone else.

In case a blogger does break an embargo, you should create a contingency plan so that all your hard work isn't lost because of one post. It's important to set up a Google Alert for the product or company so that you can track any mention online as it happens. If someone breaks the embargo, you should receive the alert almost instantaneously. It doesn't hurt to manually check each blog before the embargo time, as well. Regardless of the level of relationships you maintain with your blogger and media contacts, an immediate round of outbound responses is necessary to preserve your reputation with other bloggers and to make the case for why they should still run the story. Honesty is your only policy here.

In our experience, we've learned that, by telling the truth, we're usually able to salvage a majority of coverage. It all starts with an e-mail or a call to all your embargoed contacts to notify them that someone broke the embargo and that you're alerting them before they run at their scheduled time. Your contacts will appreciate the honesty. Usually they will ask who ran early. It's up to you whether you disclose that information, and your decision will usually vary depending on personal circumstances. By offering bloggers and reporters a new angle, a direct interview, or fresh content, such as a video demo, you can help minimize the loss of coverage you were otherwise expecting. Also, it's important that you immediately start reaching out to your additional top- and second-tier bloggers and reporters to introduce them to your breaking news. This coverage augments and expands your story's visibility and reach.

Relationships mean everything in these situations. When you have valuable news to share, you want to work with a select group of people who can really help build the community; in many cases, that means adapting to the way these influencers work.

Exclusives still have their role to play, but they're becoming rarer. Offering a story to just one writer usually limits the ultimate total visibility of that story. The more bloggers are involved, the further your reach (perhaps even a global reach). And as mentioned previously, after one blogger runs with a story, the news value of that story deflates. Most other bloggers will opt out because they don't want to appear as a "me, too" writer—they want to be part of the elite group that breaks the story simultaneously.

Remember this: *Campaigns aren't viral. People make them viral.* If Social Media has taught us anything, it's that we can empower people to help carry the word to others. However, most executives are much too impatient to sit and wait for an organic campaign to gain traction. These executives will have to learn that when people choose to make a campaign viral, it's worth the wait. Finding the right influencers takes time. The peer-to-peer influence sells products and services quicker than many other forms of marketing. This is why it's critical to extend the news push from the A-list to the Magic Middle to help the conversations permeate the Social Web.

You're Invited

We mentioned earlier that you can introduce another step into the process as a way of gaining traction sooner. Even before beta, there's alpha (or private beta). Private beta is usually an experiment in organic marketing, driven by a sense of scarcity and exclusivity. You can easily create a password-protected community to showcase and share information with your A-list before information is officially released.

Companies have found this to be an excellent way to stimulate conversations and interest. Jason Kinzler, founder of PitchEngine (www.pitchengine.com), launched his site in alpha to test a new product that helps PR professionals create and distribute free Social Media releases. Kinzler found much success when he invited bloggers, PR practitioners, communications professionals, and other media workers to enter the password-protected site. He *invited* his guests to log in with a special code to access and test the site and the product's functionality. Kinzler also set up a blog to capture comments and enable people to ask questions. Through the blog comments, many people gave favorable endorsements and praised Kinzler for developing a social networking site that provided solutions for PR people and the media. His alpha site was an excellent way for his influencers to experiment, gain firsthand knowledge, and report back on functionality and site relevance.

New companies and services are often previewed in private through invitations, opt-in reviews, or password-protected links. Bloggers, media, and enthusiasts are all included in this round of testing, and they are empowered to share information with other peers to build excitement. For example, some microblogging services became an "overnight" success after being introduced privately to a select group of influential users (in this case, highly connected geeks and bloggers). These influential users bragged about their access to the site (via invitation codes) and created a hyperactive market for invitation exchanges (with some actually going on eBay and selling them).

Socializing the News Process

Imagine breaking news organically. Wouldn't it be great if you didn't have to worry about embargoes, but instead you could use social tools and people through all channels of Social Media to share information before an official launch? Yes, you can. Some companies and communications professionals are doing it now, and are also learning how to streamline the process.

As mentioned throughout this book, Social Media is forcing an evolution in how companies share information with customers and those who act as information intermediaries to the people who depend on them for guidance. "Making news" is truly an art—one that requires talent and creativity, but also practice and experience. You must also understand the landscape in which you compete (your market, your competitors, and so forth). The most successful ways of sharing news will depend on your ability to listen and to build and cultivate relationships with those who can help break news under the "new" rules of the launch.

Many avenues are available for working with bloggers, enthusiasts, and traditional journalists, including opportunities to do things the wrong way. And if you do it wrong once, you will lose the faith and the attention of many important influencers. So you must pay attention, think, and be creative. You must have a plan and build trust to ensure that your story is clear and your intentions are honest.

Beware of Embargoes

The new rules of breaking news are intended to open your mind and unlock creativity when introducing new products and services. According to the new rules, one "audience" doesn't exist for a story or campaign, nor is it still necessary for you to share news only when something is newly available. Whether it's a derivative of the public or private beta strategies we discussed earlier, you have new opportunities beyond the usual routine of booking press tours, drafting press releases, and blasting news to reporters and bloggers.

Brian recently experienced a couple examples that made him rethink the embargo processes he employs. In two back-to-back instances, stories broke ahead of their intended time. The bloggers who broke the stories early were highly trustworthy, but they decided that they favored the scoop over the relationship. To the other lead bloggers whom Brian had brokered these launches, it appeared as if he had misled them (sending the news to others, even though he had assured them that he was giving them first rights). In both cases, Brian took brief credibility hits and had to do an exhaustive amount of repair work to ensure that these and other relationships weren't damaged because of the mistake, spite, or questionable activity of other ambitious bloggers. Brian took steps to set the record straight, and he convinced the offending bloggers to add a note or update to their posts. Ultimately, the "mistakes" were corrected, but trust is not as easily regained. Based on these experiences, Brian now practices a less-is-more philosophy. He trusts only the highest referring traffic targets with proven relationships for special private or public news initiatives.

The business of news is not only competitive—it can get downright ugly. Grumblings about foul play abound: manipulating "time stamps," copying and pasting from other blogs and sites without attribution, not disclosing any personal or professional interests, and running controversial or early stories without checking the facts first. Unfortunately, many PR professionals and the companies they represent end up the losers in what should be a mutually beneficial news process.

However, this isn't unlike the business of traditional news media, which has always been notorious for scoops. Underground rivalry will always exist among top and up-and-coming writers for authority, links, views, and the ad dollars that contribute to their bottom line. When Deirdre's firm launched RCN Metro's fiber-optic network in Philadelphia in 2008, the *Philadelphia Business Journal* learned that the *Philadelphia Inquirer* had run a brief story (as a result of an embargoed release), and the *Business Journal* wanted nothing more to do with the story. That's the way it goes with most influencers, whether traditional or new.

This is the business of news, and it's a business that is never clean. However, these enlightenments force us to rethink the process of PR launches and news distribution. Ultimately, our relationships will determine our success or failure in getting news out. Our message to you is simple: *Be careful and do your homework.* You walk a tightrope between client and company expectations and the relationships you maintain with writers and bloggers.

Your clients want to see coverage, and they want to see it everywhere, as measured by the weight of an old-school clip book. However, relationships are the foundation for all good PR, whether we're talking about traditional journalists, New Media influencers, or bloggers, and risking or compromising them should never factor into the news equation.

Many bloggers are trying to run legitimate businesses, and the privilege of receiving news early is earned based on the mutual benefits between the blogger or writer and the company. Maximizing coverage is a risky business. Unfortunately, things can quickly go south in many ways:

- Not communicating the embargo time clearly, complete with time zones

- Not receiving a documented acknowledgment of the embargo

- Not fully knowing the reputation of the blogger beforehand

- Sending the news prior to receiving an official agreement to the embargo

The reality is that some of you will learn these lessons the hard way. And many times, these lessons come at a steep price, with reputation, trust, and relationships as the currency. The most important thing you can do is keep an open dialogue with your best contacts. Talk with peers and share your experiences. You can learn plenty from others to minimize the mistakes and the steep costs associated with them.

In an attempt to earn the respect and trust of bloggers, many PR professionals are subscribing to a "blogger relations" code of ethics, which we mentioned in Chapter 4, "Traditional vs. New Journalism." It's a start in the right direction. Word of Mouth Marketing Association, known as WOMMA (www.womma.org), also lists on its Web site ten principles for ethical contact by marketers:

1. I will always be truthful and will never knowingly relay false information. I will never ask someone else to deceive bloggers for me.

2. I will fully disclose who I am and who I work for (my identity and affiliations) from the very first encounter when communicating with bloggers or commenting on blogs.

3. I will never take action contrary to the boundaries set by bloggers. I will respect all community guidelines regarding posting messages and comments.

4. I will never ask bloggers to lie for me.

5. I will use extreme care when communicating with minors or blogs intended to be read by minors.

6. I will not manipulate advertising or affiliate programs to impact blogger income.

7. I will not use automated systems for posting comments or distributing information.

8. I understand that compensating bloggers may give the appearance of a conflict of interest, and I will therefore fully disclose any and all compensation or incentives.

9. I understand that if I send bloggers products for review, they are not obligated to comment on them. Bloggers can return products at their own discretion.

10. If bloggers write about products I send them, I will proactively ask them to disclose the products' source.

Perhaps many bloggers need to think about subscribing to a blogger code of ethics. Breaking embargoes, changing time stamps, editing or barring comments, pilfering content, and so on will come back to haunt you in the long term. And the unfortunate effects of these practices will continue to destroy reputations and relationships in the process.

Tim O'Reilly, who coined the term *Web 2.0,* has an excellent series on drafting a blogger's code of ethics. Charlene Li, a former Forrester analyst previously mentioned in Chapter 4, got the conversation going almost three years ago with a call for blogging policies.

Breaking news with a few trustworthy bloggers and reporters might be more than enough to effectively align PR with business and communication objectives. After the first stories break, follow up with outreach to other primary influencers, but also find something unique for them to help them recognize a distinct angle for coverage. Some will push back for not being included in the earlier rounds, and it will be up to you to consider including them in the future—but you should do so based only on the discussions and trust.

Chapter 18
A New Guide to Metrics

How do we measure the effectiveness of PR today? How do we define *success* in the new world of socialized communications? How does any of this "social" activity affect objectives and contribute to the bottom line? These questions should sound very familiar.

In our experience, executives don't believe that the changes in our PR approach and the advent of Social Media will measurably change sales and marketing efforts that serve as the lifeblood for any business—a narrow outlook of socialized PR and community participation. They believe that no matter how much they invest in developing relationships with peers and influencers, they can never monetize the process of engagement.

This book won't make any difference if you cannot effectively convince the C-suite (corporate-level executives) not only that New PR is required to compete in today's economy, but also that it's measurable. Therefore, this chapter discusses New Media metrics that you can use to encourage business leaders to invest in PR 2.0 strategies. It is also written for executives so that they can learn firsthand how these new metrics in a new environment document influence, reach, referrals, activity, and pull.

Advertisement Deficit Disorder

Did you know that the average person sees 3,000–5,000 messages, product tag lines, and sales pitches per day? In today's PR world, we hire clipping agencies to track and clip print and online coverage. We contract brand and media-monitoring services to capture and share video or audio content as it happens. We also search Google and online sites directly to make sure that we're not missing anything.

Traditional metrics for measuring print PR coverage include the following:

- The weight of the clip books, which served as a metric and indicator of success and return on investment (ROI)

- Each "hit" or piece of coverage by the dedicated amount of real estate on the printed and online page

- A comparison of the size of the editorial coverage to the cost of a similar-sized advertisement in a hard-copy publication with the same demographics

- The reach of publications via circulation numbers and online eyeballs to capture the number of people who might have read the story

True media coverage was usually worth more than a typical advertisement because of the implied endorsement of an expert or authority.

As K. D. Paine, a specialist in New Media metrics, says, "HITS = How Idiots Track Success." Obviously, PR can continue to measure ROI and effectiveness using these dated systems and processes. However, to convince executives to experiment with Social Media, PR must introduce new metrics and processes.

David Weinberger, coauthor of *The Cluetrain Manifesto,* wrote, "There is no market for your message." He's right.

Throughout this book, we have shared our experiences and those of others to demonstrate how new influencers factor into the equation of information discovery and distribution.

New Metrics for PR 2.0

Accurately measuring the reward for our engagement is somewhat the holy grail of PR 2.0. The Social Web has both complicated and broadened our quest. It has introduced new ROI metrics, extended our options, and reset our expectations. To measure *success,* we must determine what success looks like in this new environment. For example, expecting PR 2.0 to result in direct sales (and thus pay for itself) is unrealistic. To gauge PR

2.0 success, we want to focus on momentum, in real time, and demonstrate what's working. By actively listening and continually "taking the temperature" of our various engagements, we can learn how to do things better in both the short and long terms.

Interactive marketing and Web marketers have often experimented with new methodologies and practices to measure the success of their work. We can learn much from these disciplines while also applying real-world experience that we gain through personal engagement. With PR 2.0, we can analyze, measure, and amend campaigns and long-term PR and relationship-building programs in real time. Using the same tools for measuring as we do for listening, we can track and record progress—real-world effects on market behavior. We can also respond to misperceptions or negative feedback immediately to reduce the likelihood of criticism-based flare-ups.

People, Power, Perception

"Everyday people" with access to Social Media tools, in addition to traditional experts, contribute to the public definition and perception of a brand. Perception equals the sum of all conversations in the Social Web, and those who participate steer its definition.

PR 2.0 favors engagement more than hits, referrals more than eyeballs, activity more than ad value, sales more than mentions, and market and behavioral influences more than the weight and girth of clip books.

Conversation Index

As mentioned throughout this book, conversations are pervasive in the Social Web and serve as its ever-expanding foundation. Conversations can take the form of videos, podcasts, bookmarks, blog posts and comments, tweets, pictures, reviews, meetups and events, news or story aggregation, and so on.

A conversation index indicates your placement, status, ranking, perception, and participation in the Social Media sphere. By tracking conversations based on keywords, you can measure their frequency, tonality, and locations, and create a measurable baseline with which to compare all future activity.

Almost every online conversation is trackable. You can use conversations to measure the effectiveness of your PR program. Criteria include frequency of keyword mentions over a comparable time span—for example, x number of mentions this month versus x number last month, or year-to-date equals x number in contrast to last year at x number. You can also track competitive mentions compared to conversations about your company or products.

Because Social Media is rooted in conversations, participation, and engagement, it introduces new trackable elements into our formula for determining ROI and success:

- Conversations or threads by keyword

- Traffic

- Leads or sales

- Calls to action

- Engagement

- Relationships

- Authority

- Education and participation

- Perception

- Registrations, membership, and community activity

Conversations or Threads by Keyword

Measuring the frequency and tone of conversations is the new frontier for PR and marketing, with many solutions launching as we write this book. As you'll see in the next chapter, conversations are taking place across multiple social networks simultaneously, but maybe they're not on your radar screen. The safest bet is to manually search every network to augment any automated services you might subscribe to, especially when initially listening to relevant conversations to determine which networks are host to discussions about your brand. This is the only way to specifically map the resulting data to your business and ROI metrics. Many companies are either outsourcing this process or tasking interns to listen and document benchmarks.

You can use these tools to automatically track conversations in addition to searching individual social networks:

- **Google Alerts**—A free service that monitors Google, Google News, Google Blogserach, and Google Images for your predefined keywords and sends an alert when they appear online.

- **Radian6**—A commercial suite of Social Media tools to track, analyze, and engage in conversations, and to measure and report trends based on keywords and topics. Radian6 monitors all forms of Social Media, including blogs, top video-sharing and social-networking sites, forums, opinion and review sites, image-sharing sites, microblogging sites, and online mainstream media.

- **BuzzLogic**—A commercial service that identifies influential online discussions on any topic, enabling marketers to better target their stories and insight to both opinion leaders and the engaged readers who follow them.

- **Neilsen BuzzMetrics**—A commercial service that measures consumer-generated media (CGM, a.k.a. user-generated content or UGC) and online word-of-mouth to help companies understand and track conversations.

- **Social networks and microcommunities**—Every social network includes a search box that enables you to search for conversations and activity related to keywords. For example, conversations taking place in Facebook, Plurk, MySpace, BackType, Digg, YouTube, and public customer forums will most likely go unnoticed in any of these automated listening tools. It's important that you search these services manually, especially if they've been identified as hotspots for discussions about your brand in the original listening audit. See the next chapter for a full list of services.

- **Blogpulse Conversation by Neilsen BuzzMetrics**—A free tool for assembling, tracking, and messaging threaded conversations and memes. When a blogger publishes a post and other bloggers link to it, the original post (seed) creates a thread or meme, which extends with every new post that links back to the original.

Traffic

You can track almost everything related to your company Web site or blog by using Web site analytics software. By partnering with the Web team, PR can integrate analytics to not only measure traffic and clicking patterns, but also study and process the information to formulate more market-relevant campaigns and tracking criterion.

Web traffic reports tell us how many people visited a particular Web page, where they came from, how long they were there, their click path, their activity, and also where they left. This data can prove highly educational, and it reveals almost everything we need to know about our media, blogger, and influencer relations and engagement programs.

Because success is measured in the form of unique visits and individual actions, consider the following:

- A story on an A-list blog can generate 5,000–15,000 unique visits in one month.

- Making the front page of Digg can refer more than 10,000 unique visits in 24–48 hours.

- Gaining momentum on StumbleUpon can yield 20,000–30,000 unique views in 30 days.

- Hosting an event on Upcoming or Facebook can reach and secure hundreds and even thousands of attendees.

Insight about Web activity can help you become more effective in your online marketing efforts. You can also share such information to demonstrate your value to the C-suite.

Leads or Sales

Tying marketing activity to sales is every executive's favorite way to evaluate PR effectiveness. For example, what's the ROI on distributing a news release? How do you justify the hundreds of dollars you spend on issuing your news over the wire?

We know that the likelihood of reporters finding the release on the wire and stopping what they're doing to write a story about it is a pipe dream, at best. But with the inclusion of Web distribution and hosting, we now know that a news release offers extended reach by appearing in search engines that reach not only reporters and bloggers seeking information, but also potential customers and partners.

Southwest Flying High

When Southwest Airlines realized that a greater audience could receive its news (beyond just the press and analysts), the company embarked on a series of consumer-focused press releases that included calls to action. In one such press release, Southwest announced a new fare sale and included a link in the press release to a dedicated Web page that gave consumers direct access to discounted airline tickets. The company attributed more than $1 million in sales directly from the news release's ubiquitous appearance in search engines powered by strategic keywords, a call to action, and an SEO wire distribution.

We can tie PR 2.0 strategies to lead generation or sales in a number of ways. Listening to related conversations in the Social Web will reveal various opportunities to engage decision makers, which you can then tie to customer development and loyalty building.

Calls to Action

ROI is not determined just by sales. Companies can also drive activity, which, in many cases, can prove equally important. Borrowing a page from the books of Web marketing and direct advertising, integrating a "call to action" in our communications programs produces an activity-driven metric that enables us to track response rates while also benefiting from the predefined events. For example, many social marketers are creating dedicated online landing pages to capture momentum as it happens. Landing pages are Web pages designed specifically to capture incoming traffic from a specific promotion, or they can include an area for product registration, access to special discounts or promotions, a corporate blog post, votes, community participation, direct sales, an event RSVP, and so on.

Landing Pages

Landing pages on Web sites can prove to be invaluable resources for marketers who take an active role in measuring traffic and understanding how people utilize a Web site. These pages can provide data that marketers might otherwise find difficult to mine. Information-hungry marketers, eager to know how to adjust their campaigns and how best to allocate their budget, will often lead prospects to a landing page on their site (instead of the home page) that is accessible only directly—no links to the landing page exist anywhere on the site because users have to type the URL directly to gain access. When on the landing page, a visitor's presence and subsequent actions are then tracked, giving the marketer insight into the value of the external marketing efforts.

Engagement

Engagement and relationships are probably among the most difficult to measure and are usually unique to each company. Engagement refers to the amount of time a person either participates within a dedicated or hosted Web community or service related to your brand, or interacts with a representative of your company online. Engagement can also refer to the reach of your story—the process of spreading word-of-mouth referrals and sparking new and related conversation threads.

For example, suppose that your company decides to build a dedicated social network for its brand, and host service or enthusiast conversations on Ning or as part of its corporate Web site using a service such as Leverage Software or KickApps. You can measure engagement through Web site analytics (discussed later in this chapter), such as the amount of time visitors spend interacting with each other and company representatives.

Using Social Media search tools such as Technorati or Google Blogsearch and initiating keyword alerts through Google Alerts, you can track most conversations that relate to your company. You can also research threads related to important conversations through Blogpulse.com. You should maintain records of your results so that you have baselines from which to track and compare results on a daily, monthly, and annual basis.

As PR expands its reach in social marketing, new tools for engagement are continually introduced. Widgets, virtual goods, mini applications, and fan groups in social forums are increasing in their adoption and potency.

Companies such as Coca-Cola are developing widgets for people to grab and embed on their profile pages in social networks. On Facebook, Coca-Cola developed an application that enables people to send a virtual Coke to friends. More than 51,000 people have installed this application, and the page itself currently supports 148,000 fans (and growing).

Relationships

How do we measure relationships in the real world? We typically value those relationships in which both parties draw fulfillment and inspiration (as opposed to popularity). In the world of Social Media, it's a fusion of both and always a two-way proposition. In some cases, the number of online friends and followers indicates the relationships you or your team maintains on social networks. Most don't follow or befriend you and your brand unless they deem it to be of value. It's your job after that to ensure that anything you do within these networks is based on reinforcing value instead of creating mailing or spam lists.

At the time of this writing, Web-based shoe retailer Zappos.com boasts that it's following 13,000 people and is followed by 11,000 people on Twitter. Southwest Airlines is following 2,800 people and is followed by 2,700 people. On Facebook, more than 72,000 consumers have joined the Coca-Cola fan page.

Although a company's participation is not a popularity contest, the number of people befriending these companies, and the people representing the brands, is growing because of value they receive from being part of an active, informative, and value-driven community.

Authority

One of the rewards for helping your community and becoming a resource to existing and potential customers is that your credibility, your thought leadership, and, ultimately, your authority rises above parity. Relationships and loyalty aren't cheap. So how do you define and track authority?

At the very least, corporate blogs should be part of any communications initiative. Those who are a bit more ambitious can also integrate microblogs (tumblr, Twitter, Plurk) or brandstreams (socialthing, lifestream.fm, Swurl), among many other social content–creation and hosting platforms, into their strategy. As you update any of these services with commentary, answers, feedback, and insight, you are publicly inviting others to react and respond. Several indicators will enable you to assess authority, which you can "grow" based on the value of your content and how well you promote it.

Free blog directories and search-engine solutions such as Technorati enable you to "claim" your blog, microblog, or brandstream, which then creates a snapshot of activity. When you first claim your site, your authority is zero. Proactive comments across social networks and the publishing of provocative and stellar content will increase your authority. Technorati and other similar sites and services rank the weight of the links that point back to your content, and each link contributes to a score or ranking. As the number of your inbound links increases, your blog, Web page, profile, and so on will earn a higher position in search engines results pages (SERPs). The higher the number of inbound links, the greater your PageRank, which Google defines as the index by which it weighs and factors the popularity of your site or page.

A side benefit of high authority is the organic SEO that contributes to your position in search-engine results for the keywords that define and represent your industry.

In the blogosphere, comments are used to also measure authority, meaning that the number of comments you receive per post represents your position and stature. We're not sure this is a viable metric because, although it is important, linkbacks and traffic speak volumes about your true real-world impact.

You can benchmark your authority against competition and time segments. If you enter a URL into Technorati, it will reveal the authority for that particular location and the number of inbound links to that destination.

Another way to measure authority, and also your followers, is to track the number of readers who subscribe to your RSS feeds on your blog, brandstream, newsfeeds, and so on. Everything you create in Social Media offers an RSS feed, including Twitter, YouTube, Flickr, blogs, Facebook, and so on. Tools such as FeedBurner and Pheedo enable you to manage your RSS subscriptions and measure the rate of new subscribers and the total number of subscribers. Blog and RSS feed communities such as Bloglines and Google Reader can also give you an idea of your RSS numbers.

Education and Participation

Education, participation, and collaboration are also new forms of evaluation and justification.

For example, Deirdre is working with a major food manufacturer to launch an internal innovation community to encourage employees and other groups to collaborate, and to also research and test emerging technology within the organization. In this case, it's not about measuring the ROI. The new program seeks to spark collaboration and innovation among different business groups. It also attempts to shift the culture to one of innovation and collaboration, as follows:

- Collaboration will become the new norm. The goal is to change the corporate culture so that employees engage and use peer-to-peer communication.

- Employees are encouraged to participate in existing blogs or wikis. (Some are viewing them now but not commenting.)

- The company is making Social Media tools available, and everyone is encouraged to experiment with them and perhaps discover additional utility for them.

- Increased awareness and education will lead to deeper engagement and open dialog.

To determine the success of the Social Media initiative, Deirdre and her team are monitoring the participation on internal Web pages (a viable metric). This participation includes the number of visitors on wikis and participation in wiki forums (such as wiki editing and content publishing). Measurement also consists of blog views, comments and ratings, case study downloads (podcasts and video sharing), participation in virtual tours (unique visitors), and the use of an avatar (the 3D model that answers questions in real time) to track the number of visitors who ask questions on specific topics within the Social Media portal.

Best Buy Buys In

Best Buy recently launched BlueShirtNation.com for employees to share knowledge, best practices, frustrations, aspirations, and jokes. Within a year, 20,000 Blue Shirts have registered and are actively participating. According to the BSN team, "It wasn't architected by IT professionals. It wasn't coded or designed by Web developers. It wasn't endorsed and pushed by management, and its launch wasn't unveiled by Internal Communications...In the traditional sense, it shouldn't work."

In one example, BSN has produced tremendous impact on engaging and stimulating action among Best Buy employees. The company wanted to promote 401(k) enrollment and launched "The 401(k) Challenge," a video contest hosted in the BSN network. The user-generated videos created such a buzz that the company's enrollment increased 30 percent, which equates to roughly 40,000 employees (see www.garykoelling.com/?q=node/370).

Perception

Although message control is a priority for many organizations, perception management should be the true quest of most communications initiatives. Sentiment, tone, and message integrity are easily discoverable and documentable online. Measurement is most useful when you have something to benchmark against. Running a current audit of the state of your brand perception helps you create an accurate baseline and also reveals the opportunities for engagement.

The process begins with searching keywords through free services such as blogsearch.google.com, twemes, search.twitter.com, and BackType. com. Build a grid that captures the frequency of the keyword mentions and whether the conversation was positive, negative, or neutral (which we refer to in the industry as raves, rants, or blah).

It's critical that you identify keywords that will truly capture a majority of relevant conversations. It's important to select not only words that you think would be used with your brands, but also those your customers *might* use. For example, don't forget the popular "suckometer" or "DIEometer" when running a search. You'd be surprised at how many companies use it to gauge perception management. Search *"yourcompany+*sucks" and "DIE+*yourcompany"* and chart the results. Also search *"competitorname+* sucks" and "DIE+*competitorname"* for comparison.

I Hate, It Sucks, Is Evil…

A recent study found that one in three Fortune 500 and Global 500 companies have purchased related "gripe sites" such as *www.xcompanysucks.com* and *www.ihateyourcompany.com*.

FairWinds studied 1,058 domain names for companies on the Global 500 and Fortune 500 lists. Of those companies, 35 percent already own the domain name for their brand followed by the word *sucks,* including major brands Wal-Mart Stores, Coca-Cola, Toys "R" Us, Target, and Whole Foods Market. Perhaps not surprising (but also astonishing based on what you've learned in this book), 45 percent of these domains haven't been registered by either companies or angry customers. Although some companies that do own these domain names use them as an opportunity to share positive content, most haven't published anything.

For example, Xerox has purchased roughly 20 potential hate site domain names, including xeroxstinks.com, xeroxcorporationsucks. com, and ihatexerox.net. In contrast, Dell hasn't made any moves, which is perplexing considering its proactive role in participating in online conversations. According the study, DellisEvil.com, MyDellSux.com, and IHateDell.info are for sale, but Dell is not interested in acquiring the addresses.

Over time, the idea is to use this research to serve as a reference point and to dictate the steps required to inject a positive change through strategic participation.

Registrations, Membership, and Community Activity

As mentioned previously, PR 2.0 is borrowing pages from the books of Web marketing and advertising. Not only are you extending the brand and building goodwill and trust within the communities where you participate, but you can also tie specific action and activity to your efforts to measure their outcome (and success or failure).

These efforts require PR and the Web team to collaborate in advance of any outbound activity. You want to build a back-end infrastructure to engage those who arrive at the destination to capture some form of participation, information, referrals, or content.

If you're releasing a new product, consider offering previews to boost interest. Create a registration list or fan base and offer something in return. For example, many companies offer rewards to consumers who take the time to share data (rewards such as extended warranties, T-shirts, discount codes for future purchases, access to exclusive content, and so on). Offer a demo video at a dedicated URL and encourage visitor commentary. Remember that development resources are extremely affordable (as compared to the Web 1.0 era). Many of today's communities, applications, videos, widgets, networks, and blogs are created for as little as a few hundred dollars.

Consider these examples of programs for engaging your community:

- Schedule **livestream** interviews with executives, customers, or influential personalities to share insight with visitors. You can use Veodia, Ustream, or Mogulus. Examples of this strategy include Wine Library TV, Zooomr on Ustream, and Leo Laporte on Ustream.

- Host an **online video channel** of demos, tips, and creative content on YouTube, Magnify.net, or Viddler. Examples of this strategy include HomedepotTV on YouTube, Taste of Home on Magnify.net, and Will It Blend? on YouTube.

- Create an **application** or a **widget** for visitors to download or copy and paste for embedding on social network profiles, blogs, or Web sites. Examples of this strategy include SkullCandy's "stealable" widget (which means it's portable and embeddable on Web pages, social profiles, and blog posts) developed by MediaForge, Puma's Facebook application for Usain Bolt, WWE's Fan Nation Widget, BMW's 1-Series Road Trip application on Facebook, and Acuvue's Wink application on Facebook.

- Develop a **virtual world** to captivate and cultivate your community. Examples of this strategy include Slim Jim's Spicyside.com, Discovery Channel's LA Hard Hats virtual construction site, and Coke's Virtual Thirst contest on Second Life.

- Build a **fan page** or **group** on popular social networks. Examples of this strategy include Acura's fan page for its TSX connect program on Facebook, Victoria's Secret Pink page on Facebook, Condé Nast Traveller's fan page on Facebook, Crest Whitestrips on Facebook, Ford Drive U student group on Facebook, and Jeep on MySpace.

- Create a **mashup** application or online destination that fuses your product or value proposition with readily available online tools. Examples of this strategy include Nike+ Running Route Finder and Fidelity Investments' savings rate finder and checking account comparison application.

- **Crowdsource** content creation and offer a reward for participants (such as sharing their contributions to a greater audience, promotion of content, and noteworthy prizes). Examples of this strategy include the independent Super Bowl ad challenges led by Chevy and Doritos.

- Host a **collaborative service-focused community** to brainstorm and share ideas for product or service improvements or to strategize on next-generation solutions. Examples of this strategy include Salesforce.com's IdeaExchange, Dell's IdeaStorm, Starbucks's My Starbucks Idea, and Mozilla on GetSatisfaction.com. (Actually, every company should be on the GetSatisfaction network).

- Host a community or social network to spark **hosted conversations** that focus on a series of resurfacing, relevant, and ongoing topics, events, or campaigns. Examples of this strategy include Nike's Jordan Training Program, Kleenex's Let It Out network, Best Buy's BlueShirtNation.com, Carnival's Connections social network, FujiFilm's Z2ofd network created on Ning, HSBC's Business Network for entrepreneurs, Intel's Software Network Communities, and Jeep's enthusiast social network.

You can measure these activities by Web traffic, engagement time, inbound links, user registrations and installations, and the number of mentions across the Web.

Measurement Tools

PR is moving into the inner sanctum of Web marketing and must now partner with it to measure, learn, and evolve.

One of the most common and useful tools to measure ROI of PR 2.0 strategies is Web activity analysis.

Web Analytics

To improve visitor experiences, many companies, whether PR is involved or not, run Web analytics software on their online properties to study online behavior and activity. The software runs behind the scenes and captures important data, such as the following:

- The number of unique (new) and repeat (frequency and recency) visitors and the total audience

- Where visitors were before visiting your site (referring traffic)

- The path they traveled while on your property (depth)

- Time spent on the site

- Transactions completed or abandoned

- Number of registrants and subscribers

Many Web analytics tools are available today. Many companies that we work with use a free service from Google called Google Analytics. Other providers include Ominiture, CoreMetrics, Nielsen NetRatings, and Google Urchin.

To Pay or Not to Pay

Companies new to Web tracking programs might not have the budget to pay for expensive and expansive Web analytics. Many of the free tools provide you with an excellent option: data collection and reports that you can generate on your own. The information you track and collect is a quick and easy way to review important activities and your customer's behavior on your Web site.

When your Web initiatives increase in scope or your Web site expands and budget is not a question, it's often necessary to move from the free service to the paid service provider. These commercial Web analytics tools are comprehensive, and the reports are usually generated and provided by the service company with a detailed breakdown of all customer activity.

The difference between free and paid can be substantial. Based on the metrics that are important to justifying and rewarding your activity, make sure you evaluate the service offerings of free and paid options to make a decision that serves and supports your efforts.

Offsite Analytics

You can do more than just track your online properties. Tools and services are available that enable you to analyze "offsite" activity and competitive Web traffic. These tools estimate the amount of traffic, total audience, and trends, providing comparison tools and graphs to help you capture quantifiable progress (or lack of). For example, you can measure the traffic and authority of your competition's Web sites or blogs in comparison to your visitor levels and activity. You can also track the performance of nonhosted yet relevant communities, such as fan pages, dedicated social networks, or groups within larger networks.

Several free tools are available today that enable us to track offsite services:

- **Quantcast**—The company provides media measurement services that enable advertisers to view audience reports on millions of Web sites.

- **Compete**—The company helps you benefit from click-sharing by providing free services that create a more trusted, transparent, and valuable Internet.

- **Alexa**—The company computes traffic rankings by analyzing the Web usage of millions of Alexa Toolbar users and data obtained from other, diverse traffic data sources.

Defining and Measuring Success

Engagement is more than a buzzword. It's an opportunity to connect with our influencers and the people populating and defining our target markets. It's also an index that reaches far beyond Public Relations. It absolutely affects everything from communications to sales, branding, product development, and customer service—it's no longer an option for any facet of corporate communications. Remember that every employee contributes to the public perception of the companies you represent. Therefore, your investment in engagement not only helps to positively contribute to public opinion, but also helps you procure customers, loyalty, and referrals. Most important, it enables you to instill and strengthen the emotional connection between consumers and your brand.

Defining *success* starts before anything else, including engagement. Research is the key to unlocking the metrics to define this success, and it will continue to evolve with the tools and channels that power and distribute online conversations.

When people want to find anything related to what's important to them, they first go to the Web to search. That's where you also need to start. When you first listen to existing conversations, you'll see almost immediately that they pool into related and trackable categories, including the following:

- Asking for information or help

- Answering questions related to your brand, product, and competition

- Sharing opinions or observations

- Offering suggestions

- Expressing dissatisfaction

- Promoting competition

- Reposting relevant content and market data

Defining, documenting, and monitoring these categories will enable you to accurately track conversations for benchmarking purposes and to navigate responses through predefined processes, as shown in the following subsections.

Step 1

Identify the criteria important to business leaders and decision makers within the organization.

Step 2

Based on those criteria, measure where you are today and compare it against your competition or any other data you want to benchmark against.

Step 3

Based on that data, collaboratively define realistic goals for the New PR process to justify existing or future budgets (including anticipated ROI), such as the following:

- Increase unique visitors to x

- Increase existing conversion ratios from x percent of visitors to users to x *percent*

- Enlist y number of new registered users to x

- Increase online leads or sales to x

- Reduce negative and neutral conversations by x percent and increase positive conversations by x percent

- Increase the total number of conversations by x percent

- Grow inbound links to our site or blog by x percent

- Extend our blog authority to x

Step 4

After you establish the goals, you need to reverse-engineer the actions, tools, and programs required to achieve these goals.

For example, instead of measuring the number of hits, you can measure the tonality of your coverage over a period of time, to measure message integrity through the engagement process.

Step 5

Estimate the cost of that activity and compare it against other branding activities, such as advertising, sponsorships, previous PR initiatives, trade shows, speaking engagements, and so on. To determine which have a greater impact, compare your cost of participation:

- **Objective**—Reduce negative and neutral conversations by x percent and increase positive by x percent.

- **Actions**—Identify and contact all relevant bloggers who actively cover our industry, and tell them a more meaningful and relevant story. Study, process, and determine solutions, and then engage with those customers and participants who contribute negative and neutral commentary on the Social Web.

- **Programs**—Carry out internal market education on competitive products and our own solutions. Create a new service policy that addresses issues. Modify product roadmap to address customers concerns. Create a blogger, media, and influencer relations program. Initiate direct participation in social networks and all other sites, forums, and comments sections where conversations are taking place.

- **Tools**—Google Alerts, Technorati, Blogpulse, Google Blogsearch, Twitter Search, Excel (or any other spreadsheet), Web analytics.

- **Measurement**—Quantity of conversations per month divided by positive, neutral, and negative discussions, benchmarked against previous snapshot. Also analyze the inbound referral traffic from your participation as compared to traffic from previous timeframes without it. Compare the frequency and volume of these conversations against those of your competitors—you might find that you dominate the share of conversations.

Quantifying, calculating, and justifying PR 2.0 strategies requires a new approach. And because of the existence of PR 2.0, traditional PR must also be measured against new standards using new metrics. The Social Web has resulted in an exponential growth of new influencers, widespread (even global) content distribution, shared channels and networks, and dispersed yet authoritative conversations. Therefore, PR practitioners and practices must reform to maintain relevance and ensure brand integrity. And as discussed throughout this chapter, we can now measure the success (or failure) of our PR strategies in ways that were typically absent or elusive in yesterday's Public Relations.

Through proactive and consistent listening, measurement, and refinement, PR will not only justify its role in social marketing, but also more effectively enhance relationships, build trust, cultivate communities, and increase sales (among many other benefits that will be specific to individual companies). *Remember that the benefits are limited only by your level of outbound participation.*

V

Convergence

Chapter **19**

PR 2.0 + PR 1.0 = Putting the Public Back in Public Relations

Congratulations, you've almost finished reading this book. We hope that the ideas, experiences, lessons, and examples you've read will help you for a long time to come. If you're like us, you'll continue to learn and practice a new, participatory, informed, and sincere form of Public Relations. New PR will continue to morph as we become champions for our industry.

As our professional landscape continues to evolve over time, the practices, successes, and failures shared in these pages will help you chart a new course toward a more successful, rewarding, and long-lasting communications career. And, believe it or not, industry leaders are already discussing what's next. Questions they're considering include the following:

- Will PR 2.0 give way to PR 3.0?

- Will PR as a practice dissipate and fold into a new division of Web-based relationship marketing?

- What effects will Web 3.0, or the Semantic Web, have on the communications industry?

- Will community managers and next-generation PR fuse into one all-inclusive role of listening and responding?

These are all valid questions, and their consideration will help us improve who we are, what we know, and what we practice today and in the future.

The Semantic Web

John Markoff of the *New York Times* is credited with the first mainstream article that explored the next Web. The Semantic Web, or Web 3.0, is a more intelligent Web, with natural language search

---

and artificial intelligence. Web 3.0 is meant to produce a highly intuitive Web experience by leveraging the information that already exists online with data mining, machine learning, and microformats. Many know Web 3.0 as the third decade of the Web, but many industry experts, including the World Wide Web Consortium's director, Sir Tim Berners-Lee, are referring to the next Web as the Semantic Web. Berners-Lee envisions the Web as a universal and intelligent medium for the exchange of data, information, and knowledge, enabling the Web to automatically understand and fulfill the requests of people.

According to Wikipedia, "The *Semantic Web* is an evolving extension of the World Wide Web in which the semantics of information and services on the Web is defined, making it possible for the Web to understand and satisfy the requests of people and machines to use the Web content" (http://tinyurl.com/fxdr5).

With a more intelligent Web on the horizon, perhaps today's incredibly manual processes of research, data mining, networking, and connectivity will one day adapt, learn, and streamline our work based on our individual preferences. Although PR has a lot to learn from the evolution of the new Web as it exists today, we must collectively and simultaneously grow into technologists as well as anthropologists to understand and seamlessly engage with people in online communities. We must also master the new tools and channels to effectively reach influencers today and tomorrow.

By embracing the changes outlined in this book and remaining open to future learning and growth, communication professionals can transcend traditional roles and, over time, exemplify the new hybrid of Public Relations professionals. Who we are today is not who we will be tomorrow.

As we adjust to the exigencies of New PR (as discussed throughout this book), our roles and responsibilities will adapt to recognize, understand, and satisfy the needs of the influencers who are critical to the visibility and ultimate success of your company or campaign.

We will not only create new, highly effective programs to integrate into marcom, but also document the success of our efforts to justify the investment (current and future) of resources, time, and money—all while building relationships with both new and traditional influencers. Our "job" is still being defined and reinvented. We have much work to do, and we must remember that everything begins with us.

Beware of False Prophets

Many experts will try to point to the next iteration of Public Relations as 3.0, 4.0, and so on, but the numbers beyond 2.0 are irrelevant—unless something dramatic and unpredictable occurs and a tectonic shift in PR practices forces us to reclassify (and thus distinguish) them under a higher numeral.

Brian first identified PR 2.0 as a distinguishable category because of the fundamental transformations that occurred over the past ten years. Traditional PR had to transform, too, and those changes demanded a new category: PR 2.0. And although we won't have to continue renumbering iterations of PR as it evolves (via methodologies and solutions for communicating with influencers and our stakeholders), remember that we're always learning and that technology is continually developing.

The most important lessons showcased in this book explicitly demonstrate how to merge PR 2.0 with daily Public Relations. Just as the Web 2.0 label will soon weave back into the broader and more inclusive umbrella known simply as the Web, PR 2.0 and its new methodologies will become one with PR, thus improving the overall foundations for daily communications.

PR and Its Branding Crisis

As discussed earlier in this book, PR, as an industry, is experiencing a branding crisis. Often PR practitioners must defend themselves and the industry before they can "sell it." PR has joined (for reasons discussed previously) other industries prone to continuous criticism: the auto industry (especially sales), real estate financing, and the perennial whipping boy, law. Our job is to adapt to the new world of influence, teach others around us, and, in the process, do a little PR for the PR industry. By doing so, we can fix the very things that spiraled PR into a state of crisis in the first place.

If you polled those decision makers responsible for managing communications strategies about how they characterize PR, the following common themes would undoubtedly emerge:

- PR just doesn't "get it."

- PR relies on hype and spin to "sell" stories.

- PR professionals are handlers for those who know what they're talking about.

- PR uses stunts or events to generate excitement and attract attention.

- PR spams our messages to contact lists assembled by searching keywords in databases, without considering the preferences of those on the databases.

- PR places greater emphasis on the tools than on relationships.

- PR looks at customers and influencers as their audience instead of people with individual preferences.

- PR professionals don't do their homework.

- PR runs away from metrics.

It's a pretty powerful list, and we're all guilty of contributing to it at some point in our career. The problem is that enough of us have made so many public mistakes that we have collectively earned strikes not only against ourselves, but also against the entire industry—over an entire century without any form of PR for PR itself. Some of us have even personally been dragged into the public square for ridicule and commemoration of everything that's wrong with PR. Chris Anderson's posting of the individuals whom he deemed as PR spammers is only one of many examples that hurts, seems unfair, and is an unfortunate reality. (For more information about such blacklisting, see Chapter 6, "The Language of New PR.")

PR didn't feel the need to change until it had to, for survival, and now we've reached a point where we have no choice but to transform or become obsolete. It wasn't until Social Media that we took notice of the blaring voices of those who so adamantly oppose PR (because of what we supposedly stand for and represent). In turn, it wasn't until these past few years that PR could respond in its own defense with an equally wide-spread and powerful campaign. And as we defend ourselves and our industry, we will learn more about how to improve our own practices and reputations.

We now have incredible potential to regain credibility. At the same time that we've hit an impasse, we've also reached an inflection point where we can learn and globally demonstrate our reinvention, and unveil and reinforce our new-and-improved focus on true Public Relations and service. We must commit ourselves to change things for the better, and, in the process, to recruit people to join the revolutionaries. It's up to us to stand up to our critics. In doing so, we must acknowledge our errors but also demonstrate that our collective efforts to change things for the better are, indeed, improving the dynamics of conversations between our communities and those influencers who guide them.

No longer will we fall prisoner to outdated forms of communications, expectations, and measurement. We will lead the charge for a more democratic process of sharing information and learning from our engagement. By doing so, we will create channels for two-way (and more) dialogue. We will also be able to create an infrastructure and process for assessing the valuable feedback we receive, and also for implementing the changes necessary to create more customer-driven products, services, and communications strategies.

Yes, we have hurdles to jump. Yes, we have much to learn. Yes, we will make mistakes. But you are here, learning along with us, contributing to a new, more knowledgeable, and influential class of communications professional. And this is only the beginning. For the first time, let's document our challenges to create a self-improvement checklist. By doing so, we can expedite our progression from practitioners into leaders and PR champions.

The Future of PR

Web 1.0 + Web 2.0 = New PR. What started with the introduction and proliferation of the Internet in the 1990s continues today with the interactive dynamics powering the latest incarnation of the Web. We're merely witnessing the beginning of something that will have a much greater impact and continue to transform the very fabric of how we communicate with each other. And in the process, the media industry, marketing communications, and new influencers will find more in common than those groups have found individually during the past decades. Each will now orbit around an axis defined as "we, the people." The balance of authority and power is migrating back to the center, and we have to earn the attention of customers and their loyalty by integrating into our own practices the languages, cultures, and tools they use to communicate and share with each other.

The future of PR is already underway, and it's defining who we are and what we choose to represent. Yes, it's about what we choose to represent (not what we have to or are told to do). We're empowered to make decisions that serve our best interests in the long term, as well as the interests of those companies that need our help. If you don't have room to grow within your organization because management chooses not to believe in or conform to the new era of conversations between company executives and those who represent important communities, perhaps your ambition and talents will be appreciated elsewhere.

But the future of communications and PR is inspired and powered by so much more than intentions and conviction. A true transformation is taking place that completely redefines our role. And it fuses the "best of" multiple disciplines that span everything from Web marketing to customer service to market analysis. The shift from passive, top-down, and reactive PR to proactive, hands-on, participatory engagement absolutely requires us to embody everything we represent. We must escalate our involvement, understanding, and passion to symbolize and present our knowledge in a way that's both credible and helpful. What do we have to gain by doing so? Simple: *We, too, can become media.* The smarter, more empathetic, and active we are, the more likely we are to become influencers.

New PR and Social Media strategies are not relegated solely to those elite early adopters who dwell on the edge. We're bringing this knowledge and insight back to the center to empower a new generation of communications professionals. We can't go back. The future of PR is here today. For the first time, we truly have the opportunity to put the public back into Public Relations. However, it starts from within. Everything begins with our desire and openness to step outside our comfort zones and to adapt to roles that no longer fit the traditional PR mold.

Next-generation PR professionals will exemplify a hybrid of several critical roles. These specific roles will not vanish individually, but will instead integrate themselves into best practices so that Public Relations can excel in today's social economy. PR will relearn the art of communications, listening, and interchange, and, in the process, become well versed in not only the new rules of PR, but also the following:

- Web marketing and analytics

- Viral marketing

- Customer service and relationship management

- Social tools

- Focus groups and market audits

- Cultural anthropology

- Market analysts

Perhaps most importantly, we must also become content creators and publishers to immerse ourselves in the process of discovering and sharing information, similar to those whom we're trying to engage. We need to get our hands dirty, and there's just no way to do it without doing it. We gain both professionally and personally as a result. We're consumers, too, and we will become more sophisticated in how we select and purchase products and services. Our peers will impact a wide spectrum of our decisions (not just purchasing decisions, but also the tools we use and the communities we use, join, and participate in, both online and in the real world).

As mentioned previously, we must become the people we want to reach. To do so, we must remember that our customers, influencers, and stakeholders are becoming fluent in subjects that, in the past, we might have considered our exclusive purview. So PR must now produce a stronger signal with less noise as we embrace one-on-one communications over broadcast spam, groundswells over top-down marketing, real-world benefits understood through psychographics over spin and messages to general audiences, and relatable stories over snake oil sales.

New PR Requires New Roles

If we're responsible for learning and integrating a new level of proactive, hands-on, outbound engagement, who's left to listen and to document metrics?

Next-generation PR should make room for new players on the team, players who will help PR stay on track. Many organizations will hire a community manager or a community-management team along with research managers or online curators and librarians. That role will be mostly responsible for listening, trafficking, and ensuring responses and action based on the conversations taking place across the Social Web. But it's PR's role to engage influencers, bloggers, and media using social tools at a much deeper level. Therefore, we require our own community manager of sorts who will more resemble a research librarian (one who not only tracks relevant conversations and identifies the influencers sparking them, but also documents the metrics necessary to benchmark performance).

As you learned earlier in this book, much of this work today requires manual processes, despite our desire for more effective and inclusive automated tools. Few automated solutions exist, and we must justify and prove our ROI—especially for something so new and seemingly elusive.

Some believe that there has to be a better way to listen and benchmark. At the time of this writing, however, we have yet to see something that is absolutely comprehensive. And if we've learned anything in PR during the past few years, it's that we risk complacency and laziness when the tools overautomate processes associated with identifying, tracking, and sending our stories to our contacts. In many cases, they rob us of our perspective. We lose touch with the reality of scale, human interaction, and real-world perception.

A key point is that, for PR 2.0 to fold seamlessly back into traditional PR, we must approach things differently than we have before, and new resources require sufficient financing. That money comes by adjusting existing budgets or allocating new funds. An initial audit will demonstrate the necessity. Even smaller PR agencies (as well as national and international powerhouses) will need to reengineer their financials to maintain existing services while also creating and funding these new listening and measuring roles (enabling the PR team to focus on PR). The economics work, the ROI is documented and demonstrable, and, most important, this setup doesn't steal resources from the team that's focused on results.

Ideal candidates are resourceful self-starters fluent in social tools, online search, measurement solutions, and spreadsheet or charting software. Firms should fill these positions with those who do not want to pursue a career in PR or marketing: Those who prefer data over outreach will help ensure that the training and results associated with these roles remain solid and vested for the long term.

The Conversation Prism

As we initiate the process of traversing the road from PR 2.0 back to PR, we leave you with one last important lesson: *There's much more to Social Media than Facebook, Wordpress, Blogger, Twitter, MySpace, Digg, and YouTube.*

The conversations that define our markets are expansive and beyond our reach, and are ineffective if we don't know when and where they're taking place. Although we've touched on this subject throughout this book, we haven't yet shared with you a definitive, at-a-glance map that represents the volume, scope, and diversity of the locations of conversations grouped by their nature, culture, and focus. The communities important to you span from the popular to the specific, focusing on the interests of people from the left to the right of the bell curve, and including the chasms inherent within it.

Text can certainly help convey the size and range of the social landscape, but nothing quite captures and communicates it like a good visual. In 2007, Deb Schultz introduced the Social Media Ecosystem (http://tinyurl.com/4gq2ka), Robert Scoble and Darren Barefoot debuted the Social Media Starfish (http://tinyurl.com/3aekz8), and Lloyd Davis released the Social Media Snowflake (http://tinyurl.com/3v22qh) to visually demonstrate and document the rapidly evolving landscape for social tools, services, and networks. Check them out.

If you work in marketing, Public Relations, advertising, customer service, product development, or any discipline that's motivated, shaped, and directed by customers, peers, stakeholders, and influencers, monitoring and participating in online conversations is absolutely critical if you hope to compete in the future. Having a visual map will help you know where to start listening and to benchmark audit, and it will guide you as you journey through online societies and networks.

Brian worked with Jesse Thomas of JESS3 to create a fully comprehensive social map that helps chart online conversations among the people who populate all current, active, and well-populated communities and networks that connect the Social Web. It was released as the Conversation Prism, a free tool for everyone to use and share (http://tinyurl.com/5chmt5). Brian worked with Beth Canter to contribute to a Wikispaces site that presents the information contained on the Conversation Prism in a grid format (http://tinyurl.com/6mf7wk). But Social Media is organic and will evolve as services and conversation channels emerge, fuse, and dissipate. Many will rise, many will disappear; others will merge, and several will thrive independently. Therefore, the Wikispaces site is not static. It will change over time as new channels are introduced and others wane in popularity. Appendix B, "It's Alive!" includes that grid as it exists at the time of this writing.

As a communications professional, you need to be aware of the full spectrum of conversations, whether you're observing, listening, or participating. You can then identify and better understand how to listen and, in turn, participate transparently. You can also genuinely understand where relevant conversations about your brand are occurring.

Because conversations are increasingly distributed, everything begins with listening and observing. Remember that many solutions attempt to automate the process of listening, but none are comprehensive. This is where Social Media becomes a bit more manual than you might have expected. As we pointed out earlier in the book, every social network will offer a search box where you can search for keywords to identify important exchanges. Doing so will help you identify exactly where relevant discussions are taking place—as well as their scale, volume, reach, and frequency. You can then chart this dialogue into a targeted social map unique to your brand. That map will visually remind your team where they need to monitor and participate.

Perhaps most important, listening and observing reveal the cultures of the very communities you might want to engage. You can observe how to communicate authentically without disrupting the social fabric of each network.

Brian has also introduced a sample conversation workflow to remind us of the extent and commitment required to engage, learn, adapt, reform, and improve our infrastructure to build relationships, earn loyalty, and grow our communities. He proposed the following conversation workflow steps, realizing that the workflow will change and adapt to individual companies and how they choose to implement the recommended steps:

Everything starts with the people behind the brand (brand = the organization you represent), and then

1. **Observe**—Observe the communities and cultures that define your target networks.

2. **Listen**—Discover and pay attention to important conversations related to your brand.

3. **Identify**—Identify your key communities and networks based on the frequency of those conversations and where they occur.

4. **Internalize**—Dissect, analyze, and learn from feedback and dialogue.

5. **Route**—Channel information internally to the appropriate groups (for example, Service, Marketing and PR, Community, Corporate Communications, Crisis, Product Development).

6. **Process**—Determine the opportunities to improve products or services and to implement change.

7. **Participate**—Engage with your customers, constituents, stakeholders, and influencers (both in the real world and online).

8. **Provide feedback and insight**—Consistently monitor the discussions to learn and to provide information that actively positions you

and your company as a helpful resource to the communities important to you (this is building and maintaining relationships).

9. **Repeat**—The process is always ongoing.

As we've noted throughout these pages, conversations are taking place with or without you. This conversation map and workflow process will help you visualize the potential extent and pervasiveness of the online conversations that can impact and influence those who are sharing information and making decisions related to your business and brand. These tools also remind you to listen, learn, respond, and improve over time. By doing so, we believe you can grow your business and stand out from your competitors.

Remember, participating in Social Media is more meaningful when you have a deeper understanding of the social sciences, and not just the social tools that facilitate daily interaction. You want to create, cultivate, and grow relationships with people, both online and in the real world, and these relationships are defined by mutual value and benefits. *In the social economy, relationships are the new currency.*

This is the PR industry's renaissance, so it is our chance to reinvigorate PR, to boost its valuation within marketing communications, and, more important, to instill trust and respect among the influencers who lost faith in our profession long ago. It's not just about acceptance; it's about embracing change and creating something new and valuable for your company and for your career.

Together we will put the public back into Public Relations and, in the process, spotlight the undercurrent of existing and multiplying conversations that were previously a mostly disregarded back channel. In doing so, we set a new standard for corporate communications—one that flies a powerfully visible banner that commands admiration, respect, and appreciation while exuding conviction, value, and an entirely new level of socially aware expertise and mastery.

When the people lead, the leaders will have to follow...And it's you that has the authority, for the one who is right, is the majority.
—Ben Harper

Appendix A

The SEC and the Importance of Recognizing Corporate Blogs as Public Disclosure

Major newswire services have held a lock on all financial-related press releases because their wire and Web distribution channels meet full disclosure requirements for publicly traded companies as defined by the Securities and Exchange Commission (SEC).

Introduced on August 15, 2000, Regulation FD (Fair Disclosure) addresses the selective disclosure of information by publicly traded companies and other issuers. Regulation FD states that when an issuer discloses material nonpublic information to certain individuals or entities—generally securities market professionals, such as stock analysts, or holders of the issuer's securities who might trade on the basis of the information—the issuer must make public disclosure of that information. In this way, the rule aims to promote full and fair disclosure (see www.sec.gov/answers/regfd.htm).

In the 1990s, investors typically followed their stocks through the financial section of daily newspapers, discussions with brokers, or published reports from the company, or by investing in real-time ticker-tracking services. By the mid- to late-1990s, the Internet permeated our daily lives and transformed how we interact with information (and with each other). As the Web matured, it introduced the real-time capability to buy and sell stocks and to discover rich data and relevant research to make more informed decisions. The access to this precious data and the capability to act on it immediately caught the attention of the SEC. Therefore, the government introduced regulation to prevent selective disclosure and to promote fairness in the dissemination and access of financial information.

Regulation FD fundamentally transformed how companies communicate with investors and also created processes and channels to do so quickly and efficiently.

Through Regulation FD, press release wire services such as PRNewswire, Marketwire, and BusinessWire, among others, created effective communication bridges to reach brokers and institutional, individual, and day traders equally. With the Web, everyone has access to the same information at the same time. However, Regulation FD defined the process of creating and distributing news releases, including content, context, and safe harbor—these news releases are usually governed by the legal department and investor relations (IR) team, not PR or marketing. The legal department takes the prominent role to provide critical information without hype and to prevent any potential lawsuits from shareholders because of the way information is packaged or distributed. A tremendous amount of legal expertise navigates financial press releases to satisfy disclosure and investor satisfaction.

Web 1.0 vs. Web 2.0

In Web 1.0, the Internet introduced a new way to trade stocks and access important financial information. With Web 2.0 and the introduction of Social Media, the capability to publish information and reach vast audiences is setting the stage for another high-profile, industry-changing evolution that will affect financial transactions, regulatory governance, and investor and public communications.

As blogs prominently show, Social Media is reshaping the ability to distribute information and influence decisions. Many industry leaders have petitioned the SEC to consider blogs as an alternative to wire services for disclosure (for the purposes of cost savings, ease of publishing, and the capability to centralize the content).

On July 30, 2008, the SEC announced that they will consider accepting Web sites and blogs as legitimate channels for information dissemination under the Regulation FD requirements. The next day, TechCrunch, a Web log that is coedited by Michael Arrington and Erick Schonfeld and focuses on new Internet companies and products, published Brian's response to that announcement.

SEC To Recognize Corporate Blogs as Public Disclosure. Can We Now Kill the Press Release?

By Brian Solis

For several years, Sun CEO, Jonathan Schwartz [http://blogs.sun.com/jonathan/] has lobbied the SEC to allow disclosure of financial information through corporate blogs. In a landmark announcement [http://www.sec.gov/news/speech/2008/spch073008km.htm], it seems that Mr. Schwartz may indeed get his wish, and with it, a historical decision that could break the age-old shackles that bound businesses to traditional media and distribution channels in order to satisfy full disclosure.

In a speech yesterday, SEC special counsel Kim McManus outlined new guidance the SEC is about to give companies on when they can use their Websites, including blogs, to disclose material information. What this means is that we can now finally kill the press release, at least in its current form (more on that below).

The IR Web Report [http://www.irwebreport.com/daily/2008/07/30/sec-oks-websites-and-blogs-for-reg-fd/] explains, "UNDER certain circumstances, companies can rely on their websites and blogs to meet the public disclosure requirements under Regulation FD (Fair Disclosure) [http://www.sec.gov/rules/final/33-7881.htm], according to new guidance unanimously approved by the US Securities and Exchange Commission today."

Chairman Christopher Cox opened up the discussion by recognizing that the Web has matured providing a big step forward for investors, "Ongoing technological advances in electronic communications have increased both the market's and investors' demand for more timely company disclosure and the ability for companies to capture, process and disseminate this information to market participants."

The SEC outlines boundaries for sharing information as well as holding companies and their employees liable for the information that they post on blogs and discussion forums.

Regulation FD and Social Media

The SEC is taking the right steps to embrace the new tools and services that reach people in addition to wire services. With the recognition of blogs as a viable form of disclosure, under certain circumstances of course, the SEC is officially recognizing Social Media and in a sense, socializing the rules associated with Reg FD.

Perhaps, the most significant change stemming from the new SEC guidance is that Web-based disclosure does not have to appear in a format comparable to paper-based information, unless the Commission's rules explicitly require it.

This is music to my ears as it finally opens the door for the Social Media Release [http://www.techcrunch.com/2008/05/11/the-evolution-of-the-press-release/].

For a few years, Todd Defren [http://www.pr-squared.com/], Chris Heuer [http://www.chrisheuer.com/], and I have not only defended and charted the opportunity for Social Media Releases (SMRs), but also fielded emotionally-charged questions from the financial and IR communities asking about whether or not an SMR would ever meet disclosure requirements for Reg FD, and without it, what good would it ever be...

While there have been many discussions and debates to whether a Social Media Release should cross the wire and if so, what format and design it should resemble, my belief is that SMRs should always reside on dedicated blog platforms (WordPress, MoveableType) as part of a Social Media Newsroom [http://www.pr-squared.com/2007/02/the_social_media_newsroom_temp.html]. And, Social Media Releases should only complement a traditional press release and disclosure activity and not replace it.

Originally introduced by Todd Defren [http://www.pr-squared.com/2008/04/social_media_release_template.html] in response to Tom Foremski's call for the death of press releases [http://www.siliconvalleywatcher.com/mt/archives/2006/02/die_press_relea.php], the SMR represents a new socially-rooted format that complements traditional and SEO press releases by combining news facts and social assets in one, easy to digest, and repurpose, tool.

Giving everyone what they need and how they need it, requires a different approach. Almost every press release issued today is done so without video or audio, and many still do not include links to additional information or supporting content.

While these multimedia pieces are underlying components of SMRs, there's more to the presentation than multimedia content. The value of aggregating Social Media in one digital release connects information and content across social networks with the people looking for it, as well as the conversations that bind them together.

Picture a blog post that announced corporate data (not unlike a standard financial press release) but now, along with a custom video hosted from YouTube, supporting graphs and exec images funneled from flickr, pre-recorded audio podcasts/conferences piped in from iTunes, packaged market data sourced from Docstoc, related company and landscape stories and public commentary linked from Delicious. Content can also push to micromedia services such as Twitter, Identi.ca [http://www.briansolis.com/2008/07/identica-white-label-microblogging.html] and FriendFeed to contribute to the company's brandstream [http://www.readwriteweb.com/archives/brandstreaming.php]. In a sense, the Social Media Release, hosted as an elegant and media rich blog post, acts as an aggregated hub for these disparate brand beacons, and at the same time, each piece is findable and sharable within each social network and they all point back to the Social Media Release.

Also, the SMR can feature tags and outbound links to increase exposure in social networks and blog-specific search engines.

Disclosure is an Expensive Business

Naturally, this at the very least, represents a potential harbinger of doom for each of the popular wire services.

A significant percentage of their lifeblood is tied to market-relevant or earnings content that, until now, required wire services, and hundreds of dollars (in some cases over $1,000) per announcement in order to satisfy SEC disclosure. For many companies, a fixed budget for disclosure absorbed the critical resources necessary to support the activity of sharing news and therefore relied upon wires to do their public and investor relations on their behalf.

But as many PR and IR professionals will concede, issuing releases on the wire is merely an expensive step in a process of creating and distributing news using traditional tools. If you represent a publicly traded company that is actively monitored by market influencers, it's very likely that your press release will reach their systems via the wire.

These days, it's almost certain that a reporter or analyst will, in the best case, see and file the release but most often, the very people we hope will find and in turn, report on the information discovered, will honestly never know that you released news at all unless they're proactively contacted. Any good public relations or investor relations professional will ensure that their top financial and business contacts are alerted to upcoming news, without giving away the news, in advance.

There is no substitute for the real world relationships we forge in order to bridge the right content specifically for the right people.

Do these new guidelines offer companies the ability to shift some or all of its wire budget back into the critical role of outbound support for corporate news?

Disclosure Versus IR/PR

Disclosure relates to the market—the people who may trade or act based on the information you publish. Reg FD protects the voice of the investor and guides companies on how to publish information so that it reaches a fair share of the market so that no one person has access to information before the other.

We can't deny or ignore the value and benefits associated with strategic support for connecting corporate news to market influencers. Now, to the defense of wire services, and as I've written before, wire services can bypass [http://www.briansolis.com/2008/02/wire-services-bypass-bloggers-and.html] those very influencers to reach people directly.

Not only does wire distribution meet disclosure, the art of search engine optimized press releases (SEO releases) have the unique ability to appear in search engines tied to the key words your market uses to search for related and relevant information. PR Newswire, MarketWire, Business Wire, and PRWeb offer businesses the ability to distribute news with added SEO functionality. When paired with a well-written, SEO optimized press release, wire distribution can more than satisfy disclosure, it can carry your story directly to the people looking for it.

In addition, wire services have invested over the years in the development of a secondary distribution channel that has, in my opinion, remained relevant even as the Web continues to rapidly change and evolve.

When a press release crosses a wire, many search engines and their financial properties (finance.yahoo.com or finance.google.com) and all market-powered hubs, portals and dashboards, receive wire feeds which automatically populate respective "Recent News" sections. Similar to how we receive RSS feeds to seamlessly receive the news and information we prefer, investors, analysts, press, and decision makers can see, in one place, the trading status, coverage, related news, and crowd-powered discussions around the activity. This has been the case since the days of Web 1.0 and was our first taste of the Social Web that is now becoming pervasive.

Without wire services, penetrating these valuable dashboards, that are still today, a primary source of finance information and activity, is incredibly difficult, if not impossible.

This new guidance, however, presents an opportunity to connect corporate information from sites and blogs to these powerful financial online hubs so that important corporate news can still reach people, the way they're used to receiving it.

Forcing them to change their habits isn't a realistic expectation in the short-term.

This is a Chance to Reach More People, Their Way

Not only do SMRs socialize content and link conversations across the Social Web, they also help bloggers and online journalists more effectively write a rich media post using one resource that provides them with everything they need.

Now that we don't need to adhere to a fixed form or design and presentation aesthetics, technically there's nothing holding us back from carrying the torch forward. It can only help present and share information in an alternative method that complements traditional releases, outbound contact, and market-related conference calls.

Coming back to my belief that Social Media Releases should be hosted on blogs and not cross wires, with the new rules for Reg FD, an SMR by default, could now meet disclosure—assuming that the host site is recognized as meeting the disclosure standards.

Social Media Releases offer the ability to not only share relevant financial data, but also feature social content that reinforces that data and the overall company story.

We've discussed how information can reach the market, investors, peers, and customers through search as well through articles and blog posts and also via financial portals. Search engines are manipulated by SEO (search engine optimization). Social Media is powered by SMO (social media optimization) and the results are different in how, when, and where they appear. In most cases, SEO doesn't affect the outcome of content within social networks. But, dedicated tagging, key words, and crowdsourced participation drive the "discoverability" of content in the Social Web.

Social Media Releases not only feature social content to more visually and authentically tell stories and share information, they also provide the tools necessary for people to further socialize and interact with them.

For readers of an SMR, the options for interaction are virtually endless. They can respond through a "moderated" comment system, much in the same way they do today in online financial forums. They can grab pieces of the content, such as embeddable video, audio, documentation and images, to repurpose as blog posts and online stories, which can also send trackbacks to help pool collective coverage. Stakeholders can subscribe to RSS feeds for the entire news stream or just those related to financial/market information. Readers can send the story back out to the social web through bookmarking tools such as diigo or delicious, as well as crowdsourced news communities including Digg and Mixx. As the existing social tools evolve and new services are introduced, the potential for SMRs aka blog posts, are truly a blank canvas for PR, marketing, and the community to define how they're read and shared.

Executives and marketing professionals must now weigh whether the company Web site or blog are indeed a recognized channel of distribution and more importantly, whether these online properties meet public disclosure requirements under the new rules Regulation FD.

I believe this new guidance only expands the ability to share information using a variety of approved channels. It may or may not reduce costs associated with meeting disclosure, but it will in fact, improve the infrastructure for investor and public relations by socializing the process to more effectively communicate with investors and the people who care.

The reality is that businesses can only benefit by not limiting itself to one form of communication. People seek, discover, and share information differently, and combining strategic wire, Web, and blog channels will only amplify reach and visibility.

Appendix B
It's Alive!

As discussed throughout this book, Social Media is a dynamic, organic force that transforms over time. New channels and communities are constantly introduced. The popularity of each network waxes and wanes, with some channels ceasing to exist altogether. Influence within and among channels also changes over time. The savvy PR pro monitors and participates in a variety of Social Media outlets, and thus stays "in tune" with those changes and adapts listening, observation, and conversation strategies accordingly.

Chapter 19, "PR 2.0 + PR 1.0 = Putting the Public Back in Public Relations," mentioned the Conversation Prism, a social mapping tool developed by Brian (along with Jesse Thomas of JESS3). You can view the prism online at http://tinyurl.com/5chmt5, and you can contribute to its growth and relevance at http://tinyurl.com/6mf7wk. Table B.1 is adapted from the latter site. We provide it here to introduce you to the full spectrum of the Social Web, which is representative of this moment in time but will evolve as the Social Web continues to mature. This table was developed by Brian Solis in conjunction with both Beth Kanter, a leading authority on how nonprofit organizations can benefit from the use of Social Media, and Richard Edwards, a technology research professional who works with Solis. The most important thing to remember is the source of this spectrum: the *public*. In this case, "public" refers to the people and their conversations; they are the "white light" from which the full spectrum of the Social Web emanates. Keep an eye out online for updated versions of the prism—it will change to match the tools, communities, and channels that refract the light of important conversations.

A Roadmap to the Social Web (as adapted from the Conversation Prism)

Category	Tools
Comments	**SezWho**: A social platform that enables the community of readers to not only comment on the post, but also rank the quality and insight of other commenters and the post in general. When commenting or voting, the service asks for your e-mail address and then tracks your individual comments and your ranking history, to provide interested visitors with an amalgamated representation of your views and expertise.
	Disqus: A comment and discussion plug-in for Web sites, blogs, or applications. Pronounced "discuss," the plug-in makes commenting more interactive by creating a community of discussion across the Web. It is a free service with no inline advertisements. Users create a profile and can track their comments across the Web while creating their own comment blog.
	coComment: A comment service that attempts to create conversations based on Web comments. The service notifies users when new comments are left and enables users to post new comments to their blog.
	IntenseDebate: A service that attempts to enhance and encourage commenting on your existing blog by adding features such as comment threading, the capability to reply by e-mail, and import and export of comments. Acquired by WordPress.
	Tangler: A service that enables users to embed portable, global conversations across the Web, similar to how YouTube videos are displayed in blogs and Web sites. One widget, one conversation with multiple access points.
Listening	**Technorati**: A powerful search engine for blogs. The engine tracks more than 112 million blogs. Technorati searches, surfaces, and organizes blogs and other forms of independent, user-generated content.
	Google Alerts: E-mail updates of the latest Google Web results, based on your topic of choice.
	Radian 6: Widget-based monitoring solution for managing social media.
	IceRocket: A convenient search engine for blogs.
Monitoring and Filtering	**Google Reader**: An "inbox for the Web." Subscribe to your favorite sites, and Google Reader continuously updates your inbox with updates from those favorites.
	Netvibes: (Re)mix the Web. Create a home page and add your favorite sites; Netvibes updates your home page with the newest stories every time you visit.
	Bloglines: A *free* online service for searching, subscribing to, creating, and sharing news feeds, blogs, and rich Web content.

Category	Tools
Monitoring and Filtering *continued*	**AideRSS**: An intelligent filtering assistant that updates your RSS feeds based on your interests, not just the Web site.
Crowd-sourced Content	**Newsvine**: A module-based news site that is updated continuously by those who visit the site.
	Mixx: A news site that relies on users (mixxers) to generate and vote on what content should be included.
	Hubdub: A news-prediction game (like fantasy football for the news) in which users bet on the outcome of the daily news stories.
	Reddit: A news site that lets users read, vote on, explore, and submit news stories for inclusion.
	Digg: A news tool/Web site dedicated to surfacing the best of the best of the daily news, as voted upon by members across the Web.
Blog Platforms	**WordPress**: A blog-publishing system written in PHP.
	Blogger: Google's free blog-publishing tool.
	Moveable Type: A professional blog-publishing platform.
Blog Conversations	**Technorati**: An Internet search engine for blogs. Technorati indexes more than 112 million blogs.
	Google Blogs: Google's search engine for blogs.
Blog Communities	**Blogged**: A blog directory that enables users to find and rate blogs.
	Bloglines: A Web-based personal news aggregator.
	MyBlogLog: A plug-in that enables users to leave a virtual calling card in the form of a photo left on blogs that have MyBlogLog enabled.
Micromedia	**Twitter**: A community of friends and like-minded individuals who publicly share updates, links, and thoughts in 140 characters or fewer.
	Jaiku: A Finland-based social networking, microblogging, and lifestreaming service.
	Tumblr: Effortless way to share text, photos, quotes, links, music, and videos, from your browser, phone, desktop, e-mail, or wherever you happen to be.
	Plurk: An easy way to chronicle and share with friends the things you do, the way you feel, and all the other things in between that make up your life.
	Utterz: An online text-, video-, or voice-based discussion service.

Category	Tools
Micromedia *continued*	**Seesmic**: A video microblogging Web application that gives video cam and Webcam users easy recording and uploading capabilities.
	Identi.ca: A microblogging site that enables users to post short (140 characters or fewer) text notices. It is also customizable to serve as a white label hosted community.
	12seconds: A free video-based social networking site that enables users to upload Webcam or cellphone footage.
Lifestreams	**FriendFeed**: A social aggregator that consolidates the updates from social Web sites such as blog entries, social bookmarking Web sites, and social networks, among others.
	Facebook: A social networking site.
	Lifestream.fm: A media and social aggregator that will keep you and your friends informed about what you're doing online at a glance and in real time. You can put all your profiles and activity from your favorite Web services on one page, making it easy for your friends to see your newest bookmarks, your favorite videos, your tweets, photos you've uploaded, your newest blog posts, and more.
	Life2Front: Experiments to promote the user's life, relationship, activities, and personal content, such as blogs, photos, videos, podcasts, bookmarks, or wish lists.
	Pheedo: New kinds of profit-driven advertising services through distributed content, such as RSS, for our publishers and advertisers.
	Ping.fm: Use AIM, GTalk, iGoogle, Windows Live Messenger, Yahoo! Messenger, WAP, iPhone/iPod Touch, SMS, or e-mail, and let Ping.fm relay your message to a multitude of social networking sites.
	Profilactic: A social media aggregator/lifestreaming service that pulls together just about everything you and your friends create online.
	Iminta: A service that wants to help you and your friends share what you're into (hence the name) across the different social networks you belong to.
Specific to Twitter	**Monitter.com**: A Twitter-monitoring system that enables users to follow their favorite three topics.
SMS/Voice	**Jott**: A voice-to-text transcription service. Users call a toll-free number, record a message (up to 30 seconds), and have the message e-mailed or texted to them.
	kwiry: A free service that turns text messages into reminders that you retrieve online.

Category	Tools
Social Networks	**Hi5**: A social networking site with more than 80 million users in more than 200 countries.
	Facebook: A social networking site.
	MySpace: A social networking site.
Niche Networks	**LinkedIn**: A business-oriented social networking site with more than 24 million registered users.
	Ning: An online platform that enables users to create their own social networks and Web sites.
	Plaxo: A real-time online address book that updates all your contacts when you make a change. Founded by Napster co-founder Sean Parker.
Customer Service Networks	**Yelp**: A social networking site where users rate and review vendors.
	Google Groups: Google's user-driven social networking site.
	Yahoo! Groups: Yahoo!'s user-driven social networking site.
Location	**Tripit**: An online service that helps people organize all their travel plans—flights, hotels, rental cars, trains, cruises—no matter where they booked.
	Dopplr: Travel service that enables users to create itineraries of their travel plans and spot correlations with their contacts' travel plans to arrange meetings at any point on their journey.
	brightkite: Location-based social network that lets you track your friends and meet people around you without GPS.
Video	**YouTube**: A video-sharing Web site where users can upload, view, and share video clips.
	Vimeo: A video-centric social network site (owned by Connected Ventures) that launched in November 2004. The site supports embedding, sharing, and video storage, and allows user comments on each video page.
	DailyMotion: A video-hosting service Web site, based in Paris, France.
	Viddler: An online video-hosting service founded in 2006. It was noted for the introduction of inline commenting and tag annotations in online video, as well as on-the-fly video recording.
	blip.tv: A video-sharing service designed for creators of user-generated content. blip.tv provides content creators with free hosting, support for a variety of video formats, distribution using technologies such as RSS, and an opt-in advertising program with a 50/50 revenue share.

Category	Tools
Curation/ Aggregation	**Magnify.net**: Magnify's video platform enables users to easily add and monetize custom branded video channels to their existing sites based on topics or brands for the community to view and share all video related to that topic.
	Wonderhowto.com: Browse, search, or network your way into the expanding universe of free video tutorials.
Documents	**docstoc**: Provides the platform for users and businesses to upload and share their documents with all the world, and serves as a vast repository of documents in a variety of categories, including legal, business, financial, technology, educational, and creative. All documents on docstoc can be easily searched, previewed, and downloaded for free.
	scribd: A San Francisco start-up company changing the way people share documents online.
Events	**Zvents**: A local search engine to discover things to do. Zvents helps you quickly find out what's going on, wherever you are. Find local events, movies playing nearby, the perfect Indian restaurant, or where your favorite band is playing next.
	Madelt: Service that helps users make personalized invitations, share photos after the party, and connect with friends.
	Empressr: The first Ajax/Flash-based presentation Web application.
	Socializr: A new Web service offering free online event invitations and innovative ways to share event and party information with your friends.
	Acteva: An event-registration service provider for event organizers. Acteva automates the entire event-registration process and brings it online, where it can be easily accessed any day or night.
Music	**Last.fm**: A music-recommendation system called Audioscrobbler. Last.fm builds a detailed profile of each user's musical taste by recording details of all the songs the user listens to, either on the streamed radio stations or on the user's computer or some portable music devices.
	Pandora: An automated music-recommendation and Internet radio service created by the Music Genome Project. Users enter a song or artist that they enjoy, and the service responds by playing selections that are musically similar. Users provide feedback on the individual song choices—approval or disapproval—which Pandora takes into account for future selections.

Category	Tools
Music *continued*	**ODEO:** Home to millions of audio and video episodes from thousands of podcasts and media sites across the Web. Odeo.com is part search engine, part media directory, and part social network. Users can search and explore media channels covering just about any topic or area of interest, from automotive to technology, comedy to cooking, education to entertainment. With Odeo, it's easy to subscribe to channels and be alerted when new episodes are published, save favorites, and create playlists to share with friends.
	Mufin: Mufin stands out because of its advanced access and retrieval functions for large music content pools. The company was founded on the belief that each level of content complexity—structured data, text, audio, video, and other forms of rich media—requires specific, adequate access and manipulation functions.
Wiki	**WetPaint:** A free wiki-hosting service (or wiki farm) founded in October 2005. All wiki URLs are a subdomain of wetpaint.com. WetPaint targets nontechnical Internet users who want to collaborate online and, therefore, attempts to include easy-to-use features, such as a three-step wiki-creation wizard.
	MindTouch: An open source software-development company.
	PBWiki: PeanutButterWiki, a commercial wiki farm started by three graduates of Stanford University: David Weekly, Ramit Sethi, and Nathan Schmidt.
	TWiki: A structured wiki, typically used to run a collaboration platform, knowledge- or document-management system, knowledge base, or team portal, developed by Peter Thoeny. Users can create wiki applications using the TWiki Markup Language, and developers can extend its functionality with plug-ins.
Livecasting (a.k.a. Lifecasting) Video and Audio	**Qik:** Service that enables users to stream live video to the Web from a cellphone.
	BlogTV: Service that lets users create live video shows and chat with their audience.
	Kyte: A universal digital media platform that enables brands and communities to easily produce live and on-demand digital content, distribute it to multiple online and mobile destinations simultaneously, engage with an audience through multimedia communications, and monetize their brand assets.
	Justin.tv: The leader in live video, and the place to broadcast and share video online. This community consists of more than one million registered users, and the site receives millions of unique visitors per month and hundreds of millions of page views per month.

Category	Tools
Livecasting *continued*	**Ustream**: Free, live interactive Web broadcasting. **Mogulus**: Service that enables users to mix videos in real time to create their own live broadcast with Mogulus. You can blend your Webcam, video clips from YouTube, and your own original content into your own unique TV program. And you call all the shots. When you're not broadcasting live, turn on the autopilot and let it drive your play list. **BlogTalkRadio**: Create your own live talk show, which can be heard around the world, without the need for fancy equipment or downloads. Freedom of speech meets social networking.
Pictures	**SmugMug**: A digital photo-sharing Web site, founded by Chris and Don MacAskill in 2002. **Flickr**: An image- and video-hosting Web site, Web services suite, and online community platform. It was one of the earliest Web 2.0 applications. In addition to being a popular Web site for users to share personal photographs, the service is widely used by bloggers as a photo repository.
Social Bookmarks	**Diigo**: A Web site made for people to discover and share content from anywhere on the Internet, by submitting links and stories, and voting and commenting on submitted links and stories. Voting stories up and down is the site's cornerstone function, respectively called digging and burying. Many stories get submitted every day, but only the most dugg stories appear on the front page. **StumbleUpon**: An Internet community that enables its users to discover and rate Web pages, photos, and videos. It is a personalized recommendation engine that uses peer and social networking principles. **De.licio.us**: A social bookmarking Web service for storing, sharing, and discovering Web bookmarks.
Social Productivity	**Google Docs**: A Free Web-based word processor and spreadsheet that enables you to share and collaborate online.

Index

S